The Miegunyah Press

The general series of the
Miegunyah Volumes
was made possible by the
Miegunyah Fund
established by bequests
under the wills of
Sir Russell and Lady Grimwade.

'Miegunyah' was the home of
Mab and Russell Grimwade
from 1911 to 1955.

Shannon Bennett's

P·A·R·I·S

A PERSONAL GUIDE
TO THE CITY'S BEST

REVISED & UPDATED

SHANNON BENNETT,
SCOTT MURRAY
& FRIENDS

THE
MIEGUNYAH
PRESS

THE MIEGUNYAH PRESS
An imprint of Melbourne University Publishing Limited
187 Grattan Street, Carlton, Victoria 3053, Australia
mup-info@unimelb.edu.au
www.mup.com.au

First published 2009
This edition published 2011
Text © Shannon Bennett and Scott Murray, 2011

Design and typography © Melbourne University Publishing Limited, 2011

This book is copyright. Apart from any use permitted under the *Copyright Act
1968* and subsequent amendments, no part may be reproduced, stored in a
retrieval system or transmitted by any means or process whatsoever without
the prior written permission of the publishers.

Every attempt has been made to locate the copyright holders for material
quoted in this book. Any person or organisation that may have been
overlooked or misattributed may contact the publisher.

Designed by Trisha Garner
Typesetting by Megan Ellis
Printed in Hong Kong
National Library of Australia Cataloguing-in-Publication entry:

Bennett, Shannon.
Shannon Bennett's Paris: a personal guide to the city's best /
Shannon Bennett and Scott Murray.
2nd ed

9780522858136 (pbk.)

Includes index.

Restaurants—France—Paris—Guidebooks.
Cooking, French.
Paris (France) —Guidebooks.

647.9544361

Contents

Preface

Wandering the streets of the Marais for the first time, I became enamoured with the history of food and fascinated by the way it is associated with who and where I am today. Food and its evolution not only represent me as a chef, they have shaped the great city of Paris. That is why this book is not so much a guide as a collection of stories and opinions about why Paris means so much to me.

Sometimes we forget that life is not about what we have to look forward to; it is about enjoying the now. What is more enjoyable than working hard and saving money, then dressing up and going out with friends to eat fine food and drink fine wine in great surroundings? Some people can afford to do this weekly or even daily, but for most of us it is a once-in-a-while experience that brings a certain purpose to our lives. It balances out the days when there is seemingly no light at the end of the tunnel.

I wrote this book because I want to celebrate the special dining experience Paris provides, to help convey what makes that city so unique: from its fine restaurants with Michelin stars to the simple bistros and brasseries, from the take-away baguettes and macarons to the local restaurant that makes you feel more at home than in your own dining-room. I want to celebrate the wonderful food shops where you can buy chocolates and caviar, hundreds of different cheeses, and the finest breads and butters you will ever eat. I want to acknowledge centuries of French cooking—from the traditional onion soup and steak with frites to the latest culinary and artistic inventions of Pierre Gagnaire and Le Meurice.

But I haven't done this alone. I asked my mate Scott Murray to help out, along with other friends who have added their personal comments. Scott has been going to Paris almost every year since 1976 and has eaten in more than a few great restaurants. What he and I share is a passionate conviction that, at its best, French food is the finest in the world. We adore the thrill and creativity of three-star restaurants, just as we love the simpler places offering more traditional fare. We love to talk about past and future food experiences. We regularly plan overseas trips, usually based around restaurants we have just heard about (Le Chateaubriand) or ones that have been famous for decades (La Tour d'Argent), where a meal becomes part of our understanding of the evolution of French cooking. Scott and I have been fortunate to eat together in France many times, but sometimes we have eaten separately. For example, I went to La Tour d'Argent in 2007, while Scott was last there in 1980. It may seem a little unusual to include accounts of both experiences, separated by decades, but a restaurant is more than just one visit or one meal. It has a history.

In this book, there are both stories we have lived and told others, and stories others have told us. Some of our comments are short; some will feel like a chapter of a full-length memoir. But that is how those restaurant experiences live in our minds. All we want to do is share them with you.

It also may seem a little unusual that we have concentrated on French cooking in a city with an extraordinary range of ethnic cuisines. But whenever I travel I concentrate on the indigenous food and wine—I don't go to Italy to eat Chinese, or to China to eat Portuguese. Sometimes I may miss out on some great culinary experiences as a result, but a visitor to a foreign city only ever has a limited time in which to eat and drink.

For anyone concerned by our highlighting so many 'expensive' Michelin-starred restaurants, I have three things to say: only a bad meal is an expensive meal; you cannot take it with you when you go; and expensive restaurants can employ up to 100 people, so every diner there is actually helping support the lives and dreams of a lot of people.

As well as restaurants, we look at Parisian hotels, ranging from the simple and reasonably priced to the opulent and expensive. There are also sections on where to buy food (at markets, in specialist stores) and how to cook more than a dozen classic Parisian dishes (with just a twist or two).

Interspersed throughout the book are some (hopefully) informative lists, including our favourite parks and museums, what foods to take on a picnic, and the best books and films set in Paris.

I hope this book will inspire you to love Paris just as much as I do. It certainly is the great city of Light and Love and, most of all, of Food!

Happy eating!

Shannon Bennett

Friends with Opinions

Shannon would like to thank all his friends and family who contributed their thoughts to this book:

STEPHANIE ALEXANDER

HARRY AZIDIS

UTE BIEFANG

ELIZABETH BRIMER

STEVE FELETTI

CRAIG FINLAYSON

GEOFF GARDNER

ADAM GARRISON

JEREMY HOLMES

CHANTAL HOOPER

STEVE JONES

PAUL KALINA

BRYAN LLOYD

SIMON MEADMORE

MATT MORAN

SUE MURRAY

SARAH REAICH

MADELEINE WEST

DAVID WILLIAMS

RAÚL MORENO YAGÜE

A Note about Venue Details

The names of restaurants and hotels (which have countless variations in guide-books) are as given on the official website or the signage by the front door. That is why, for example, some hotel names have a circumflex over the 'o' in 'hôtel' and others do not.

The prices of set menus and à la carte meals (three courses, not including wine) are based on recent visits, the restaurant's website and the latest guides. Be warned, however: this is not an accurate science, due to regular changes to menus and seasonal ingredients. A mountain of black truffle is probably going to increase the cost!

Room prices are taken from the respective hotel website (choosing 15 July as the standard, when all-year rates are not shown) and, sometimes, guidebooks (which usually give rates well under the rack rates shown on a hotel website). You may find many of the rates discounted, either by the hotel or on a booking site.

All the details (addresses, phone numbers, etc.) were correct as of March 2011, but may have changed since, so please check first.

Conventions for quoting prices and rates are Menu: 75 (lunch)/210€, À la carte: 140–360€.

Where venue names are highlighted in burgundy, you'll find a fuller description elsewhere in the book. Names highlighted in blue refer to entries in *Shannon Bennett's France* (2011). Only the first reference in a section is highlighted.

Restaurants, bars, hotels, etc., are listed in alphabetical order within districts.

What Paris Means to Me

At the age of 11, my strongest memory is of not being very good at accepting the simple fact that, as individuals, we are never going to acquire the skills to be good at everything. For me at that time, it was about my inability to comprehend the French language. (Modern times have brought different challenges, such as learning to change nappies, to keep my opinions to myself and to play golf.) Back then, I had no idea why I wanted to learn French, apart from the fact my uncle Tom could speak it and he was a chef, so I thought I'd better get onto it. But the feminine–masculine rules just did not compute to a boy from Westmeadows.

My French teacher, Mr Jarnet, was defiantly in the authentic French mould, with a beautiful moustache (it looked like he glued it on every morning), traditional dapper dress and a very calculated accent (think Inspector Clouseau in *The Pink Panther*). He was very skinny, but food was his first love. I took five years off this poor guy's life in Year 7, but he seemed to feel sorry for me, to take pity on me. He demonstrated this by making me the example. Whenever a difficult question was put to the class, I was always chosen: 'Shannon, please finish the sentence.' After looking at every other class member for a muted answer, I would slowly turn my eyes towards him and say, 'Masculine'. Pity the question was 'Please finish this sentence'. Basically, I was bloody useless.

However, there was a shining light in all this because I actually liked French class. It was not like my weekly religious studies class with Reverend Clegghorn, whom I really did give a hard time and so often spent longer outside the classroom than inside. I have mixed emotions about that now: though religion plays no part in my life, I do love history in its every aspect, including the huge part that religion played in building the world as it is today. I used to let poor old Clegghorn have it when there were areas I did not agree with, yet there was a link with my French lessons. I actually used to get quite excited by our monthly French history class, hearing about Paris and its people and architecture. I loved to hear how important food was to the pride of Parisians; and of their connection to and appreciation of the farmers outside the city who, despite very tough living conditions, managed to produce poetry in their products and make the people of Paris sing.

There was also a connection here with my home-economics class. A few, though certainly not many, of the dishes we cooked were French: *crêpes suzette*, *tarte tatin*, *coq au vin*. The pieces of a puzzle were beginning to come together and my life during high school filled up with thoughts on cooking and travelling. I struggled along with French for four years, mainly because it was compulsory but also because both my French teachers were passionate, which used to annoy and frustrate me. I had a tremendous envy of their freedom. They travelled to and from France, and had this chameleon gift of speaking this amazing language, which instantly changed the way they lived. Unbeknownst to me, the embryo of my future was forming right there and then.

My first trip to Paris was when I was 16. It was not love at first sight, to be honest. Montmartre can do that to you, as it is full of cheap tourist hotels, seedy shops and overpriced and overhyped bistros. But two days into my trip I suddenly felt a strange connection. A farmers' market, of all things, caught my attention: it was a punnet of *fraises des bois* and some mangos from Africa that gave me butterflies in my stomach. All at once, I realised that the people around me were of different colours and shapes and sizes, from different cultures, but they were all talking this amazing language I had never bothered to learn. Mr Jarnet had been right and I was wrong. This geeky French bloke had preached, 'You have not been to a market until you have been to one in France.' I felt a swell of excitement. The approach I took to the remainder of that trip was gathering information: What was foie gras? What was the difference between a bistro and a brasserie? How many people live in Paris? I also fell in love with plane travel that year. Turning left in the plane made me think: What's out to the right? How do I get there? Which airline has the best seats and the newest planes and the best food (i.e., caviar and Krug)?

That was the beginning of my drive to succeed and to one day be able to experience what hard work can enable you to enjoy: freedom. The only setback was my failure to reach my goal of speaking French fluently. Yes, I can speak it, but not in a full-flowing conversation and I don't have the confidence to attempt it with my colleagues at Vue de monde. But that is all going to change: the only way for me to succeed in French is to travel to Paris more often and immerse myself in the language. I hope you do the same after reading this very personal book, which aims to make travelling through Paris fun. Don't forget: life really is far too short to hesitate.

My First Great Paris Experience

I ate at my first Michelin-starred restaurant in Paris when I was 20, and found the experience enthralling. I was lucky, though, as it was the legendary Joël Robuchon's Jamin. He was famous for many dishes and ingredients, but his *pommes mousseline* was something no other chef had quite worked out.

How do you turn mashed potatoes into a three-star dish? Easy, really. Take a kilo of the nearly extinct potato variety called Ratte and sponsor a grower to grow them in perfect red-rich soil. Boil them in salted water, drain them, peel when dry, then put in the oven for 5 minutes. Pass them through a mouli with 250 g of Échiré butter, then pass again through a fine drum sieve. Place one-third of the potato purée into a skillet (press the rest into a container, cover with cling film and store at room temperature). Warm 200 ml of organic full-cream milk, while whisking into the purée over a very low heat another 200–300 g of diced Échiré butter. Gradually add just enough of the warmed milk to keep the butter and potato together. Season with salt: the mixture should taste like pure silk—if it doesn't, add more butter. Do not serve too hot and certainly at no more than 45°C. It should not be oily or split; the texture must be smooth and thick. Serve in a beautiful bowl, fanning the top with the back of a spoon to create a floral effect. And there you have three-star potato mash. It is great with grated truffles, as it was served the day I went to Jamin.

Paris Dining

I have always felt intimidated by Paris and its chefs. Maybe it is being from the other side of the world, but I have trouble believing I could be as good as chefs such as Alain Ducasse. Yet, my confidence rises each year upon returning to Paris, mainly to check or benchmark where I believe Vue de monde sits and compare it to the likes of Astrance, Pierre Gagnaire and Restaurant le Meurice. I come back with more belief each year that Australia still has much to admire and learn, but also has much to offer.

It may seem to the non-professional that running a restaurant is a straight-forward task, but in inner Paris the first thing that comes into the equation is that rent is the highest in the world. Everything about running a restaurant there reeks of money—particularly around place de Madeleine and rue Royal. While big traffic numbers pass through this area every day, they do not necessarily include the sort of diner who decides on a whim to spend 400€ for lunch. For that, a restaurant requires consistent marketing and great reviews, and years of experience in how to handle the Michelin inspectors, and an absolute dedication to training and inspiring a team of around 70 staff (to 50 seats). You can see why I am so passionate about, and in awe of, any successful Michelin-starred chef operating in Paris.

When you're dining in a fine restaurant, have a think about that side of things and appreciate everything around you. Take the silverware—particularly the cutlery. Laguiole and Christofle are my favourites, as both styles allow chefs to design bespoke ranges—at a cost, of course! A chef's personality can be found not only on the plates but in them, and in the accoutrements such as salt-and-pepper holders, napkin holders, cutlery rests and, of course, the table art.

Then there is the glassware, whose size and shape are chosen to enhance the temperature and aromatics of each wine. They are handled ever so delicately, but you just know that by the end the week a $100 Riedel sauternes glass will be chipped or broken.

Shannon's Favourite Fine-dining Restaurants

1. Pierre Gagnaire
2. Restaurant le Meurice
3. Restaurant Guy Savoy
4. Le Bristol
5. Astrance

Shannon's Favourite Neighbourhood Restaurants

1. L'Atelier de Joël Robuchon
2. La Brasserie Thoumieux
3. Le Chateaubriand
4. Brasserie Bofinger
5. Le 114 Faubourg

Then, as the show-plates are taken away, even before you have had a real chance to inspect them, you wonder whether all this passion and amazing class isn't just some stupid business idea. Why bother? You are talking millions of dollars to complete a restaurant setting. It is mind-boggling and many critics of this sort of dining would say it is a waste. But for the most part these critics are insecure failures who forget that life is about giving your best. Then your moment of doubt fades as quickly as it came, to be replaced with a burst of excitement. Observing how well the Parisians work their magic, I start wanting to change things back home at Vue de monde.

I spend at least half an hour every day thinking about these details. I live for this sort of creativity, because working with artists to design show-plates and table art gives each restaurant a distinct identity and purpose.

A Short History of French Food

So many Parisian chefs helped shape the architecture of French cookery as we know it today.

The best-known French chef of the Middle Ages was Guillaume Tirel, also known as Taillevent. He worked in numerous royal kitchens during the 14th century, his first position being as a kitchen boy. He was later chef to Philippe de Valois and then to the Dauphin, who became King Charles V in 1368. Taillevent's career spanned 66 years, and on his death he was buried in grand style between his two wives. His tombstone represents him in armour, holding a shield with three cooking pots on it.

The next most important figure is undoubtedly Antoine Carême (1784–1833). He started out as an apprentice pastry chef, before being discovered by the influential diplomat and nobleman, Talleyrand. Carême went on to become one of Napoléon's head chefs and had a hand in many famous banquets. His greatest contribution was in refining French cuisine. The basis of his cooking style was his identification of four 'mother sauces': now referred to as *fonds* ('foundations'), these base sauces—espagnole, velouté and béchamel—are still used today. Each was made in large quantities in his kitchen, forming the starting point for multiple derivatives: in all, Carême had more than 100 sauces in his repertoire. Soufflés also appear in Carême's writings for the first time. His final contribution didn't become a commercial success until well after his death, which was the discovery and implementation of preserving food in jars and cans—particularly the tomato. You will eat Carême's food in some form or another all over Paris.

The late 1800s to the early 1930s saw the rise of modern French cooking that drew on the inspiration of the past, through chef, restaurateur and culinary writer Georges Auguste Escoffier (1846–1935). While Escoffier's technique was based on that of Carême, his particular achievement was to simplify and modernise Carême's elaborate and ornate style, and transform many peasant dishes into ornate meals by replacing everyday ingredients with hard-to-find and luxury ingredients, such as truffles, caviar and foie gras, as most three-star restaurants do today.

Alongside the recipes he recorded and invented, Escoffier elevated cooking to the status of a respected profession, introducing ordered discipline in his kitchens. He adopted the *brigade de cuisine* system, with each section—cold larder, pastry, fish, meat and vegetables (garnish)—run by a *chef de partie*. He also replaced the practice of service à la française (an elaborate buffet) with service à la russe (serving one dish after another). His legacy is evident when you dine at the Hôtel Ritz Paris (which he opened with Swiss hotelier César Ritz), which still honours the great man with certain of its dishes.

There are many other great chefs, such as Fernand Point and, more recently, Paul Bocuse, who added to this legacy, along with many of the contemporary chefs we write about in this book. But you can still feel the spirit of those pioneers every time you have a great three-star meal.

Fine dining is to mere eating what
Swan Lake is to a local barn dance
And never is that art more celebrated
Than when one dines in France
MADELEINE WEST

Fine Dining: THE BEST OF PARIS

Fine dining is very difficult to categorise. It can mean any number of things to different people and cultures, from the classical and expensive to the spontaneous and inventive. What few would dispute, though, is that it is the French who made restaurant dining an art form.

What to Look For

Tablecloths should be perfectly ironed, with no creases, and be placed on an underlay. The napkins should be linen, the cutlery silver and/or artisan-made. Show-plates should be used to enhance the room and give each setting a purpose when it is vacant. Water glasses should be stemmed or styled. The table centrepiece can be anything from a piece of driftwood with the chef's name engraved on it to a Rembrandt Bugatti sculpture. The tables should be spaced appropriately—which normally means no more than 10–22 tables and a maximum of 70 covers. All staff must be appropriately dressed and their roles identifiable: there should be at least one staff member to every two guests.

The wine list—of a minimum 450 different bins/labels—should be managed by a team of fully qualified sommeliers. Different wine varieties need different and appropriate glassware. There should be apéritif and digestive lists.

In a top-class restaurant, everything is made on the premises. As soon as a food is brought in from somewhere else, it becomes generic. Bought puff pastry is an obvious example, and bread is another: it should be a freshly baked artisan product that reflects the personality of the restaurant proprietor, not of a commercial baker. There should be a choice of several breads. If the chef does not want to serve bread, there must be something similar with which to start the meal. Butter should be of excellent quality and be served at room temperature, with a choice of salted or non-salted available (upon request).

Every dish should use the finest ingredients and be carefully crafted by a well-trained team of chefs (a minimum of 10). Ingredients that one would not find in standard supermarkets or food stores—such as caviar and truffles, aged cheeses, line-caught fish and organic or free-range meats—should be highlighted. Pastries and desserts should be of the highest *wow* factor.

If a restaurant serves food that you know the average home cook could make just as well, it should not describe itself as a fine-dining establishment. But be careful before making that sort of judgement, as a dish may seem simple but require much effort behind the scenes; many a great chef strives to create dishes that are served modestly but cooked to perfection. Last but not least, coffee and tea should always be served with handmade chocolates and/or *petits fours*.

Some Fine-dining Tips

You should have your budget planned before you go to a fine-dining restaurant; you don't want to get there wondering, 'What is this going to cost me?' and 'What am I going to get for it?' Don't plan ahead what you are going to eat, apart from any dietary requirements. Look on the website for the cost of the wine dégustation and the menu, then go there and forget about it. Don't worry about exchange rates, don't worry about anything else. This is your big night out in Paris, and you need to deal with that in your mind before you arrive.

Here are a few ideas on how to choose the perfect fine-dining experience in Paris.

Selecting a Restaurant

You will either keep visiting the places you know and love, or you will be brave and try new ones. You don't do this by walking down a street and taking a chance—you may get lucky, but the odds aren't good. Anyway, a true fine-dining restaurant is usually booked out weeks in advance. It is far better to plan ahead: talk to friends, visit restaurant discussion websites or investigate the cornucopia of guidebooks and magazines on sale. I particularly like *gastroville.com*, *gastromondiale.com*, and magazines like *Etoiles et tois* and *Restaurant* (UK).

USING A RESTAURANT GUIDE

There are two principal guides to eating out in France, the annual *Michelin France* and *GaultMillau France*. Michelin also produces a smaller annual Paris guide.

Michelin For more than 100 years, Michelin has ruled supreme. It is a guide both to hotels and to restaurants across France, broken down alphabetically by towns. The stars refer only to the food, not to the service, environment, etc.

Michelin pioneered the star rating system (technically, they are rosettes but almost no one uses that term). The three categories are explained by Michelin as follows:

★   A very good restaurant in its category.

★★   Excellent cooking and worth a detour.

★★★   Exceptional cuisine and worth the journey. (One always eats extremely well here, sometimes superbly.)

The rating 'Bib Gourmand' indicates exceptional value.

In Paris, the matter of taking a detour isn't an issue; what is important is the relative merits of the restaurants on offer. Everyone has their own point of view, but there is a fair degree of agreement on the city's truly great restaurants.

There will always be a debate about whether a two-star restaurant deserves three, or whether a three-star has faded slightly and ought to be downgraded. Michelin stars are hard-won over years and decades, and they are not changed on whim. The loss of a star can cause economic difficulty for the restaurant concerned, but rarely the ruin that journalists like to prophesy.

GaultMillau GaultMillau is the controversial upstart (first published in the 1960s) in the ratings business and is still treated dismissively by some, especially as it has changed hands several times. Many ask, 'Who is behind GaultMillau and what qualifies them to judge French restaurants?' The answer to that is its excellent track record over the past few decades.

It is generally acknowledged that GaultMillau has long been way ahead of Michelin in discovering and promoting new talent. Arguably the greatest chef in France, Michel Bras in the village of Laguiole, received GaultMillau's highest rating in 1988; it took Michelin till 1999 to finally give him three stars. GaultMillau got it right; Michelin did not. One suspects not even Michelin would dispute that today. The downside of GaultMillau's enthusiasm for the new is that it often has to downgrade the very people it lauded only a year or two earlier. A Cuisinier de l'Année (chef of the year) may even drop right out of sight.

These days, *GaultMillau France* exists only in a French-language edition, so if French is not one of your preferred languages grab a dictionary and calmly work your way through it.

GaultMillau traditionally rated restaurants out of 20, but in 2009 the guide changed to a rating in toques, or chef's hats, from five down to zero. There is also a lengthy description, which is quite often provocatively written. The one thing you can never accuse GaultMillau of is a lack of passion.

Most of its reviews are very fair and detailed. Any restaurant with four or five toques is definitely worth going to, plus their Cuisinier de l'Année award is a guarantee of a great meal.

GaultMillau also uses the symbol of a heart to mean 'coupe de cœur' or 'We love it!'

Michelin or GaultMillau? The answer to the eternal debate of which is the better guide is easily settled: use both.

While Michelin remains the best way to source an 'all round' experience, GaultMillau leads the way for accessing future directions in fine dining.

USING THE INTERNET

There are several websites that are fun to read (though, sadly, the number has been dropping of late). These sites can be a great guide, especially the ones where reviewers spend a thousand words or more on a meal.

Bernard Loiseau and the Guides

The most famous 'incident' involving food guides is that of Bernard Loiseau at his restaurant, La Côte d'Or (now Le Relais Bernard Loiseau) in Saulieu, Burgundy. In 2003, GaultMillau downgraded the restaurant from 19/20 to 17/20 and there were rumours that Loiseau was about to lose one of his three Michelin stars, with complaints he had spread himself too thin with consultancies around the globe and a line of frozen foods. That month, Loiseau committed suicide and some journalists blamed Michelin, though the guide had actually maintained his three-star rating. GaultMillau championed Loiseau long before Michelin gave him the highest accolade and it made very little difference to his bottom line. A Michelin rating means money; a GaultMillau rating does not. So to claim that the downgrading in GaultMillau led to the suicide is wrong. As Loiseau's wife Dominique has often said, it was financial pressures that were the problem.

To Dominique's great credit she has (with chef Patrick Bertron) kept the restaurant open—and it still has three stars. Along with Anne-Sophie Pic at Pic in Valence, Dominique Loiseau is one of the heroic female stories of French dining. That is the real message of this incident, not any fantasies about the influence of critics.

These reviews also tend to be illustrated with photographs of the different courses. However, as the camera of choice is usually a low-pixel mobile phone, the images can make even the greatest dishes look unappetising.

Beware, too, what you read on the Internet. There is no guarantee a site has any critical standards that it is trying to live up to.

Some sites that *are* worth looking up are:

luxeat.com—reviews the world

gastroville.com—a great site

gastromondiale.com—covers restaurants, wines and hotels

andyhayler.com—especially good for young chefs

tripadvisor.com—has some great reviews and rankings, but it is a little hard to use as the opening page lists by popularity. What you need to do is sort them in order of their rating (out of 5) to see what readers consider the best restaurants in Paris.

Booking a Restaurant

Essentially, you have two choices. One is to ring: it is almost certain the person answering the phone will speak English, so be brave and go for it. The alternative is to book via the website. Some restaurants (such as L'Ambroisie) only take bookings by phone.

Dealing with Waiters

The chance of getting a difficult waiter in a fine-dining restaurant these days is fairly remote. Parisians seem to have realised that they need tourists and that they should be nice to them.

On recent visits, I have found the wait staff to be fabulous in just about every restaurant I ate in. The best of them are better than any you'll encounter elsewhere in the world. They turn looking after restaurant guests into an art form (look at my comments on Pierre Gagnaire).

If you do come across a difficult waiter, just relax. Don't let anyone ruin your meal. You have travelled thousands of kilometres to be there; enjoy what there is to enjoy and forget the rest.

My mate Scott has a slightly different point of view: he doesn't tolerate rudeness or lack of service in any way; he stands up for his rights, no matter what. He has put me on the edge of my seat several times, but he gets the right response in the end. The French always treat him with more respect after he has complained than they did before; to a certain extent, the French expect it.

Be firm but charming. Rudeness will only make things worse.

The Menu

Most fine-dining restaurants have a menu in English. Just ask for it. If there isn't one, ask the waiter to help guide you: if you are still at a loss, just play 'Pin the Tail on the Donkey' and randomly choose an entrée and something from Poissons or Viandes. Best of all, go for one of the set menus and let the chef decide for you.

Basically, it is inconceivable that you will find a top-class restaurant in Paris where lack of French is an issue. In rural France, it can still be.

And while on the subject of menus: it is still a tradition in fine-dining restaurants not to have prices on the menus handed to female guests. There is no point getting hot under the collar. If the man is paying, just sit back and relax; if it is the woman, then just swap menus unobtrusively. The staff will not make the same misjudgement twice.

À LA CARTE OR SET MENU?

I love selecting one of the dégustation menus. It makes everything so much more relaxed. I am happy to walk into any restaurant in the world and tell the chef to cook me whatever he or she likes. Rather than studying up on what is in season in

Le Fooding

Shannon: A great new iPhone application has been brought out by Le Fooding. It has reviews and locator maps for all areas in Paris. It only lists restaurants it likes and is not based on revenue-raising initiatives such as advertising from restaurants in return for listings. The application rates visits and reviews out of 1 to 3 BLINGS! It has a usage fee.

France, at fine-dining restaurants simply put your trust in the chef to be using what is fresh that day at the markets. The French remain absolutely committed to using seasonal ingredients.

If you have a strong desire to eat certain foods, then try and plan your next trip to coincide with when they are in season. For me, that is probably *fraises des bois* (wild strawberries), which start appearing in late May but are better a few weeks later. And then, of course, there are the fresh truffles in December, the asparagus from February to June, and so on.

Restaurants usually offer one or more set menus. Choose the number of courses you feel like, or the one with the dishes that most inspire you. If you want to swap a course from one menu to another, don't hesitate to ask. I have never had a refusal. Just remember that most restaurants these days insist on everyone at the table having the same menu, though they will replace a dish or two for a diner with specific dietary requirements.

Wine

Dealing With a Huge Wine List

Don't. Unless you are a true wine connoisseur, forget about trying to wade through 100 pages of wines and vintages you have never heard of or tasted. Call over the sommelier.

The other problem with a big wine list, which people don't tend to talk about, is that it removes at least one person from the conversation for up to 15 minutes. That puts a real dampener on the start of a nice meal.

Some restaurants do list a range of wines on their websites. Download the list and study it at your leisure in the comfort of your own home; that way, you will arrive prepared. But I still think it is better to ask the sommelier.

But Can I Trust the Sommelier?

If you are not going to trust the sommelier, you shouldn't be in the restaurant. He or she may appear imperious or impenetrable, but they know more about what's on the wine list than you do. They know better than any critic what will go with the food. Just ask for their advice and, if concerned about cost, either mention a budget limit or, better still, point to a wine on the list and suggest the sommelier look for something around that price. That way, the cost of the wine doesn't have to be part of everyone's conversation. In my restaurant, I have seen more disputes about how much should be spent on wine than about any other single issue.

Food and Wine Matching

Many restaurants now offer a flight of wines to match a dégustation menu. The obvious first advantage of this, when with a group of people, is that everyone knows from the start what the total cost will be. It lessens the chance of someone ordering a wine out of the budget range of other guests.

I also prefer food and wine matches because it makes the restaurant experience so much more relaxing. The chef and sommelier work out these pairings together; they may have spent months getting it perfect. How can you hope to compete with that when handed a large wine list and not yet knowing how the food will taste?

Regional Versus Big-name Wines

Scott and I chat about this all the time. Scott loves regional wines whereas I tend to go for the great wines of France. And, in Paris, you have access to great and rare wines you won't find anywhere else. The prices aren't cheap, but you only live once.

Should I Only Drink French Wine in Paris?

Well, you shouldn't drink Parisian wine, that's for sure. The only vineyard is in Montmartre and the wine is only good as a fun present. As to whether wines from outside France can complement the food—of course they can. But when faced with the greatest collection of French wines in the world, why would you want to drink anything else?

Wines to Drink in Paris

As recommended by Vue de monde sommelier Raúl Moreno Yagüe

Paris is not only France's capital, it is also its gastronomic and vinous epicentre. When dining in Paris, I try to drink wines that I cannot source in Australia, wines which only French people drink. Local wines from lesser-known appellations are great value: these can only be found in their region of origin—or in Paris.

Fresh and Crisp

1. Muscadet Sèvre-et-maine AOC
   Named after the grape from which it is made, this is the main wine of the region of Nantais.
   Domaine de L'Ecu 'Expression de Gneiss'—look for 2008, 2007 and 2005 vintages
2. Muscat d'Alsace AOC
   Blend of Muscat Blanc, Muscat Ottonel and Muscat à Petits Grains. The wine is floral, dry and less spicy than Gewürztraminer or Pinot Gris.
   Maison Trimbach—vintages 2009, 2007, 2005

A Different Sauvignon

1. Entre-Deux-Mers AOC
   A vibrant Sauvignon Blanc born 'in between two seas' (that is, between the Dordogne and Garonne rivers), without the herbaceous intensity of Loire Valley wines.
   Moulin de Launay—2008, 2007, 2006, 2005
2. Bergerac AOC
   From South-West France near Bordeaux, this includes Semillon-Sauvignon blends, wood-matured with the intensity and complexity of the great wines of Bordeaux, at a more approachable price.
   Grand Maison 'Cuvée Sophie'—vintages 2007, 2006, 2005

Something Quirky

1. Vin Jaune, either Arbois AOC or Château Chalon AOC
   A forgotten treasure from the Jura region, made from the local Sauvignon grape. It is similar to a dry sherry, but is not fortified.
   Domaine André & Mireille Tissot—vintages 1999, 1996, 1993

Light, Red and Perfumed

1. Sancerre AOC
   From the central vineyards of the Loire Valley, these red wines based on Pinot Noir have nothing to envy from Burgundian Pinot Noir.
   Lucien Crochet 'La Croix du Roy'—vintages 2007, 2006, 2005
2. Crus Beaujolais
   Based on Gamay Noir, the Cru Beaujolais from selected sites can produce

extremely interesting wines. Look for Moulin-à-vent AOC, Morgon AOC and Fleurie AOC.
Domaine Jean Foillard Morgon 'Côte du Py'—vintages 2009, 2008, 2007

Medium, Red and Rustic

1. Costières de Nîmes AOC
   You cannot go wrong with these wines, a southern Rhône-style red based on
   Grenache, Syrah and Mourvèdre.
   Château Guiot—vintages 2006, 2005, 2004
2. Bandol AOC
   Located west of Toulon in the heartland of Provence, Bandol produces wines based
   on Mourvèdre, with a density and rusticity that makes them ideal to pair with tradi-
   tional country dishes such as cassoulets and game.
   Château Pradeaux—vintages 2005, 1998, 1995

Red, Rich and Supple

1. Cahors AOC
   Some of the oldest vineyards in France, situated in the south-west, they produce
   deep wines based on Malbec fruit; best drunk only after long cellaring.
   Clos Triguedina 'Prince probus'—vintages 2000, 1998, 1990, 1971
2. Minervois AOC
   From the Black Mountain, between Aude and Hérault, these wines are based on
   Carignan, Grenache and Cinsault.
   La Tour Boisée—vintages 2008, 2002, 1998, 1996

Sweet and also Fresh

1. Bougey VDQS
   A pink, sparkling sweet wine made according to the *méthode ancestrale,* using
   Poulsard and Gamay Noir varietals from the Savoie region.
   Alain Renardat-Fache (non-vintage)
2. Côteaux du Layon AOC
   Bright style of botrytised Chenin Blanc from the Anjou region of the Loire Valley.
   Château Pierre-Bise—vintages 2008, 2005, 1993, 1985

A Little Fortified, Perhaps?

1. Rivesaltes AOC
   A legend still alive, a *vin doux naturel* with an extremely long ageing potential.
   Raisins and dates dance together in the glass, under the direction of honey and
   caramels!
   Domaine Sainte Croix—vintages 1948, 1938, 1909
2. Banyuls AOC
   One of the most southerly vineyards in France, producing very dark and sweet wines
   from the Grenache grape in a *vin doux naturel* style. Think chocolate? Think Banyuls!
   Vial Magnères Rancio (non-vintage)

Casual Dining: BRASSERIES, BISTROS AND NEIGHBOURHOOD RESTAURANTS

How to distinguish a brasserie from a bistro is a common dilemma. Traditionally (reflecting its origins), a brasserie is Alsatian in its atmosphere and style of food, with beer on tap (*brasserie* is the French word for 'brewery'). One expects hearty food such as choucroute, sausages and foie gras, helped along with pints of beer or wines like Gewürztraminer and Riesling. A bistro, on the other hand, is usually a small husband-and-wife restaurant, with a limited menu; there will be daily specials, or a good-value set menu. House wine is usually served by the carafe and is often from the region of the owners' childhood; the wine list should be strong in Burgundy and Vallée de Rhône. In some bistros, you may be asked to share a table with others. If you are lucky, there will also be a zinc-top bar. Some say the word *bistro* (sometimes spelt *bistrot*) comes from the Russian word *bystro*, meaning 'quickly', but no one really knows.

Accommodation

Hotels

The Ratings

Anyone who has travelled to Paris has probably been totally confused by the star ratings of hotels. This is because the ratings given by the major guidebooks don't correspond with the official government ones (which focus on room sizes and basic facilities). Unless otherwise noted, the ratings given in this book are ours and take a consensus approach.

Choosing the Perfect Hotel

Here are some tips on how to choose the hotel that suits you best.

DECIDE WHAT YOU WANT

First, of course, you must ask yourself if you want to stay in five-star luxury near the Champs-Élysées or tuck yourself away in the romantic atmosphere of a boutique hotel in Saint-Germain-des-Prés. In one sense it doesn't matter, because the Métro and bus systems can easily and swiftly get you anywhere. But why take public transport if you can walk? And there are fewer better cities to walk in than Paris.

If you're not sure whether you are a three-, four- or five-star person, go for four stars. These hotels have more than enough luxury and generally none of the stiff formality of some five-star establishments.

DO YOUR RESEARCH

Always go to the website of any hotel you're considering, and look at all the photographs. Try and work out how large each room actually is and don't be fooled by obvious photographic tricks such as the use of wide-angle lenses.

See if the rest of the hotel has what you want: a restaurant, a breakfast room, a private garden or courtyard, public rooms where you can relax and meet friends, and so on. Most important, check what Internet services it provides (Wi-Fi, LAN) and at what cost.

Then go to a commercial booking site, such as *venere.com* or *booking.com*, to check out their photographs, ratings and reviews. Then visit *tripadvisor.com* to read the reviews there (but don't be put off by the terrible photographs taken by guests; they could make Le Meurice look like a slum). Remember also that American tourists invariably complain about the size of French hotel rooms, especially in the Marais and Saint-Germain-des-Prés: they tend to have unrealistic expectations about rooms, facilities and services, and often seem unaware that many of the buildings were constructed for less-tall people several centuries ago.

The site *mrandmrssmith.com* is great as it recommends actual room numbers.

Note: Unless you know a travel agent made in heaven, you should do the research yourself. An agent is not going to study photos on the Internet to make sure a room is exactly what you want; they won't know if bright-pink wallpaper will thrill or depress you.

BOOKING

First check the prices on the hotel website. Note if breakfast is included or an extra charge: this can make a huge difference, especially for two people. An apparently expensive hotel that offers free breakfast may in the end actually cost less than a cheaper one where breakfast is extra.

Once you've decided on one or more likely hotels, go to *venere.com* and all the other commercial sites to see if you can get a better price (often you won't). Some online booking services, like *hoteclub.com*, require you to pay up-front. You get a refund, minus a small deduction, if you cancel. Such sites often claim that by paying ahead you have got the painful bit out of the way before you travel, that you're not at the mercy of currency variations, and that their buying power enables them to give bigger discounts. You can test that last one out for yourself.

Other sites, such as *venere.com* and *booking.com* (and many, many more) charge you nothing to book through them and you can usually cancel up to 24 hours beforehand without penalty of any kind. You only pay when you check out of the hotel. What you must remember to do is cancel any booking you are not going to take (the hotel or booking service will tell you how far ahead you must do this to avoid a penalty). This is far easier to forget than you might think. However, if you do you will usually be charged for one night, not the whole booked stay.

The main advantage of booking directly with a hotel as opposed to through a commercial booking service is that you are dealing with the very people who will be looking after you when you are a guest. A request for a room at the back, or a bath instead of a shower, is more likely to be met. You also get a reply to a request, which you don't from most booking sites.

Have fun choosing!

Apartments

Apartments are the perfect way to spend an extended time in Paris, especially with a family. They are also worth considering for a short stay, especially for those who will be dazzled by the food produce on sale and wish to rush back to a kitchen and cook up a feast. There is no doubting that even a moderately talented cook can eat brilliantly after spending a few minutes at the stove. This is especially true of the prepared food available from a range of stores, from Fauchon and Hédiard down to the simplest corner store (and they still do exist in Paris, especially in the 5th and 6th arrondissements).

Apartments are much cheaper than a hotel, but you have to make sure making beds and doing housework isn't going to spoil the fun. Of course, several apartment firms can supply maids and cooks.

A group of people can also share a travel experience without being confined to cell-like rooms in a hotel and hampered by a total absence of a private communal area.

Shannon's Favourite Luxury Hotels

These are my fantasy hotels—where you go for an once-in-a-lifetime experience, for one or two nights—rather than where I stay every time I am in Paris. They embody everything Paris is about: old-world luxury.

1. Hôtel Le Bristol
2. Hôtel Plaza Athénée
3. Le Meurice
4. Four Seasons George V
5. Hôtel de Crillon

Shannon's Favourite Boutique Hotels

1. L'Hôtel
2. Pershing Hall
3. Hôtel Fouquet's Barrière
4. Hôtel François 1er
5. Duc de Saint-Simon

Another obvious advantage is that you can entertain guests in a way you can't in a hotel, unless you are paying for a multi-room suite. It is also wonderful to be able to have a great wine on chill and a feast at your fingertips, and not be dependent on the poor-quality items found in minibars or on pricey room-service menus.

The disadvantage of an apartment is that if you don't like it you may be trapped. It is much easier to trade one hotel room for another, or simply change hotels. However, the better rental firms really do have your happiness as their primary goal. They thrive off returning customers and great word of mouth. Specialist firms such as Guest Apartment Services on the Île Saint-Louis will do whatever they can to make your Paris visit special. This can mean arranging opera tickets and babysitting to limousine hire and specially prepared breakfasts. The gap between hotel and apartment services is narrowing.

Four firms I and readers have found to be excellent, and thus worth highlighting, are:

apartrental.com
guestapartment.com
parisaddress.com
parissimo.fr

Cooking Dinner in Paris

Cooking dinner at home is fun. For me, the most opportune time is usually a Sunday. The process is like having a magic box: I go to the fridge and see what we have, then to the cupboard and see what will work, and then to the garden for herbs and for a few vegetables. Out of this I like to replicate classic dishes, like Couscous Royale or a cassoulet in winter, but with a modern twist.

Cooking in Paris brings a new level of excitement, not least because apartments are often so small and kitchens even smaller. You can buy fresh food every other day from the markets that travel from neighbourhood to neighbourhood. These markets are amazing during all seasons. I particularly like the end of spring, where fresh morels and white asparagus are scarce but at their best. *Fraises des bois* and raspberries are everywhere and white peaches are not far away.

I also love the hundreds of providores around Paris. As soon as an inspirational idea comes to mind, I closely follow it up with a foie gras idea and race off to get fresh foie gras. Fresh fish is easily available: I quite like the gourmet food section in Le Bon Marché on the Rive Gauche, purely because it is reliable. However, there are better places and some that are cheaper. A few of the most famous are L'Océanic (1st arrondissement), Poissonnerie du Bac (7th), Poissonnerie Lacroix (11th), Poissonnerie du Dôme (14th), Daguerre Marée (15th) and Bayen Marée (17th).

My ideal menu would be only three courses, because finding basic ingredients can the most challenging logistic in a foreign kitchen and, for every course, more of these basics will be required.

FIRST COURSE

Foie Gras with Roast Peach

The first course would be a slice of fresh foie gras pan-fried with peach. When choosing foie gras for the first time, remember there are two types: *canard* (duck) or *oie* (goose). I prefer duck foie gras as it is smaller, cheaper and has a more pronounced flavour. Look for livers with no bruises or blood spots, and of a light creamy colour; they should be firm to touch. Keep refrigerated. When slicing the liver, use a very hot, thin sharp knife: slice it just before cooking, to prevent oxidisation. *Serves 2*

1 peach	Cut the peach in half and then cut it into 3-mm slices, as you would an apple. Sauté the slices in a hot pan with 1 tablespoon of the butter until warm and cooked through (about 2 minutes) and remove to a bowl. Flavour with the fennel and shallots. Dress with hazelnut oil and sherry vinegar. Leave to the side for 5 minutes and then place in the centre of the plate. Bring a heavy frying pan (no oil) to a very high heat. Fry the foie gras slices until coloured, then remove and deglaze the pan with the sweet wine. Whisk in a tablespoon of the very best butter until a sauce has formed. Adjust the sweetness with a squeeze of lemon or lime juice.
2 tablespoons butter	
1 small bulb fennel, very thinly shaved	
1 shallot, chopped	
1 tablespoon hazelnut oil	
1 tablespoon sherry vinegar	
2 x 100 g fresh foie gras	
100 ml sweet wine such as Madeira, Marsala or port	
1 lemon or lime	Place the foie gras on top of the salad and spoon the sauce over.

SECOND COURSE

Roast Farm Chicken with Cèpe Mushroom Sauce

The second course is based on what is for me France's most underrated product: the humble chicken. Bresse is the most famous breed and well worth its relatively high price. French supermarkets generally stock great-quality poultry and there is a great variety of (less expensive) poussins to choose from as well. Look for *poulet fermier* (farm chicken) and choose a plump, free-range or organic bird. I hate the way we store our poultry in plastic bags here in Australia, and I applaud the French for their basic packaging that allows the skin to breathe and look presentable. Wild cèpes are available in both autumn and spring, but tinned cèpes are available all year round and, while nothing compares to the flavour of wild ones, the tinned versions are very good. To make shopping easier, pass this note to the assistant when ordering: '*Pourrais-j'avoir un poulet fermier [farm chicken] de 1.5–2 kg et 500 grams de graisse d'oie [goose fat], s'il vous plaît? Je voudrais quelques cèpes frais aussi, mais pas verreux [no worms]. Avez-vous du beurre (doux ou salé)?*' Serves 4

1 free-range chicken, about 1.5–2kg

500 g goose fat

salt and pepper

2 tablespoons cultured butter

PERSILLAGE (HERBED BREADCRUMBS)

2 tablespoons finely chopped curly-leaf parsley

1 teaspoon fresh thyme leaves

2 cloves garlic

4 tablespoons olive oil

50 g breadcrumbs

The day before you plan to serve the dish, preheat oven to 140ºC. Remove the chicken neck, wishbone, wing-tips and legs. Put everything except the legs in the refrigerator. Preheat goose fat to 120ºC in an ovenproof pot with a lid. Season chicken legs with salt and pepper, place in the pot, cover lightly with foil, put lid on and bake for 1–1½ hours or until the meat starts to fall off the bone. Remove from oven, allow to cool in the fat, then refrigerate.

To complete the cooking, preheat oven to 180ºC.

Make the persillage: put all the ingredients in a food processor and pulse until finely chopped. Set mixture aside.

Place the chicken on a board with the neck towards you. With poultry scissors or a sharp knife, remove the underside of the bird, leaving the breast section (crown). Chop the backbone, neck and wing-tips into 5-cm pieces, put in a baking tray and set aside. Run your fingertips carefully under the skin of the breast, starting at the neck, separating the skin from the meat. Take a large handful of persillage and press this into the gap between meat and skin until completely filled.

Rub butter over the skin, place chicken crown on top of the bones in the tray. Season well, cover tightly with foil and roast in preheated oven for 1 hour. Remove tray from oven, put crown on a rack or plate, cover with foil and rest in a warm place.

CÈPE MUSHROOM SAUCE

1 tablespoon chicken fat

1 tablespoon chopped shallots

1 clove garlic (crushed)

20 g dried cèpes (porcini)

4 medium fresh cèpes (cut in half)

1 cup Madeira, Muscat or Marsala

1 cup chicken stock

50 g butter

lemon juice and salt and pepper to taste

Take a roasting tray and add fat, shallots, garlic and cèpes and cook over medium heat for 1 minute. Deglaze with alcohol, reduce until almost evaporated. Add stock and stir around tray. Drain into a saucepan and simmer for 10 minutes, then add butter. Season and serve.

A Fish Alternative

If you prefer fish, simply pan-fry in olive oil until golden and cooked through. Add butter, lemon juice and parsley. Make sure the butter is Échiré.

THIRD COURSE

Blueberry Cream with Hazelnut Praline

You can serve this dessert in a goblet or even a traditional glass. I also like the fact that you can change the fruit to anything that is in season, such as prunes, cherries, berries or even poached apples or pears. *Makes 12*

HAZELNUT PRALINE
100 g sugar
200 ml water
100 g hazelnuts, roasted and peeled

To make the praline, heat the sugar and water in a small saucepan over medium heat until a golden caramel is formed. Fold in the hazelnuts, then pour onto a tray lined with greaseproof paper and leave to cool. Once the mixture has set, remove from the tray and place in a food processor. Blitz to a fine powder, and reserve in an airtight container.

BLUEBERRY JELLY
250 ml water
2 teaspoons lemon juice
250 g blueberries
4 leaves gelatin, soaked in cold water

For the jelly, bring the water, lemon juice and blueberries to the boil in a medium-sized saucepan. Reduce to a simmer and cook for another 10 minutes, then pour into a food processor and blitz until smooth. Place mixture in a saucepan over low heat, add the gelatin and stir to dissolve. Remove from the heat and pass through a fine sieve into deep glasses for serving.

CRÈME ANGLAISE
560 ml milk
560 ml double cream
seeds from 2 vanilla beans
10 egg yolks
75 g superfine caster sugar

To prepare the crème anglaise, put milk, cream and vanilla seeds in a heavy-based pan and bring to the boil. Remove from heat. Beat yolks and sugar together until pale and creamy, gently combine with the milk–cream mixture and return to the stove over a low heat, stirring constantly with a wooden spoon for 10 minutes or until mixture thickly coats the back of the spoon (it should have a custard-like consistency). Strain through a fine sieve into a bowl set over ice. Stir occasionally.

BISCUIT MIX
6 savoiardi biscuits, roughly crumbled, and soaked in 100 ml sweet sherry

To assemble the dish, take the glasses of jelly and put approximately ½ cup of the sherry-soaked biscuit crumbs in each. Pour in approximately 50 ml of the crème anglaise, then place in the fridge until set. When ready to serve, dust lightly with the ground praline.

Accompanying Wines

Choosing wines that would match this sort of menu is a little tricky, but I would recommend an Alsatian late-harvest style such as Gewürztraminer *vendage tardive*, which will go with both the foie gras and the dessert. I'd also go for a nice red burgundy such as Clos Vougeot Domaine J Confuron-Cotetidot, but at the end of the day choose whatever wine takes your fancy. This meal is all about being in Paris and living as the Parisians do.

The Arrondissements of Paris

For those unfamiliar with the Parisian arrondissements (or districts), they are arranged in a clockwise spiral from the centre of Paris, or 1st arrondissement. That is why the pattern is known as The Snail (see drawing).

Furthermore, Paris is divided by the River Seine into the Rive Droite (Right Bank) and Rive Gauche (Left Bank), with the islands of the Île Saint-Louis and the Île de la Cité in between.

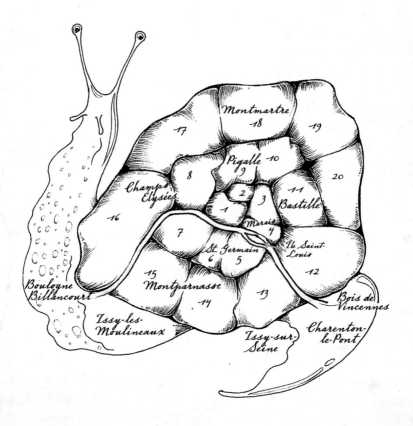

Drawing by Madeleine West

Rive Droite

RIGHT BANK

Tuileries, Place Vendôme, Palais-Royal, Louvre, Les Halles

1ST ARRONDISSEMENT

TUILERIES

FINE DINING (WITH LUXURY HOTEL)

Le Meurice's staggeringly beautiful 17th-century dining-room was reopened in 1990 after an ignominious interlude as a conference room. More recently, designer Philippe Starck was brought in to subtly modernise the space with little touches here and there. The real challenge, though, was to have the restaurant's food and service equal the hotel's exalted reputation. That it now does is primarily due to one man: 35-year-old Yannick Alléno, a former *chef de partie* at the hotel, who was brought back as head chef in September 2003. The restaurant now has three stars and deserves every one of them.

Restaurant le Meurice

Chef: Yannick Alléno
228 rue de Rivoli, 75001
01 44 58 10 55
lemeurice.com
Michelin: ★★★
GaultMillau: ☻☻☻☻☻
Menu: 78 (lunch)/220/320€
À la carte: 175–325€

Shannon: My favourite recent dining experience would have to be **Restaurant le Meurice**, because of its opulence. When you walk in to the dining-room, it is like entering another era. I didn't realise until I began eating, from all the minute details, that it was actually 2008. Philippe Starck's touches highlight the best of the two centuries that the dining-room has been open.

The people-watching was just amazing: these were modern Parisians, with obviously busy lives, who had taken three or four hours out of their day to eat three-star food. It was as enjoyable as watching the theatre provided by the wait staff. Whatever stress there may have been in the kitchen, they were very calm in their presentation of the food. The dishes were taken to the table, on trays the young staff carried on their shoulders; the dishes were passed to the *chef de range*, who then delivered them to the maître d', who introduced the dish. It was really spectacular old-style service, backed up with Yannick Alléno coming out and meeting everyone at each table, and talking to us honestly and openly. He has a great personality.

The restaurant has had a chequered history as far as the food is concerned. Alléno has done an amazing job in turning around its reputation, particularly in its style of cuisine—great produce with touches of French technique and Oriental flavours. The food had a modern feel—there was no cream anywhere in the meal—and the portions were perfect.

My most vivid memory was of one of the first courses, a little miso soup served with crunchy radishes dipped in French butter. The butter had been thickened with some ingredient—perhaps gelatin, perhaps seaweed extract—and set hard, like an icing, after the vegetables were dipped into it. The dish was complemented beautifully by a little curry spice and sea salt.

I tried the foie gras—simply pan-fried and served with poached cherries—and thought it exceptional. There was a Red Mullet dish that I felt was beautifully put together with the tiniest of mussels: I remember a clean white plate with the perfectly cooked Mullet on it. I had shoulder of lamb, accompanied by a little bit of loin, which was pretty mind-blowing with its extraordinary almond sauce.

The little pre-dessert came out with a lot of theatre. The dessert wasn't my favourite dish, but it was intriguing and the presentation superb. It was a fig that had been hollowed out and stuffed with a quite spicy mixture that included nuts, and was then shaped into a ball and dipped in white chocolate. It was served with a light mascarpone cream. The chocolates at the end of the meal were perfection.

I can't say there was any dish that was the most memorable I have ever tasted, but the balance of the meal was amazing: eating here is about the whole experience, and anyway the menu changes regularly. I would sum up the experience as sophisticated, clean and seasonal, with beautiful presentation.

There is a certain stuffiness at Le Meurice, but it's the kind you want when you go to Paris. The waiters were so polished they did not understand our sense of humour when we tried to have a bit of fun, but this was balanced by the maître d', who picked up on it and indulged us. We felt very comfortable.

I walked in with long daggy hair, in a suit I had bought that day from CoSTUME NATIONAL (a label I had never heard of before, but which one of my trendier mates, Adam, had convinced me to buy). I probably looked 'not the part', but they accepted me straightaway. They never spoke down to us and I liked that. At some other three-star restaurants, I have felt inhibited because the maître d' let us know implicitly but in no uncertain terms that this was an expensive, upmarket restaurant where we didn't seem to belong. French restaurants are renowned for this kind of attitude and, while you expect a certain degree of *hauteur*, you do want to feel accepted. You need to book at least a month out, if not two. That's really important.

Scott: I visited Restaurant le Meurice in August 2007 with my mother, Gillian. Today, there is a direct entrance from the rue de Rivoli, but for many years you had to enter via the hotel's main entrance on rue Mont Thabor. You then wandered down a long dim corridor and across the open-space café (the Restaurant le Dali). It was a long walk, but worth it. The grand-siècle splendour that awaits you is almost heart-stopping. There is no more dazzling dining-room, surely, in the world.

The experience was perfect from the start. The staff were all charming and did not mind speaking French when I tried to, or switching to English when I stumbled (which was often). When they returned with the next course, they would try French again. This may sound like a small courtesy, but as someone who has had several potentially great meals scuttled by arrogant waiters who refused to speak English, or pointedly ridiculed my attempts, the elegant young men and women of Le Meurice go straight to the top of the class. This is the easiest three-star to feel totally relaxed in, despite the empiric glory of the surroundings.

The maître d', a master of his art, arrived each time with the faintest click of his heels. Indeed, one could just detect the faintest theatrical cheekiness in all he did—which was to supervise the serving of *every* course. Sometimes he did the plating himself; at other times, he just stood back and observed.

We opted for the dégustation menu. From memory, there were 14 courses in all, including the *amuse-bouches* and

extra delights. I cannot recall all we ate, but it doesn't matter in the sense that no course was better than any other. It remains the only long meal I have eaten where it as impossible to rate any dish below 20/20.

Our surprise at the brilliance of each course led us to repeatedly express praise to the waiters. Used to the French habit of diners saying nothing, they were at first puzzled by these eccentric Australians, but soon shared the joy. After the third course, Yannick Alléno came out, just to meet us. He was utterly charming and happily chatted in English, and came again before the end, to thank us for our praise and enthusiasm.

At one point I did think I had finally found a minor weakness. It was the sixth or seventh course: lamb with an orange-blossom sauce. It was a little shy at the start; but, by the end, I could only rate it one of the greatest dishes I have ever tasted.

The most unusual dish, and magnificent, was the cheese course: the maître d' shredded the cheese and then served it with jam. Extraordinary.

Having chosen the dégustation menu, we did not get to select from the dessert trolley (but I'm sure we could have, had we asked). I have never seen anything so visually stunning paraded around so elegant a dining-room. It was berry season and everything on the trolley was either blazing red or pristine white (such as poached and moulded egg whites, and cubes of the lightest-looking meringue). There were myriad choices of each colour, with equally varied textures. Pure theatre.

The wine list is a masterpiece, a tome. I opted for a remarkable 1999 Rasteau (a small appellation in the Southern Rhône) from Domaine de la Soumade. It was a near-perfect accompaniment to an astonishingly perfect meal.

Le Meurice

Rating: 5★+
228 rue de Rivoli, 75001
01 44 58 10 10
lemeurice.com
Rooms: 137
Single: 540–665€
Double: 540–665€
Suites: 23

While the Hôtel de Crillon (travel west along the rue de Rivoli to the 8th) still reigns as queen of the grand-dame hotels, **Le Meurice**, after decades of fading into near-insignificance, is now back to its rightful place at the acme of Parisian hotels. Its position on the rue de Rivoli is commanding, with some rooms offering spectacular views across the Jardin des Tuileries.

If you are able to book a Deluxe Garden Double or a Junior Suite, with a balcony, do so. At the absolute pinnacle, though, is the Belle Étoile Suite, which has a 300 m² private terrace and a 360° view of Paris. Nothing can compare with it. But no matter the size, all the rooms are beautifully designed in the Louis XVI style and have generous bathrooms. Most look over the rue du Mont Thabor (where the hotel's main entrance is) or the inner courtyard. The service is exemplary and the eponymous restaurant is one of the two or three finest in Paris—and, therefore, according to the French, in the world.

Scott: I stayed here decades ago. It was my first experience of a top-class hotel and, despite my youth and obvious lack of resources, the staff treated me as if I had been a regular for years. The bedroom was gorgeous. I love how the French often place the head of a bed into an alcove, with lamps and bookshelves at a handy distance on either side. The bathroom was twice the size of the bedroom. I thought this absurd at the time, but have since learnt that few things can wreck a hotel experience faster than a too-small bathroom. The location is exceptional with the Tuileries gardens across the street, the place Vendôme around the corner, a station on Paris' main Métro line a few metres away and, perhaps best of all, one of the world's finest bookshops, the **Librairie Galignani**, almost next door.

Great Paris Bookshops

Librairie Galignani
224 rue de Rivoli, 75001
galignani.com

This is one of the world's most irresistible bookshops. Hours will pass unnoticed as you wander delightedly through its hallowed spaces.

On the rue de Rivoli, not far from Le Meurice, it occupies a large street-level area with books arranged on elegant wooden bookshelves reaching to the rather high ceiling. (Ask the staff to reach for the unreachable; they all speak perfect English.) The front part of the shop is devoted to French literature and non-fiction (the range of photographic, art and fashion books is impressive). It is also strong on French cookbooks, especially specialist editions from the likes of Olivier Rœllinger and Michel Bras.

About halfway down, the books change to American and some British hardbacks (mostly non-fiction), then to an extensive range of serious paperback fiction. Near the back on the right is a cubbyhole of travel books and guides. Air-freighted magazines are also available from a small news-stand area in the middle.

The website is superb and offers a complete tour of the shop.

W.H. Smith
248 rue de Rivoli, 75001
whsmith.fr

W.H. Smith is the antithesis of Galignani, a chain bookshop aiming at a less erudite reader. It stocks only English-language books, usually in UK editions. Downstairs houses paperback fiction, a small hardback fiction area and a huge news-stand at the back, which is always crowded. It is one place to get the Sunday editions of *The New York Times* and *The Times*, though they will be missing several sections and the colour magazines.

Upstairs is a wide range of non-fiction, mostly in hardback, and a selection of (expensive) UK DVDs. This area used to be a tea-room, which is missed by older-generation clients.

Virgin Megastore
52–60 avenue des Champs-Élysées, 75008
virginmegastore.fr

In the crowded Virgin Megastore on the bustling avenue des Champs-Élysées, there is a huge book section to the right and downstairs as you enter. Almost everything is in French, except for a small collection of fairly low-brow paperbacks (and the odd hardback) in the most distant corner to the left. For the non-linguist, it is a must for latest editions of guidebooks and a wide range of art and photographic books. Lovers of French cinema will also find something of interest.

Shakespeare and Company
37 rue de la Bûcherie, 75005
shakespeareandcompany.com

Founded in 1951, this is a haunt of literary romantics. Many of the books on sale have seen better days, and it is always packed, but few places have the history of this small shop, where regular visitors included Henry Miller, Anaïs Nin and Lawrence Durrell.

BISTRO

Lescure

7 rue Mondovi, 75001
01 42 60 18 91
no website
Menu: 23/45/62€
À la carte: 30–55€

This tiny bistro, hidden away in a small street off the rue de Rivoli near the place de la Concorde, specialises in the cuisine of the South-West.

Scott: The room was packed when our party of five came in out of the pouring rain. It was a scene that might have come from *The Three Musketeers*, where d'Artagnan and the boys ride across a desolate countryside at night and arrive at a deserted-looking inn, only to enter and find half the population of France happily eating there. The owner greeted us most charmingly and then squeezed us into one of the very long rustic tables (forget separate ones). We were packed so tightly it was almost impossible to move our elbows: eating the largest chunk of confit of chicken I have ever been served wasn't easy, nor was trying to hear what anyone was saying. But the food was hearty and the bottles of dark-red Cahors delicious. We all adored the experience.

 LUXURY HOTELS

Hôtel Costes

Rating: 5★+
239 rue du faubourg
Saint-Honoré, 75001
01 42 44 50 00
hotelcostes.com
Rooms: 82
Single: 400–750€
Double: 550–750€
Suites: 3

The **Hôtel Costes** is one of the chic-est hotels in Paris, even if its lustre has been slightly diminished by relentless brand marketing. It was opened in 1991 by Jean-Louis Costes, famous for his Philippe Starck–designed Café Costes in Les Halles. The Napoléon III–style building is shaped around perhaps the most lively hotel courtyard in Paris. It is a beautiful Italianate space, with creepers cascading down the walls. The hotel bar is always in vogue.

The charming hotel staff are, or are rumoured to be, models filling in time between photo-shoots, which means a lot of people come just to look (as they should). The décor by that tongue-in-cheek lover of excess, Jacques Garcia, is predictably over-the-top; it's a bit like staying in a brothel. The 18-metre Moroccan-style swimming pool is a masterpiece.

The only real query is whether you want to stay in a hotel that releases almost as many albums as Kylie Minogue; it also produces a range of perfumes, accessories and packaged food. In other words, the Costes has become a brand rather than a hotel; the owner has also opened the Hotel Costes K Paris on avenue Kléber in the 16th.

Scott: Haven't stayed here, but visited just after it opened. Had a drink in the fabled courtyard, where the staff were as beautiful as rumoured and all surprisingly charming. There was absolutely no hint of attitude. We were happily shown around and visited the swimming pool and sauna area. My only concern was how noisy the rooms facing the courtyard might be, especially as many people tell stories of the late-night revelry. This is a hotel for those who want to stay in the epicentre of the action and would rather party than sleep.

. . . .

Hôtel Costes Bar
239 rue du faubourg
Saint-Honoré, 75001
01 42 44 50 00
hotelcostes.com

Experience the glories of designer Jacques Garcia in full flight at the bar of the super-cool Hôtel Costes. *Worldsbestbars.com* calls it a 'den of opulence' and 'a Lounge Lizard's Mecca'. The atmosphere is super-chilled, and, if you like the background music, it will turn up soon on one of the Costes CDs.

. . . .

The Westin Paris
Rating: 5★
3 rue de Castiglione, 75001
01 44 77 11 11
thewestinparis.com
Rooms: 440
Single: 340–750€
Double: 340–750€
Suites: 29

On the corner of the rue Castiglione and the rue de Rivoli, opposite Le Meurice, this imposing grand luxe hotel has been recently and superbly restored. The location is unbeatable, even if it is a bit dead at night. But with several of the best fine-dining restaurants nearby (Restaurant le Meurice, Les Ambassadeurs), and with the Hôtel Costes just around the corner for a drink, you don't need to travel far. If you want simpler food, either walk to bustling Lescure or take the Métro outside your front door and head off to Brasserie Bofinger. The hotel does have its own restaurant, Le First Restaurant Boudoir Paris, a typically bold statement from Jacques Garcia. With modern-style rooms as low as 249€ on the Internet, this is one of the most affordable five-star hotels in Paris.

Shannon's Favourite Parisian Treats

Macarons

Shannon: What makes a good macaron is simple: a well-defined flavour, and a shining and bright natural appearance. It should be round, not too thick, with a rough footing around the bottom and very chewy and not too delicate on the inside, with a well-made butter cream that is light and at a good temperature. It's pretty easy, and more places get it right than get it wrong.

Most of the wankers who have set up websites and blogs on these subjects are missing the point by taking a biscuit that reminds me of fun and decadence, and turning it into a sport for people who belong in Siberian labour camps. If I have joined their ranks, I will say one thing: Fauchon's macarons always disappoint me. They are very cakey and don't last very long, and you pay for the packaging.

The three best macarons in Paris are, in order:

1. Pierre Hermé. I love most the banana spilt and the lychee with raspberries.
2. The next-best macaron is from Pâtisserie Sadaharu Aoki. This man is really turning it on, especially with influences from Japan, such as wasabi. Don't squirm, because balancing really obscure flavours with traditional ones brings an incredible excitement and contrast to what could otherwise be a boring cup of tea and a biscuit. Aoki's salted butter caramel flavour is a real winner.
3. Ladurée was a shock for me. Since staying at the rue Jacob quite a few years ago, I discovered real hot chocolate at Ladurée and have always loved the pistachio macaron that came with it. In my mind, the experience has not changed: Ladurée still has the best pistachio macarons in Paris.

Jean-Paul Hévin

Since 1988 (La Petit Boulé), 2002 (Hévin2)
231 rue Saint-Honoré, 75001
01 55 35 35 96
3 rue Vavin, 75006
23 bis avenue de la Motte-Picquet, 75007
jphevin.com

In 2005, Jean-Paul Hévin's chocolate macaron was voted the best macaron in Paris ('traditional' category). Lovers of La Maison du Chocolat's version might disagree, but no one can dispute the magnificence of Hévin's macarons, with their dark-chocolate ganache and crystallised pistachio chips, or liquid raspberry jelly, or mango and coriander. The truly brave can try the goat's cheese from Charolais, the Époisses from Burgundy and the Roquefort from the Aveyron.

Ladurée

Since 1862
16 rue Royale, 75008
01 42 60 21 79
21 rue Bonaparte, 75006
75 avenue Champs-Élysées, 75008
62 boulevard Haussmann, 75009
laduree.fr

A Parisian institution, **Ladurée** was founded in the 19th century by a miller from the South-West. Including the original store on rue Royale, there are four shops across Paris. Ladurée has always been known for the elegance of its tearooms and its extraordinary macarons, including mint, chocolate, raspberry, lemon, rose petal and violet. Some macarons come in an oversized form.

Paul

Since 1889
8 rue Tronchet, 75008
01 40 17 99 54
25 avenue de l'Opéra, 75001
77 rue de Seine, 75006
paul.fr

With more than thirty shops in Paris, **Paul** is the most convenient place to locate a decent macaron when the desire suddenly strikes.

Pierre Hermé

Since 1998 (Tokyo), 2001 (Paris)
72 rue Bonaparte, 75006
01 48 74 59 55
4 rue Cambon, 75001
63 rue Montorgueil, 75002
89–91 rue Saint Antoine, 75004
185 rue Vaugirard, 75006
14 boulevard Saint-Germain, 75006
84 avenue des Champs-Élysées, 75008
pierreherme.com

Many believe Pierre Hermé is the world's best maker of macarons. His caramel is not just salted like most people's, but uses the best fleur de sel. The vanilla pods come from Mexico, Tahiti and Madagascar, while the chocolate is the finest grand cru (Porcelana, Venezuela Ocumare and Mexican). And let's not forget the white truffle and hazelnut or the wasabi and grapefruit.

Pâtisserie Sadaharu Aoki

Since 2001
35 rue de Vaugirard, 75006
56 boulevard de Port Royal, 75005
Galeries Lafayette Gourmet
40 boulevard Haussmann, 75009
25 rue Pérignon, 75015
sadaharuaoki.com

Sadaharu Aoki is a master pâtissier, who also makes divine macarons.

La Maison du Chocolat

Since 1977
225 rue du faubourg Saint-Honoré, 75008
99 rue de Rivoli, 75001
19 rue des Sèvres, 75006
52 rue François 1er, 75008
8 boulevard de la Madeleine, 75009
Printemps Haussmann, 75009
120 avenue Victor Hugo, 75116
lamaisonduchocolat.com

Though world-famous for its chocolate macaron, **La Maison du Chocolat** seems to have allowed its standards to slip. The macarons now have a machine-produced feel and several flavours are close to indistinguishable when eating them with one's eyes closed. That said, it is a regal experience to take a coffee and a chewy macaron in one of its stores, or be served by the immaculately trained staff.

Stephanie Alexander's France

In the years when I made such pilgrimages to France (the 1980s), the establishment far above all others was Alain Chapel, in Mionnay. I can still see and taste my salad of roasted guinea fowl, with a deep-red wine reduction streaked through the jus and a salad of tiny oakleaf lettuce leaves on the plate. It was the first time I had seen this idea of a little posy of greens with rich meat, an idea I freely copied for years (duck salad with peaches and parsnip crisps, etc., etc.). And just to reinforce how subjective all of this is, and how a disgruntled diner tends to remember incidents forever, my booking at Lucas Carton, made from the Australian embassy in Paris and accompanied by six bottles of good Oz plonk, somehow got lost. There was no table available when we arrived, and they were extremely rude. When I did visit a year later, the waiters were still incredibly rude. I hated Ambassade d'Auvergne: dark, depressing and too heavy. Adored Au Trou de Gascon (01 43 44 34 36) until they stuffed up the Belle Époque décor and turned it into a pale-grey, sad place. L'Ambroisie served perfect roast chicken with truffles. I had the best time last year at Le Villaret, Le Dôme, Brasserie Bofinger and Benoît—more my price range these days. Also, it should be said, I cannot eat all that food, and who needs five desserts?

Stephanie Alexander
Best-selling author and former chef

PLACE VENDÔME
FINE DINING (WITH LUXURY HOTEL)

L'Espadon

Chef: Michel Roth
Hôtel Ritz Paris
15 place Vendôme, 75001
01 43 16 30 80
ritzparis.com
Michelin: ★★
GaultMillau: ♥♥♥♥
Menu: 80 (lunch)/225€
À la carte: 165–250€

For as long as one can remember, the Hôtel Ritz Paris' restaurant, **L'Espadon**, had just one star. With both Restaurant le Meurice and Les Ambassadeurs just a short walk away, it was hard to imagine why a hotel guest ever ate in-house. However, the arrival of chef Michel Roth has seen a major turn-around, GaultMillau now rating L'Espadon one of the great dining-rooms of Paris and Michelin adding a second star. The Ritz should never have accepted anything less for this sumptuous space (a gorgeous greenish room with a trompe-l'œil ceiling), given that the hotel's first chef was none other than Auguste Escoffier, one of the most influential in history (and, among other things, inventor of Peach Melba. He also trained Ho Chi Minh as a pastry chef, but that's another story).

Hôtel Ritz Paris

Rating: 5★+
15 place Vendôme, 75001
01 43 16 30 30
ritzparis.com
Rooms: 124
Single: 770–870€
Double: 770–870€
Suites: 37

This legendary hotel has been synonymous with Parisian luxury for more than a century. It was opened in 1898 by César Ritz, its position on the place Vendôme one of the most iconic in Paris. It is also regarded as the most 'feminine' of the top-class hotels, Ritz having been a great lover of women: he reputedly chose apricot lampshades as they best flatter the female skin. The hotel's reputation was greatly enhanced by its partnership with chef Auguste Escoffier, who lifted its restaurant to a culinary pinnacle it has since struggled to equal. Ernest Hemingway did his bit for the **Ritz** legend when staying here, draining the bar and famously writing, 'Whenever I dream of paradise and the beyond, I find myself transported to the Ritz in Paris.' The hotel has also become a cinematic icon, starring in such classics as Billy Wilder's *Love in the Afternoon*, with Audrey Hepburn and Gary Cooper. The swimming pool is considered one of the finest in Paris (along with those at Le Bristol and the Hôtel Costes).

Simon: The Ritz suffers from an inadequate renovation in the 1980s that took too many short-cuts, which in Paris—where, for example, Philippe Starck has made **Restaurant le Meurice** a must-visit experience—is a bit sad. To think this was the best Princess Di could get on her last night. Strangely, I find I think of her often when I'm in the tiny lifts, where the grainy cameras captured her final hours. Your thoughts become twisted for a few moments in those cramped boxes.

....

It's not easy to find (head through the hotel lobbies and down the endless corridors, then turn left), but this tiny bar has as much history as any drinking-hole in Paris. Ernest Hemingway made it famous when he lived on and off at the Ritz in the 1920s. (His books *A Moveable Feast* and *The Sun Also Rises* were both set in Paris during that decade.)

The Bar Hemingway

15 place Vendôme, 75001
01 43 16 30 30
ritzparis.com

Simon: The Bar Hemingway has lost all its Hemingway, though it is still plush and wood-panelled. The main Bar Vendôme has a garden setting, which is worth stopping in for a drink.

20 Non-fiction Books about Paris by Foreigners

A chronological list; only one book per author.

1. *A Moveable Feast* (Ernest Hemingway, 1964)
2. *The Seine* (Anthony Glyn, 1966)
3. *The Diary of Anaïs Nin* (7 volumes, 1966–1974)
4. *Paris* (Julian Green, 1991)
5. *Our Paris: Sketches from Memory* (Edmund White, 1995)
6. *A Corner in the Marais: Memoir of a Paris Neighborhood* (Alex Karmel, 1998)
7. *A French Affair: The Paris Beat 1965–1998* (Mary Blume, 1999)
8. *The Piano Shop on the Left Bank: Discovering a Forgotten Passion in a Paris Atelier* (Thad Carhart, 2000)
9. *Paris to the Moon* (Adam Gopnik, 2000)
10. *Almost French: A New Life in Paris* (Sarah Turnbull, 2002)
11. *Seven Ages of Paris* (Alistair Horne, 2002)
12. *Sixty Million Frenchmen Can't Be Wrong: Why We Love France But Not the French* (Jean-Benoît Nadeau and Julie Barlow, 2003)
13. *True Pleasures: A Memoir of Women in Paris* (Lucinda Holdforth, 2004)
14. *My Life in France* (Julia Child, 2006)
15. *Paris: The Secret History* (Andrew Hussey, 2006)
16. *The Sharper Your Knife, The Less You Cry: Love, Laughter, and Tears in Paris at the World's Most Famous Cooking School* (Kathleen Flinn, 2007)
17. *Paris Then and Now* (Peter and Oriel Caine, 2007)
18. *Naughty Paris: A Lady's Guide to the Sex City* (Heather Stimmler-Hall, 2008)
19. *Paris: Memories of Times Past* (Solange Hando, 2008)
20. *The Hare with Amber Eyes: A Hidden Inheritance* (Edmund de Waal, 2010)

FINE DINING

In a city where many a convent has become a hotel or restaurant, none has been so brilliantly modernised as the 17th-century convent of the Feuillants order, now known as **Carré des Feuillants**. Owner-chef Alain Dutournier employed the artist Alberto Bali to completely redesign the space, and the modern minimalist interior is something to behold. The restaurant is situated on rue Castiglione, between the Jardin des Tuileries and the place Vendôme (how historic can one get?).

Dutournier has been a master chef for more than three decades. Patricia Wells predicted his success in her seminal *The Food Lover's Guide to Paris* (1984), writing: 'Alain Dutournier is, unquestionably, one of Paris' most talented young chefs. Season after season, he continues to astonish and surprise, for he's always creating ...' (She was reviewing Au Trou Gascon in rue Taine, whose name references Dutournier's roots in the South-West.) Wells still thinks him a star.

Carré des Feuillants

Chef: Alain Dutournier
14 rue de Castiglione, 75001
01 42 86 82 82
carredesfeuillants.fr
Michelin: ★★
GaultMillau: 🍴🍴🍴🍴
Menu: 58 (lunch)/
160/220/225€
À la carte: 135–200€

 LUXURY HOTELS

The **Mandarin Oriental** was one of the most anticipated hotel openings of 2011. Michelin-starred chef Thierry Marx (formerly of Château Cordeillan-Bages in Pauillac) will be introducing his award-winning cuisine at his first gastronomic venture in the French capital.

Mandarin Oriental

247–251 rue du faubourg Saint-Honoré, 75001
mandarinoriental.com
Rating: 5★+
Rooms: 99
Single: 850–1050€
Double: 850–1050€
Suites: 39

L'Hôtel Mansart

Rating: 4★
5 rue des Capucines, 75001
01 42 61 50 28
paris-hotel-mansart.com
Rooms: 57
Single: 165–365€
Double: 165–365€

For those who want to be near the place Vendôme but baulk at the prices of the Hôtel Ritz Paris and the Hôtel de Vendôme, the **Mansart** is an excellent choice. Jules Hardouin Mansart was architect to Louis XIV and this classical hotel's refurbishment pays tribute to him. All the rooms represent extraordinary value, but the Superior rooms at 210€ are simply a steal. The somewhat-plain breakfast room is rescued by a fascinating leadlight window. The hotel is superbly located just north of the place Vendôme, and thus close to the Opéra Garnier.

Best Western Premier Opéra Richepanse

Rating: 4★
14 rue du Chevalier de Saint-George, 75001
01 42 60 36 00
richepanse.com
Rooms: 35
Single: 160–400€
Double: 160–400€
Suites: 3

You don't need to go to Prague to find an Art Déco gem; here is a beauty. Built in the early 19th century and recently restored, this boutique hotel is a few steps from the place de la Madeleine. It has three grades of double rooms, with the VIP rooms the finest. Avoid the rather plain Classic rooms, which are only 14 m² (way too small for a four-star hotel). The three spacious suites have views of the Madeleine. Breakfast is served in a vaulted 17th-century salon. Some people might be put off because it is a Best Western hotel, but don't be.

Hôtel de Vendôme

Rating: 5★+
1 place Vendôme, 75001
01 55 04 55 00
hoteldevendome.com
Rooms: 19
Single: 300–550€
Double: 350–700€
Suites: 10

Almost unnoticed, the **Hôtel de Vendôme** has accelerated to the top level of Parisian hotels. Built in 1873 for Pierre Perrin, secretary to Louis XIV, this former townhouse has one of the most exclusive addresses in Paris, on the corner of the place Vendôme and the rue Castiglione. It is not a subtle statement, with chandeliers, burnished wood and gilt greeting you loudly as you enter the rather small lobby. (It is curious how many grand hotels in Europe have small entrances and few public rooms; it often takes a while to get over the initial sense of claustrophobia.) The bedrooms, though, are spacious, even if a little routinely decorated. This is a civilised boutique hotel in a stunning location, and makes a good alternative to the large five-star ones nearby.

PALAIS ROYAL
FINE DINING

. . . .

Le Grand Véfour, which claims to be the oldest restaurant in Paris (there are many claimants), was established in 1784 and formerly known as the Café de Chartres (the name can still be seen on the façade facing the Palais Royal garden). Famous early guests included Napoléon and Joséphine. The interior is in the Louis XVI style, with intricate woodwork and square pillars where glass covers exquisite silk paintings. It has, not surprisingly, been called the most romantic dining-room in Paris.

But things have not all been plain sailing. The restaurant became a ruin after 1905 and it was not until 1948 that Raymond Olivier brought it to back to its former glory. In 1991, chef Guy Martin took over the restaurant, immediately causing a minor scandal by pairing lamb with chocolate (this, after all, is France, not Mexico). He has continued to be the subject of much public debate, losing his third star in 2007 amid claims that he was too often away from his stove overseeing far-flung projects. Most bet that he will regain the missing star soon.

Le Grand Véfour
Chef: Guy Martin
17 rue de Beaujolais, 75001
01 42 96 56 27
grand-vefour.com
Michelin: ★★
GaultMillau: ♕♕♕♕
Menu: 88 (lunch)/268€
À la carte: 215–265€

Paul: For the full dramatic impact of dining at Le Grand Véfour, enter the glorious Palais Royal from rue Saint-Honoré to the south. The sumptuous dining-room can make some people feel intimidated, especially when one's daywear is hastily dispatched behind a velvet curtain and a black dinner jacket is offered instead. (Yes, at least 50 per cent of the suit-and-tie rule still prevailed in July 2007. For whose benefit, one wonders?) But your dread that this is the mere prelude to a parade of antiquated formalities (what next, a slap over the knuckles for holding a fork incorrectly?) is quickly forgotten. Sure, the setting exudes the elegance and pomp of a regal age, but the silver-haired maître d' quickly puts us at ease with his geniality, charm and humour. The dress code, I realise, is just part of the theatre in this monument to an era when refinement was more treasured than it is today (not that we should feel regret at its passing).

Each setting in the intimate dining-room is named after one of the establishment's renowned regulars. Victor Hugo's seat turns out to be prophetic in view of the society scandal that will be played out at the adjoining table over the next couple of hours, where a couple are less-than-discreetly playing out their less-than-secret affair.

We opt for the set lunch menu, which includes an entrée, meat or fish main, dessert and a selection from the breathtaking and grandiose cheese trolley. We have starters of duck pâté and seasonal vegetables, followed by poached Bream and—the standout dish in this limited sampling—a plate of soft and sweet pork done two ways (poached and roasted, if memory serves me correctly). I barely remember dessert, having gorged so much cheese, courtesy of the encouraging waiter, who seemed to have a sixth sense for which cheeses warranted a second, third and subsequent extra portion. We linger for hours, happy to languish in the atmosphere, and in the discovery that formality isn't necessarily stuffy or stulti-fying. It's just a dress rule that doesn't really make sense (then again, how many do?) and is not there to be debated. The comedy of the unfolding soap opera at the next table makes sure of that. Within moments of the diner bravely remov-ing his jacket, the vigilant maître d' arrives with a polite request. You can guess the rest.

32 Novels Set in Paris

A chronological list; only one book per author.

1. *La Cousine Bette*
   (Honoré de Balzac, 1846)

2. *Ange Pitou*
   (Alexandre Dumas, père, 1853)

3. *A Tale of Two Cities*
   (Charles Dickens, 1859)

4. *Les Misérables* (Victor Hugo, 1862)

5. *Le Ventre de Paris*
   (*Savage Paris*, Emile Zola, 1873)

6. *Bel-Ami*
   (Guy de Maupassant, 1885)

7. *Claudine à Paris* (Colette, 1901)

8. *The Ambassadors*
   (Henry James, 1903)

9. *Le Bal du Comte d'Orgel*
   (*The Ball of Count d'Orgel*,
   Raymond Radiguet, 1924)

10. *Le Paysan de Paris*
    (*Paris Peasant*, Louis Aragon, 1926)

11. *L'ombre Chinoise*
    (*Maigret Mystified*,
    Georges Simenon, 1932)

12. *Tropic of Cancer*
    (Henry Miller, 1934)

13. *Nightwood*
    (Djuna Barnes, 1936)

14. *Madeline*
    (Ludwig Bemelmans, 1939)

15. *Good Morning, Midnight*
    (Jean Rhys, 1939)

16. *The Razor's Edge*
    (W Somerset Maugham, 1944)

17. *L'âge de Raison* (*The Age of Reason*,
    Jean-Paul Sartre, 1945)

18. *Madame de …*
    (Louise de Vilmorin, 1951)

19. *Les Mandarins*
    (Simone de Beauvoir, 1954)

20. *Un Certain Sourire* (*A Certain Smile*,
    Françoise Sagan, 1956)

21. *Zazie dans le Métro*
    (Raymond Queneau, 1959)

22. *La Cœur en Désordre* (*The Passionate
    Ones*, Anne Rolland-Jacquet, 1963)

23. *The Merry Month of May*
    (James Jones, 1971)

24. *Rue des Boutiques Obscures* (*Missing
    Person*, Patrick Modiano, 1978)

25. *La Vie mode d'emploi* (*Life: A User's
    Manual*, Georges Perec, 1978)

26. *The Man Who Lived at the Ritz*
    (A.E. Hotchner, 1981)

27. *Natural Victims*
    (Isabel Eberstadt, 1984)

28. *Le Divorce* (Diane Johnson, 1997)

29. *Les Particules Élémentaires* (*Atomised*,
    Michel Houellebecq, 1999)

30. *Ensemble, c'est tout* (*Hunting and
    Gathering*, Anna Gavalda, 2004)

31. *L'élégance du Hérisson*
    (*The Elegance of the Hedgehog*,
    Muriel Barbery, 2006)

32. *Harm's Way*
    (Celia Walden, 2008)

LOUVRE

CAFÉ

. . . .

Le Café Marly

Cour Napoléon, Palais du
Louvre, 93 rue de Rivoli,
75001
01 49 26 06 60
no website
À la carte: 40–70€

On an arcaded terrace of the Musée du Louvre, Jean-Louis
Costes' **Le Café Marly** overlooks the courtyard highlighted
(or ruined) by IM Pei's modernist glass pyramids. While
eating an expensive club sandwich, you can count the glass
panes in the main pyramid and see if Dan Brown got it right
(he didn't). The simple food is pleasant enough, but the view
is sublime.

BAR

. . . .

Le Fumoir

6 rue de l'Amiral de Coligny,
75001
01 42 92 00 24
lefumoir.com

Opened by Rita Blade, an ex-mannequin, **Le Fumoir** is a
haven filled with sweet nostalgia ... and very nice drinks!

Shannon: Finding a good stand-alone bar in the central area of Paris, close to
all the major hotels, can be a challenge. This quite large 'everything to everyone'-
style establishment is a refreshing and convenient change to the opulent and
bustling Champs-Elysées. The front area is a meet-and-greet cocktail bar. There
is a large seating area to the right, with well-appointed furnishings, including
mafi flooring. The bar has a great wine list, French and Flemish beers, and
classic cocktails such as brandy sours and margaritas. To the back of the eating
area there is a quiet room/library with a more extensive menu. Here there are
communal tables for families with kids. Free Wi-Fi streams around the bar.

HOTEL

The **Hôtel Britannique** is English through and through, which is not surprising given it was established by a British family (in the 1860s). The guest rooms are small but comfy, full of comforting fabrics and cushions and plush drapes. It is located on the avenue Victoria to the left of the busy and charmless place Châtelet, south of Les Halles. Michelin doesn't always print that part of the street in its guidebook maps, so check the directions carefully before setting out.

Hôtel Britannique
Rating: 3★
20 avenue Victoria, 75001
01 42 33 74 59
hotel-britannique.com
Rooms: 39
Single: 160–230€
Double: 180–230€

Liz and Craig: This was our first hotel in Paris, recommended to us by parents who had stayed there many years earlier. The hotel is small, but the rooms are well appointed. The guest rooms are inviting, especially those overlooking avenue Victoria: they are light and airy but, like many in Paris, not air-conditioned.

There is a beautiful traditional-style lounge, set below street level, where we would start the evening with a glass of champagne. The breakfast room is one of the best we have experienced. It is small, though the tables are well spaced. However, it is the selection of foods that stands out: boiled eggs cooked to your preference; yoghurts in glass jars, served with homemade preserves; and a wide choice of cereals, toasts, cheese and meats. When we initially travelled on a small budget, we could feast ourselves on breakfast and forget lunch!

We have stayed at this hotel twice. It is in a great location and the hotel staff were very helpful in recommending a number of good local restaurants.

LES HALLES

BRASSERIE

Tourists tend to think Paris never sleeps, but it is actually an early-to-bed town where most restaurants shut their doors indecently early. The ultimate Parisian brasserie could therefore be said to be this fabulous Belle Époque eatery, which has never closed its doors since 1947. It is busy at all hours of the day and night, and is the perfect place for a pick-me-up snack at 4 a.m. You can get seafood, steak and a traditional French onion soup, but it is most famous for the many pork dishes, including, of course, its namesake: pigs' trotters.

Au Pied de Cochon
6 rue Coquillière, 75001
01 40 13 77 00
pieddecochon.com
Menu: 27€
À la carte: 40–100€

Shannon's Parisian Recipes

Some Parisian Classics

I have not observed in any other city in the world the extent to which, in Paris, different areas have very strong identities, with restaurants grouped according to the regions their cooking come from. Even Tokyo, for all its amazing variety of food and ingredients, does not have the same cultural diversity. Each food region in France has a history that has helped shape its people. Take Alsace: Alsatians are very proud and protective of their food and wine culture, and are equally proud to share and export it. Hence, Paris has built up a huge array of restaurants featuring Alsatian specialties such as choucroute and beer-on-tap, and healthy quantities of foie-gras terrine washed down with a late-harvest pinot gris. Places like Brasserie Bofinger (Alsatian influences) and Benoît (Lyonnaise) are great examples of traditional, regional cuisines that flourish in Paris today.

The recipes interspersed throughout this book are for me what French food is all about. And Paris is the only place in France where all these dishes and ingredients can be consumed in one meal—if one has the stomach and time.

Beef Tartare with Quail Eggs and *Pommes Pailles*

Beef tartare has been replicated around the world, and bastardised around the world too. Traditional beef tartare is made with top-quality meat: it really should be the finest fillet, preferably the cut used for châteaubriand steak, but seems to have been replaced by secondary cuts. There is also a tendency now to cut the meat less finely, but I believe it needs to be well minced: that way, you get all that flavour out of the meat. The best way to get a good beef tartare is to have it 'mixed' at the table or in the kitchen 'à la minute'; it's all about freshness.

Typically added in are capers, chopped onion or shallot, parsley, Tabasco sauce, Dijon mustard, and sometimes raw egg yolk. A modern way I like to make it is to add egg mayonnaise. I like to add a spoonful of tomato ketchup, which is accepted. At Le Châteaubriand recently, I had a tartare with some fresh spiced tomato purée, which I really enjoyed.

Beef tartare is traditionally accompanied by thinly sliced baguette, which has been toasted with butter or olive oil in the manner of a croûton; or by *pommes gaufrettes*, which are very thinly sliced and then deep-fried. Here I've suggested *pommes pailles* (potato straws).

350 g beef fillet, finely chopped
50 g capers, drained and finely chopped
80 g cornichons, chopped finely
1 shallot, chopped finely
50 ml tomato ketchup
2 tablespoons mayonnaise
½ tablespoon Dijon mustard
1 tablespoon Worcestershire sauce
2 drops Tabasco sauce
1 tablespoon chopped parsley
salt and pepper

POMMES PAILLES
1 large Désirée
(or good frying) potato
vegetable oil for deep-frying
salt

GARNISH
4 quail eggs, boiled
salt
50 ml white wine vinegar

To make the tartare mix, combine the beef, capers, cornichons, shallots, ketchup, mayonnaise, mustard and Worcestershire sauce in a bowl. Mix well until evenly combined. Add the Tabasco and parsley, and season to taste with salt and pepper.

For the *pommes pailles*, slice the potato very thinly, using a mandolin slicer. Stack the slices and cut into very thin bâtons (julienne). Rinse in cold water, then pat dry on absorbent paper.

Preheat a deep-fryer to 180ºC, or half-fill a small saucepan with vegetable oil and place over medium heat. Deep-fry the potato straws in batches until golden-brown and crispy. Drain on absorbent paper and season with salt.

To cook the quail eggs, place 500 ml of water in a small saucepan and season with the salt and vinegar. Bring to a rapid boil, add the quail eggs and cook for exactly 90 seconds. Remove from pan and place in iced water to stop the cooking process. Once the eggs are cold, lift from the water and carefully remove the shells. Set eggs aside until required.

To serve, divide the tartare mixture into four equal portions. Pack one portion into an egg ring in the centre of a round white plate (or spoon neatly onto plate with a serving spoon), ensuring the mixture is smooth on top. Remove the ring, if using, and repeat process with the three remaining portions. Arrange an egg on each plate and accompany with some *pommes pailles*.

Serves 4

Bourse

Passage 53, named after the alley in which it is situated, is the hottest restaurant in Paris. Chef Shinichi Sato (ex Astrance) is dazzling with his contemporary cuisine, using the finest produce sourced by owner and maître d' Guillaume Guedj, stepson of Hugo Mugaritz, the most famous butcher in town. Sato hates menus, so you'll get what he decides. Expect, though, dishes like white truffles on a slow-cooked egg or a Cévennes onion with slices of chorizo.

Passage 53
Chef: Sinichi Sato
53 passage des Panoramas, 75002
01 42 33 04 35
passage53.com
Michelin: ★★
GaultMillau: ♟♟
Menu: 53 (lunch)/95€

BRASSERIES, BISTROS, NEIGHBOURHOOD RESTAURANTS

This classic bistro was opened in 1890, and since 2002 has been run by Alain Ducasse and his partners. As the name implies, it serves hearty Lyonnaise food, with a lot of pork dishes, including *cervelas pistaché* (cured sausage with pistachios). The wine list is strong on Burgundy and Vallée de Rhône.

Aux Lyonnais
Chef: Frédéric Thévenet
32 rue Saint-Marc, 75002
01 42 96 65 04
auxlyonnais.com
Michelin: Bib Gourmand
GaultMillau: ♟♟
Menu: 28€
À la carte: 40–52€

Matt: It is a very simple bistro, with easy service and an impressive wine list. You go for the classic dishes: foie-gras terrine with great brioches and some chutney jam; eggs and jelly; veal with a persillade; quenelles of fish; and a filet mignon with fresh girolles (it was that time of the year). My wife had a veal blanquette, which was to die for. It is really simple, easy food.

After handing over Buerehiesel in Strasbourg to his son Eric in 2007, Antoine Westermann came to Paris to revitalise several restaurants. One is this famous brasserie, where the Goncourt literary awards are handed out each year. It has been completely renovated and the food is back to the standard of the days when Patricia Wells raved about it in her *Food Lovers Guide to Paris* (1984).

Drouant
Chef: Antoine Westermann
16 place Gaillon, 75002
01 42 65 15 16
drouant.com
GaultMillau: ♟♟
Menu: 43€ (lunch)
À la carte: 68–89€

La Fontaine Gaillon

Chef: Laurent Audiot
1 rue Gaillon, 75002
01 47 42 63 22
la-fontaine-gaillon.com
GaultMillau: ☻☻
Menu: 43€
À la carte: 60–90€

La Fontaine Gaillon is a glamorous restaurant owned by actors Gérard Depardieu and Carole Bouquet. The building was constructed in 1672 and has been owned by a series of historic personages ever since. Opened in 2003, the restaurant bucks the trend of ultra-modern food (even mocking it on the website as 'Coke Chicken' and 'Vache-qui-rit Granita'). You are more likely to eat *Pressé de queue de bœuf aux blancs de poireaux* (pressed beef tail with leeks) and *Cochon de lait farci aux herbes et rôti à la broche* (milk-fed pork stuffed with herbs and roasted on a skewer). The impressive cellar includes, not surprisingly, wines from Depardieu's own vineyards. The chef, Laurent Audiot, was formerly at Marius et Janette.

Le Vaudeville

Chef: Jean-François Thorel
29 rue Vivienne, 75002
01 40 20 04 62
vaudevilleparis.com
Menu: 30€
À la carte: 40–85€

Overlooking the Bourse (the historic Paris stock exchange), **Le Vaudeville** is another beautiful Art Déco brasserie. The bustle inside is inviting, the battle to get a waiter's attention thrilling, the food invariably heart-warming. The *Tranche morue cuite à la planche, purée de pommes de terre à l'huile de truffe* (Cod with truffled mash on the side) is unbeatable. On a warm night, try to get one of the few tables on the tiny terrace lining the street.

Scott: This is a favourite brasserie of Pierre Rissient, one of the dearest friends the film industry has ever had (he helped discover Jane Campion, among many others). Le Vaudeville is uncorrupted by the floods of tourists that have convinced too many restaurants to degrade their standards. This is pure Paris and one of my first ports of call on arriving.

 BAR

Harry's New York Bar

5 rue Daunou, 75002
01 42 61 71 14
harrys-bar.fr

The name may make this sound like a place to avoid, but **Harry's** is a classic American bar with white-coated waiters and a long list of butane-strength cocktails. The Bloody Mary is said to have been invented here.

On the rue de la Paix, which joins the place Vendôme with the Opéra Garnier, stands the **Park Hyatt Paris—Vendôme**. Consisting of five Haussmannian buildings, now restructured into one, this hotel has skilfully become part of Parisian heritage rather than defacing it. It was the brainchild of Paris-based architect and interior designer Edward Tuttle, well known for his design of luxury boats and for his work on opulent Asian hotels (Amanresorts in Bangkok, the Chedi in Phuket). The hotel is an eclectic mix of classicism, Louis XVI and Art Déco. Mostly, though, it is strikingly fresh and modern. The bedrooms are works of Oriental-inspired art, in the suites small glass-shaded lamps lighting up the lacquered wood-panelled walls and stark-white bed coverings. The limestone bathrooms have heated floors. For those in need of relaxation, there is Le Spa.

Park Hyatt Paris—Vendôme

Rating: 5★
5 rue de la Paix, 75002
01 58 71 12 34
paris.vendome.hyatt.com
Rooms: 168
Single: 630–820€
Double: 630–820€
Suites: 36

Shannon: I haven't stayed here yet. I find that its yacht architecture really suits Paris. Park Hyatt hotels are famous for not having big open spaces, rather offering plenty of smaller spaces that you can hide away in to read a newspaper or escape the crowds. You can obtain good rates through travel agencies or on the Internet.

A few steps from the place Vendôme, the **Hôtel Westminster** has a very impressive façade. The hotel was named for the Duke of Westminster, who used this building as his personal residence in the 1840s. The lobby is rather American in feel and is unusual for its spaciousness. The Duke's Bar has an enormous fireplace and is packed with green leather chairs. As for the guest rooms, there are a wide variety of period styles, from Louis XV and XVI to Napoléon III and Regency; the rates are surprisingly low. There is a fitness club that overlooks the roofs of Paris, and a Moorish hamman (steam bath), where Australians will feel at home as it is scented with eucalyptus. The Westminster is also home to the one-star Le Céladon restaurant, situated in the ravishingly pretty Regency-style dining-room-cum-library: the subdued lighting makes it a very romantic place to dine—and you can dine well here.

Hôtel Westminster

Rating: 5★
13 rue de la Paix, 75002
01 42 61 57 46
warwickwestminsteropera.com
Rooms: 102
Single: 270–350€
Double: 270–350€
Suites: 22

Chantal's Paris

Rive Droite

Le Restaurant du Palais Royal
110 Galerie de Valois, Jardin du Palais Royal, 75001
01 40 20 00 27
This is my favourite restaurant for lunch, sitting on the terrace in the gardens of the Palais Royal. It is medium priced and elegant. Definitely go if there is great weather!

'Little Tokyo'
rue Sainte-Anne, 75001
Begin your trip down 'Little Tokyo' at the junction of rue Sainte-Anne and rue Thérèse, where you will find a myriad of Japanese inn-style restaurants serving such favourites as *mabo-don*, *gyoza* and even *katsu-don*. Join the locals in the queue for a seat at many of these small but popular restaurants.

Aux Lyonnais
32 rue Saint-Marc, 75002
01 42 96 65 04
Michelin: Bib Gourmand
An institution that opened in 1889, Aux Lyonnais is now the small unpretentious bistro of Michelin-star chef Alain Ducasse. With classic dishes from Lyon, it is not good for vegetarians but is for those who like offal!

Chez Georges
1 rue du Mail, 75002
01 42 60 07 11
Classic restaurant (a must-go), only open Monday–Friday and very popular with the locals. It is medium priced, with excellent food and wine, but you definitely need to book. It is close to the place des Victoires, near Opéra.

La Fontaine Gaillon
1 rue Gaillon, 75002
01 47 42 63 22
Owned by actor Gérard Depardieu, La Fontaine Gaillon is a medium-priced, elegant restaurant just off the avenue de l'Opéra. It is wonderful to sit outside on the terrace in the evening for dinner in summer.

Restaurant Julien
16 rue du Faubourg Saint-Denis, 75010
01 47 70 12 06
Julien is a charming restaurant away from the tourist spotlight. It has an authentic setting truly representative of a bygone era, with a classic Art Nouveau interior and a floral-glass roof. Try the homemade goose cassoulet or slivers of duck foie gras panfried with green lentils from Le Puy-en-Velay.

Le Marais
(one of my favourite neighbourhoods)

MARKETS
The market, which is a 'must-do', is located on boulevard Richard Lenoir, and is open on Thursdays and Sundays until around 2.30 p.m. The closest Métro is Bastille and it is very close to place des Vosges in the Marais. It is one of the loveliest ways to enjoy a morning and then prepare a picnic lunch … or take the cheat's option and savour some of the takeaway gourmet treats on offer.

RESTAURANTS
L'Ami Louis
32 rue Vertbois, 75003
01 48 87 77 48
Located near Métro Arts et Métiers in the Marais, this famous bistro is small and quaint, with gingham curtains and French classics. L'Ami Louis is quite expensive, but a wonderful gastronomic experience.

Chez Janou
2 rue Roger Verlomme, 75003
01 42 72 28 41
This busy, fun and inexpensive restaurant is just behind the place des Vosges. There are two dinner settings at 8 p.m. and 10 p.m. It is also open for lunch. Chez Janou was my local café when I was living in Paris. It is very casual and great for Sunday night dinner or supper. Go more for the atmosphere than the food.

Le Petit Marché
9 rue de Béarn, 75003
01 42 76 00 03
Also in one of the side streets off the place des Vosges, this has great food, is medium priced and has a casual setting. It is very popular with locals.

Brasserie Bofinger
5 rue de la Bastille, 75004
01 42 72 87 82
Located in the Marais and close to Bastille, Brasserie Bofinger is a charming Art Nouveau bistro with French classics.

OTHER MARAIS 'FINDS'
Good streets to stroll, with plenty of cafés and casual lunch spots:

rue des Rosiers
World's 'best' falafels, plus Jewish pastry shops.

rue des Francs Bourgeois
For shopping and cafés; closed on Mondays.

place du Marché Sainte-Cathérine
For casual restaurants; a group of restaurants placed around a square.

rue Saint-Paul and the little streets near Church St Gervais
There is a charming romantic restaurant called Chez Julien, just opposite the Seine.

rue Vielle du Temple
Lots of cafés, with a great Italian ice-cream place, Amorino (no 31), plus a restaurant with an open grill, Robert et Louise (no 64). Try and book a table upstairs.

rue Saint-Louis-en-l'Île
Just a 10-minute walk across the Seine from the rue de Rivoli, this is a great place to have a coffee near the bridge that links to Notre Dame, along with a famous Berthillon ice-cream.

Rive Gauche
Brasserie Lipp
151 boulevard St Germain, 75006
St Germain des Prés
01 45 48 53 91
Brasserie Lipp is a brasserie with lots of pomp; a real institution. The waiters are generally rude, but the place is good for people watching. It is across the road from the famous cafés Les Deux Magots and Café de Flore.

Oil

It is impossible to cook well without fine oil, and Paris has some of the best traditionally produced fruit and seed oils.

Huilerie Artisanale J. Leblanc et Fils

Since 1878
6 rue Jacob, 75006
01 46 34 61 55
huile-leblanc.com

What else would you expect in the prettiest street in Paris but one of the world's finest makers of stone-ground oils. Anyone who has used Leblanc oils (the walnut and pine-kernel are a must) knows how great they are. The shop also sells soap, mustards and vinegar. All the produce is manufactured according to century-old practices in Burgundy.

La Tête dans les Olives

2 rue Saint Marthe, 75010
09 51 31 33 34
latetedanslesolives.com

Cédric Casanova specialises in Sicilian oils.

Ute: All the really interesting chefs, Iñaki Aizpitarte included, use Cédric's carefully chosen products. He is a fairly eccentric, wonderful, passionate man who runs the tiniest shop in a very offbeat part of town.

Classic Bouillabaisse with Rouille and Garlic Croûtons

The manner in which bouillabaisse is prepared varies between towns, and I think that is a huge part of its charm. Ingredients, too, can vary according to the local fisherman's catch (for the non-shellfish component, small, oily fish are best). This is a soup hearty enough to be served as a main meal. Rouille is a red garlic mayonnaise.

BOUILLABAISSE
5 Red Mullet carcasses
500 g crab shells
500 g crayfish shells
1 carrot, diced
1 stick celery, diced
2 onions, diced
1 bulb fennel, diced
1 leek, diced
1 head garlic, chopped in half
3 sprigs thyme
2 bay leaves
pinch of cayenne pepper
2 pinches saffron threads
4 star anise
2 cups dry white wine
150 ml pastis (Pernod)
150 ml dry vermouth (Noilly Prat)
5 ripe tomatoes, roughly chopped
150 g tomato paste
1 cup olive oil
salt and freshly ground pepper
12 cups fish stock

ROUILLE
1 large sebago potato
1 bird's-eye chilli
pinch of sea salt
2 cloves garlic, crushed
pinch of saffron threads
3 egg yolks
200 ml olive oil
juice of ½ lemon

GARLIC CROÛTONS
1 sourdough baguette
2½ tablespoons extra-virgin olive oil
1 clove garlic, peeled
1 cup finely grated Gruyère cheese

First prepare the soup. Remove the eyes from the Mullet carcasses (they will impart a bitter flavour to the soup). In a large container, combine the mullet, crab and crayfish shells with the vegetables, herbs, spices, wine, pastis, vermouth, tomatoes, tomato paste and 100 ml of the olive oil. Cover, and leave to marinate in the refrigerator for 24 hours. Strain and reserve the bones and marinade separately.

Heat the remaining olive oil in a heavy-based saucepan, add the drained fish bones, shells and vegetables and cook for 4–5 minutes or until the bones are golden. Season with salt and pepper. Add the reserved marinade and reduce over low heat until it evaporates. Add the fish stock and simmer for 2 hours. Using a hand blender, roughly purée the soup (do not be too concerned about the bones and shells, as they will be strained out). Pass the soup through a coarse sieve, then through a fine sieve

To make the rouille, preheat the oven to 180°C. Place the potato (unpeeled) on a baking tray and bake in preheated oven for about 30 minutes or until cooked through. Remove from the oven, allow to cool, and then peel. Using a mortar and pestle, crush the chilli, salt, garlic and potato to a paste. Transfer to a bowl, beat in the saffron and egg yolks, and then gradually whisk in the olive oil (in three stages, to stop the mixture splitting). Continue to whisk until it resembles a thick mayonnaise. Add the lemon juice and set aside for 2 hours before using.

To make the croûtons, slice the baguette into thin rounds on the diagonal. Place on a tray and drizzle with olive oil, then put in the preheated oven for 10 minutes or until golden-brown. Remove, and rub one side of each slice with garlic. Reserve croûtons along with the grated cheese.

To serve, reheat the soup and serve with rouille, garlic croûtons and Gruyère cheese on the side.

Serves 8

Shannon's Favourite Parisian Treats

Wine Stores

Though some try, it is difficult to enjoy great food—from eating a simple picnic to visiting a three-star restaurant—without pairing it with great wine. Fortunately, Paris is filled with excellent wine shops, even if they can be hard to find, discrete exteriors giving no hint of the treasures within.

Caves Augé

Since 1850
116 boulevard Haussmann, 75008
01 45 22 16 97
cavesauge.com

One of the joys of Paris, this wine store has an astonishing range of the very best: Latour, Romanée-Conti, d'Yquem and much more. If you feel as if you have walked into the past, you're right: this shop hasn't changed since it opened in 1850; only the labels and vintages are different. Apart from stocking all the great names, Augé highlights new discoveries and organic wines.

Caves Taillevent

199 rue du faubourg Saint-Honoré, 75008
01 45 61 14 09
taillevent.com

If you adored what you drank at Taillevent the night before, you can return the following morning to raid its boutique cellar. It is particularly strong on great and rare Burgundy. Some consider it the finest wine cellar in Paris.

La Dernière Goutte

6 rue Bourbon-le-Château, 75006
01 43 29 11 62
ladernieregoutte.net

Run by an affable American, this gorgeous wine shop on the Left Bank is tiny but full of treasures, particularly lesser-known wines from Languedoc-Roussillon and Corbières. When you don't feel as if you have three hours to spend selecting a wine, this is the place to go. Whatever you grab will be delicious.

Lavinia

3 boulevard de la Madeleine, 75001
01 42 97 20 24
lavinia.fr

A few steps from the place de la Madeleine (and thus in competition with Hédiard and Nicolas, among others) is Lavinia. Unlike the historic Caves Augé, this is modern Paris, with the wines sitting in polished metal racks and pigeonholes, the displays curved as if designed by the man responsible for the circular terminal at Charles de Gaulle airport. (Lavinia's architect was actually Morales de la Peña.) It offers 65 000 different wines including 2000 from outside France. There is a restaurant where the wine is served at the same price as in the shop.

Legrand Filles et Fils
Since 1880
1 rue de Banque, 75002
01 42 60 07 12
caves-legrand.com

The U-shaped bar in Legrand Filles et Fils is as romantic a spot as you will find in Paris, glass in hand. Most wine-lovers haunt places that have a nose for the new and the great, a reputation Legrand has long proudly held. It mostly follows the French tradition—pretty well abandoned in the New World—of storing wine flat so that it doesn't go off by drying out the cork. The only challenge is that the wine is stacked up very high walls, which leaves you wondering what is tucked away up there, just out of view. Legrand is well known for sourcing rare bottles from around the world on request.

Nicolas
Since 1822
31 place de la Madeleine, 75008
01 42 68 00 16
Also at (among others):
142 rue de Rivoli, 75001
30 rue Rambuteau, 75003
5 rue Monge, 75005
21 rue des Archives, 75004
13 rue de Buci, 75006
nicolas.com

With countless stores across Paris (and a total of 522 in France), this excellent chain has plenty of wines to choose from, with a good number regularly discounted. Nicolas tends to be looked down on by wine snobs, which is silly given the enormous range of famous and rare wines on offer here.

Le Marais

Ambassade d'Auvergne

3RD

Chef: Françoise Petrucci
22 rue du Grenier Saint-Lazare,
75003
01 42 72 31 22
ambassade-auvergne.com
Michelin: Bib Gourmand
GaultMillau: ♙
Menu: 28/38/55/65€
À la carte: 32–48€

This unofficial ambassador for all that is good from the Auvergne—*aligot* (whipped potatoes with Cantal cheese), in particular—has long been a cherished part of the Parisian culinary landscape. Some think it has become too popular, even a little touristy, but few deny it is a wonderful place to visit and enjoy both the food and the sense of theatre. Certainly, it seems impossible these days—even at the great restaurant Bras—to be served *aligot* without some theatre attached. Sometimes with one Michelin star and sometimes not, Ambassade d'Auvergne is an undisputed star of the 3rd arrondissement.

Shannon: This is a great bistro, which is located very close to the Centre Georges Pompidou. It is not in the prettiest part of the Marais, so don't expect a romantic walk from your auberge—it's a bit more quotidian than that.

Ambassade is the place on which I modelled Bistro Vue, because it reminds me of the old Paris; the dining-room dates back more than 200 years. It has the great asset of a very good maître d', who commands the floor with great care and integrity. But it is not a place where you should expect outstanding food or service; instead you get *real* food and *real* service; the wine list is modest, yet complete. Come for lunch, book lateish and make no plans afterwards.

I tried a bowl of sautéed girolles and duck leg with *aligot*. The food is heavy, but this is a great dish for those who love wild mushrooms. For dessert, it was a simple burnt cream with fresh *fraises des bois* (wild strawberries). There was also a poached peach with vanilla syrup—simple and satisfying. I loved the magnums of Armagnac that are offered to each table after 2.30 p.m., and the great prices.

L'Ami Louis

32 rue Vertbois, 75003
01 48 87 77 48
no website
À la carte: 120–180€

On one of the least pretty streets in Paris sits one of the world's most expensive bistros, **L'Ami Louis**. It is a legendary place— everyone famous has eaten here, from Chirac and Clinton to Gorbachev and Francis Ford Coppola—and it is always packed, often with American billionaires. The roast chicken with a side dish of shoestring potatoes (the pile is so high and delicate it almost looks like spun sugar) has long been considered as perfect as a simple meal can be. (Some insiders, though, insist you must order the potato galette instead.) Michelin has never liked it, though; and GaultMillau, once its most passionate advocate, doesn't list it any more. This has not deterred the restaurant's devoted fans—especially after a lacerating review by A.A. Gill in *Vanity Fair* (April 2011), where he called it the 'worst restaurant in the world'. A-list Hollywood is outraged.

Matt: I ate at L'Ami Louis twice on my last trip to Paris. Absolutely brilliant. Being a cook, I just love it for what it is: there's no fuss—they just put the food down in front of you. If you order foie gras, you get a slab of foie gras. If you order snails, you get a massive bowl of snails. It's total, absolute excess. The beef ribs for two are just unbelievable. Massive portions. And the chicken, too. You pay for it, obviously.

Every time I go to Paris I go there. There is always someone famous there: my wife was trying to take a photograph of me and a mate, and she asked us to leave a gap between us. We couldn't work out why, so we turned around and there was Matt Damon sitting behind us. It also has an amazing cellar.

Over the years, I've got to know the guys a little bit, and the last time I was there I went underground and saw the vaults: the tunnels are so small you can't stand up in them. The Romanée-Contis and so on were absolutely amazing. L'Ami Louis is the place I always tell people not to miss.

Near the place des Vosges, this is a classic French bistro. Full of film posters, it has even made a cheeky film about itself which runs on its cute website. The food is traditional bistro: *Petit chévre rôti au romarin, Moules gratinés à la provençale, Entrecôte bistro, Brandade de morue, Tartlette aux fruits*. The wine list is strong on Côtes du Rhône and de Provence and, most unusually, serves more than 80 pastis, from the traditional Ricard to some obscure labels, and a 72 per cent absinthe.

Chez Janou

2 rue Roger Verlomme,
75003
01 42 72 28 41
chezjanou.com
Menu: 15 (lunch)/24€
À la carte: 25–35€

3ʳᵈ

Shannon: I sat outside with my friend Simon looking at all the university students acting as if they were the only people in the world. Simple cocktails, beer or wine are the go. I found the food too big in size, and old-fashioned, but I wanted to include this place because the atmosphere is fantastic. Sit outside to capture Parisian life; sit inside if you prefer a longer and more intimate meal. The décor reminded me very much of Melbourne. The Toulouse-Lautrec posters are the cherry on top for what is my favourite neighbourhood hangout. The set-lunch menu is good value at 14€, but do please remember that this place is for atmosphere over food. You will love it.

Matt's Favourite Parisian Treats

Kebabs

The kebab may not at first be thought of as French food (and hence not within the ambit of this book), but it became part of the culinary scene after France established colonies in Africa, and with the arrival of Middle Eastern immigrants.

One great experience of Paris is to have a kebab in the Marais. They are the best kebabs in the world. There and in Berlin. They are the perfect snack if you are going to have a big dinner that night. In New York, you can always go and have sushi for lunch, but in France I don't think they do sushi that well. So, it's good to walk around the Marais and then go to the area around rue des Rosiers, where there are about 10 kebab shops. The queues are unbelievable, but the kebabs are to die for.

BAR

Andy Whaloo
69 rue des Gravilliers,
75003
01 42 71 20 38

The cute name of this bar, seemingly a word-play on the artist Andy Warhol, is actually Arabic for 'I who have nothing'. Regarded as having the best mojitos in Paris, this bar was opened by the owner of London's Momo and Sketch. In the heart of the Marais, it serves Turkish and Moroccan mezze and wines. In summer, you can sit in the small courtyard, but will need to book.

 LUXURY HOTELS

Murano Urban Resort
Rating: 5★
13 boulevard du Temple,
75003
01 42 71 20 00
muranoresort.com
Rooms: 49
Single: 310–900€
Double: 310–900€
Suites: 2

The **Murano** is a challenger to the Hôtel Fouquet's Barrière as the trendiest luxury hotel in Paris. It is also one of the most controversial (and most disliked). Located, rather surprisingly for luxury accommodation, in the Marais, it bills itself as an urban resort, not a hotel.

The hotel entrance is a blaze of white marble, steel and glass; in your room, however, you can change the colour scheme to match your mood, from sky-blue to sunshine-yellow or emerald. Guides like *Wallpaper** rave about the Murano's design, but others feel it has been at the expense of common sense. The gym is small and located in a basement room, but is adequate for those who want to keep fit or counter any overindulgences provoked by the restaurant recommendations in this book. If you do fall in love with the place, you will be pleased to know there is also a Murano Resort (not Urban this time) in Marrakech.

Shannon: I was attracted to the Murano by a fabulous image on their website of a room with an individual lap pool. Paris always inspires me to be physically active, so the lap pool would have been a great benefit. Unfortunately, it was not a benefit that came with the room I was allocated. The gym was small and located in a basement room, but was adequate for those who want to counter any overindulgences provoked by the restaurant recommendations in this book.

My room—a Murano Room—was quite spacious, the bathroom nearly one-third of the total space, with a central, stand-alone bathtub. I did find the rooms lacked character, however: they were stark and cold. I was also most annoyed by the bed, which sat on a plinth and I had to remember to take care and not to sprain my ankle when jumping out of bed. The room had only one window, overlooking the courtyard two floors below, where there were plenty of parties going on. Room service was non-existent.

The hotel guests we met in the public areas were very positive and there was a great atmosphere there. Those we spoke to commented particularly favourably on the hotel's restaurant, which serves Mediterranean-style food.

I really liked the area around the Murano, which is a good springboard for exploring the Marais. The street it's in is a bit dingy, but provides good insight into day-to-day Parisian life.

Madeleine: To ensure the myth that the French are as famous for their rudeness as their pastries is not needlessly perpetuated, I would recommend that first-time visitors to Paris avoid this hotel—or at least its '24-hour room service'. My request for a 7 a.m. espresso from said service was met with 'Non, we no do coffee yet.' I would have queried this had they not immediately terminated the call. So profound was my bewilderment I almost tipped them!

The Murano, all brilliant white exteriors and Art Déco flourishes, well placed on the boulevard du Temple and central to many great tourist hubs, is über-stylish. Therein perhaps lies its fundamental flaw: the place is all style and no substance: so busy are the staff playing cool they seem to have forgotten they are actually running a hotel.

Our junior suite was lush and spacious, but would want to be at 1100€ a night. The rooms are awash with avant-garde detail, but the slate floors remain resolutely chilly. The mammoth bathroom, with its magnificent bath, while impressive in scale, swallows the entire studio space; and soon small details, like the fact the rotating Bang & Olufsen television doesn't rotate far enough to be watched from the bed, start to grate. The bar and dining spaces on the ground floor are plush and costly, with menus to match, proving the perfect congregation point for Paris's nouveau riche and upwardly mobile. The array of specialty vodkas and cocktails on offer had us dazzled, but parting with 70€ for a single shot left Shannon a little dazed and confused. Poor acoustics and a badly thought-out floor plan ensure that guests get to join in the Murano's frequent all-night parties, even when they are in their rooms trying to sleep! When at 5 a.m. we finally complained to the concierge about the fracas below, we were summarily dismissed with a few conciliatory sighs. A similarly condescending reception met our 'concerns' as we were departing. You cannot buy attitude like that! In hindsight, considering the prices the Murano commands for fairly poor service, perhaps the abundance of attitude is precisely what you are paying for.

....

Murano Urban Resort Bar

13 boulevard du Temple, 75003
01 42 71 20 00
muranoresort.com

Brightly coloured egg-shaped chairs are ranged along a lengthy grey bench and a ledge topped with an array of empty green bottles, above which are video screens. You need to twist your head to talk to anyone.

Shannon: This is a great bar, like Sydney's Establishment but smaller and with cooler background music. On a Sunday afternoon, there is live music for the hip young crowd. The food is really quite good. (The Murano has a sister bar, Ice Kube, in the 18th arrondissement; the hotel driver can take you there.)

For decades the **Pavillon de la Reine** ruled unchallenged over the Marais and Beaubourg districts. It is located on the northern edge of arguably the most perfect space in Paris: the place des Vosges. Built by Henry IV and opened in 1612, the arcaded square is filled with history. And the hotel makes full use of its position and past: the entrance, its high walls completely covered in vines, with splashes of scarlet from window boxes, is one of the most enticing in Paris. There is a beautiful library-retreat-cum-bar, with a huge fireplace, off the lobby. Some of the rooms have four-poster beds and, if you are lucky, exposed-beam ceilings (though these may be painted, as was the fashion at one time). Lovingly if conservatively refurbished in a country-house style, this is a haven of calm and restful space in the claustrophobic jumble and noise of the Marais' back streets and half-timbered houses. Bernard Pacaud's three-star L'Ambroisie restaurant is just across the square (in the 4th).

Hôtel Pavillon de la Reine

Rating: 5★+
28 place des Vosges, 75003
01 40 29 19 19
pavillon-de-la-reine.com
Rooms: 38
Single: 330–600€
Double: 330–600€
Suites: 16

3RD

The restful and elegant **Villa Beaumarchais** is situated on the corner of the rue du Grand Veneur, next to a former royal hunting pavilion; the hunting theme is echoed throughout. Some rooms are spacious and all are comfortably furnished. The hotel created quite a sensation when it opened, but today it basks contentedly in its solid reputation (and cheaper prices). It was the setting for much of Jacques Rivette's joyous comedy film about life and love in the Parisian theatre, *Va Savoir*.

Villa Beaumarchais

Rating: 4★
5 rue Arquebusiers, 75003
01 40 29 14 00
villa-beaumarchais.com
Rooms: 50
Single: 170–330€
Double: 170–330€

Geoff: Villa Beaumarchais has the great virtue of being close to a major boulevard but just far enough away to ensure it's almost completely protected from traffic noise. The room we stayed in was very small and the bathroom even smaller (we were on a budget and the smallest room was right on our limit), but the comfort was there. The foyer, where drinks could be taken, and the breakfast service, were both exquisite. The rooms occupied by Camille (Jeanne Balibar) and Ugo (Sergio Castellitto) in Rivette's movie were definitely bigger than ours. Or maybe Rivette used a wide-angle lens to give them a spacey feel.

Great Paris Museums

Musée National Picasso

Hôtel Salé, 5 rue de Thorigny, 75003
musee-picasso.fr

In the stunning 17th-century Hôtel Salé
(once the mansion home of a collector
of the salt tax) is the Picasso Museum.
The collection includes more than 260
paintings and 1700 drawings by the
Spanish master, along with many of his
private collection of works by friends
such as Braque and Cézanne. This is an
extraordinary tribute to a man and an era.

Musée Carnavalet

23 rue de Sévigné, 75003
carnavaletparis.fr

Hidden away in the Marais, this is a jewel
of a museum that offers a surprisingly
rich and enjoyable history of the city of
Paris. The two buildings which make
up the museum (the 16th-century Hôtel
Carnavalet and Hôtel Le Peletier de
Saint Fargeau) are both gems, but the
exhibits—150 000 photographs, 2600
paintings, several re-created boudoirs
and salons, 800 pieces of furniture
and countless objets d'art—are superb
and a remarkable evocation of earlier
times. Carnavalet is a refuge of calm
and culture.

Cité de la Mode et du Design

3 quai d'Austerlitz
en.parisinfo.com

The 'City of Fashion and Design' is
one of Paris's most modern (and
most green) buildings, from architects
Jakob + MacFarlane. Its long-delayed
opening kept Parisian gossip bubbling
along. This new home for the Institut
Français de la Mode is a must-visit
shrine to French design (and yet another
restaurant and shopping hub).

Centre Georges Pompidou

place Georges Pompidou, 75004
centrepompidou.fr

Once the most controversial building in
Paris (designed collaboratively by Renzo
Piano and Richard Rogers and opened in
1977, then renovated in the late 1990s),
the Centre Georges Pompidou (often
simply called Beaubourg by locals, as it's
in the Beaubourg district) is now one of
the city's top tourist attractions. If staring
at this work of genius/monstrosity is not
enough in itself, inside are collections
from the 20th and 21st centuries of
design, sculpture, painting, photography,
books, music and graphic arts. There
are always long queues and it is faster to
buy tickets well in advance or via one of
the credit-card machines in the entrance,
although they aren't always overly friendly
to cards from outside France.

Musée Rodin

79 rue de Varenne, 75007
musee-rodin.fr

The Musée Rodin is both a stunning
tribute to the great sculptor's work and a
garden of rare peace and beauty. Most of
the Rodin collection is in the Hôtel Biron,
a magnificent 18th-century mansion

where Rodin (and other artists such as Jean Cocteau) lived at one time. There is always a crowd around *The Thinker* and *The Kiss*, but take your time to explore every nook and cranny … and then do it again. There are several thousand sculptures alone, so don't be surprised if you return a few days later; many do. Don't miss the rooms devoted to the sculptor Camille Claudel, Rodin's lover of more than a decade and who, some believe, contributed to many of Rodin's major works. Outside is a ravishing garden of nearly three hectares, with lawns, a fountain and glorious rose-beds and, lest one forget why one is here, great pieces by Rodin (including *The Gates of Hell*).

Musée du Louvre
Entry via the large pyramid, 75001
louvre.fr
What is there to be said about the world's most famous museum? Just don't try to beat the record for sprinting down its galleries (9 minutes 45 seconds in Jean-Luc Godard's *Bande à Part* and later 9 minutes 28 seconds in Bernardo Bertolucci's *The Dreamers*). The Louvre won't be amused.

ANOTHER HOTEL

The second of Christian Lacroix's hotels (the other is Le Bellechasse), the **Hôtel du Petit Moulin** is strictly for the fun-loving and adventurous. It really is like living in one of his dresses: the wallpapers are beyond loud, the contrasts bolder than anything you could ever imagine, the frescoes eccentric. No other stay in Paris will ever feel like this. To get a good sense of the place, check out the website, which recalls Richard Williams's animated credits for the movie *What's New Pussycat*. If you can't work the site properly (it's more interactive than it seems at first), call in a child to help.

Hôtel du Petit Moulin
Rating: 3★
29-31 rue de Poitou, 75003
01 42 74 10 10
paris-hotel-petitmoulin.com
Rooms: 17
Single: 190–350€
Double: 190–350€

APARTMENT

5 Rue de Moussy

5 rue de Moussy, 75004
01 44 78 92 00
no website
Single: 400€
Double: 450€
Triple: 500€

Located in the historical heart of Paris, **5 Rue de Moussy** consists of three modern apartments (known as '3 Rooms') created by Tunisian fashion designer Azzedine Alaïa, in a traditional Parisian 18th-century building. It has hi-speed Internet and a Bang & Olufsen entertainment system. Breakfast is available at 28€. The building is non-smoking.

Shannon: I actually found the apartment a little cold: it just didn't click for me. The designer furniture was more about style than comfort, but I did like the kitchen. We took the two-bedroom apartment, but one of the bedrooms was way too small and more like a kid's bedroom or a study. Also, the bathroom did not work well and the super-strong showerhead flooded the joint (I suppose that's one advantage of having a concrete floor throughout).

The building is very close to Pain de Sucre, which may be reason alone to rent it. But with the likes of *Wallpaper** and several Condé Naste publications raving about this place, I really wonder if they have actually stayed there.

Le Marais Apartments

Here are three sites specialising in apartments in Le Marais:

apartmentsactually.com

alacarte-paris-apartments.com

specialapartments.com

Shannon's Parisian Recipes

Caviar Served with Pancakes

The classic combination of blinis and caviar is successful on account of both the texture and the flavour of its components. I respect this way of serving caviar that has been practised by generations of great chefs. Using traditional pancakes just makes the dish a little more quirky.

100 g caviar

PANCAKES
180 ml milk
1 egg
165 g plain flour
1 tablespoon sugar
1½ teaspoon baking powder
pinch of salt
50 g unsalted butter, melted

ACCOMPANIMENTS
4 hard-boiled eggs
100 g cornichons, finely diced
2 shallots, finely chopped
1 tablespoon chives, finely chopped
3 tablespoons fromage blanc
1 lemon, cut into wedges

Preheat the oven to 180°C.

First make the pancakes. Whisk milk and egg until just combined. Mix the flour, sugar, baking powder and salt in a bowl, then slowly pour in the milk–egg mixture, whisking until smooth. Mix in half of the melted butter, then leave mixture to rest for 30 minutes.

Separate the yolks and whites of the hard-boiled eggs, chop finely and then aside. Heat twelve pancake or blini moulds (4-cm diameter) on a flat grill. Add the remaining melted butter and 3 tablespoons of the batter to each mould and cook over medium heat for 30 seconds. Remove from heat, and place pancakes on an oven tray and cook in preheated oven for a further 4 minutes.

To serve, arrange some of the chopped egg, cornichons, shallots and chives on each plate. Place three pancakes, evenly spaced, next to the garnishes, then top each pancake with a teaspoonful of the fromage blanc, formed into a quenelle shape. Place a teaspoon-sized quenelle of caviar on each of four traditional mother-of-pearl teaspoons, arrange these on the plates, next to the pancakes, with a lemon wedge on the side.

Serves 4

Saint Paul

FINE DINING

The place des Vosges is one of the treasures of Paris, a small but perfect garden square surrounded by beautiful arcaded buildings. At one corner, in the former Hôtel de Luyens, is chef Bernard Pacaud's discreet and elegant sanctuary, **L'Ambroisie**. It is a temple to delicate classical cuisine: the food is so subtle that many insist it takes a few visits to fully appreciate the cooking, a view that even Pacaud publicly espouses. Dishes that have reached legendary status include a red-pepper mousse and a *Feuillantine de langoustines aux graines de sésame, sauce curry*. Pacaud started at Le Méditerranée in Paris, before serving (as did many other famous chefs) under Claude Peyrot at Vivarois. In 1981, aged 33, Pacaud opened the first L'Ambroisie on the rue Bièvre (just off the quai de Montebello), gaining his first star in 1982 and the second a year later. Few restaurants and chefs have risen to such prominence so quickly. In 1986, Pacaud moved to splendid new surroundings on the place des Vosges, gaining his third star in 1988. Opinions oscillate between those who think he is the sublime master of French food and those who find his cooking a little dated.

L'Ambroisie

Chef: Bernard Pacaud
9 place des Vosges, 75004
01 42 78 51 45
ambroisie-placedesvosges.com
Phone bookings only
Michelin: ★★★
GaultMillau: 🍴🍴🍴🍴
À la carte: 225–290€

4ᵀᴴ

Matt: Four of us went to L'Ambroisie for dinner, which was the only three-star I visited on a recent trip to Paris. It's one of my favourites: I love it, though it's stupidly expensive. It was white-truffle season when we were there and the entrées were priced between 120€ and 160€! The main courses weren't that much more expensive, at 180€–200€. I had scallops with a broccoli purée and white truffle over the top. I then had Bresse chicken with a piece of foie gras and a little more white truffle. Then we had chocolate cake, which looked heavy but just melted in your mouth—it was like air, like a soufflé. It's flourless and contains no egg whites; I don't know how they do it (they will tell you what's in the cake, but not how they make it). It's like their trade secret—they are famous for this cake. I actually find it a bit weird, because most three-star restaurants are very open, but L'Ambroisie won't let you into their kitchen, no matter what: they say the chef is embarrassed by the size of it, but I think that's rubbish—they just don't want you in there.

L'Ambroisie cost us about $1000 per head; most of that was food, with very little wine. There is no doubt L'Ambroisie is one of the greats, but do book well ahead, because it is very hard to get into.

BRASSERIES, BISTROS

Brasserie Bofinger

5 rue de la Bastille, 75004
01 42 72 87 82
bofingerparis.com
GaultMillau: 🍴🍴
Menu: 28€ (lunch)
À la carte: 35–65€

In 1864, an Alsatian by the name of Frédéric Bofinger set up his first beer pump in Paris and established a small restaurant at 5 rue de la Bastille. It rapidly gained a reputation for the quality of its sauerkraut and for serving beer on tap, which was then still basically unheard of in Paris though commonplace in rural France. **Bofinger** is the most spectacular brasserie in Paris, with its wood panelling, velvet banquettes, stained-glass windows and, best of all, glorious glass-dome ceiling. A particular draw-card for Paris's élite, the ceiling was designed by stained-glass artists Néret and Royer, who were responsible for many cultural landmarks throughout Paris.

The oysters are perfect and the rest of the classic food is fine, but this place is so theatrically thrilling that even an ordinary meal will not dampen your pleasure.

Get a group together and enjoy Brasserie Bofinger (pronounced, by the way, 'bo-fahn-jay', with a soft 'j'). The Alsatian bent of the menu ensures it even has kugelhopf.

Shannon: This place resonates in my mind because it reminds me of the television series *Bewitched*, which I used to watch whenever I was kept at home during my younger primary-school years. The same episode always seemed to be on, with the snooty-but-somehow-likable mother (Agnes Moorehead) taking Samantha (Elizabeth Montgomery) on a trip to Paris for half a day. A twinkle of the nose and they would be magically transported to the famous boutiques of the Champs-Élysées. After spending their morning shopping, another twinkle of the nose would have them sitting in an opulent, male-waiter-dominated restaurant, sipping champagne and eating Niçoise salad. These were the types of venues you could only, as a kid, imagine ever eating in if your parents won the lottery or some long-lost relative left them a fortune in a bank in Paris. The food didn't matter; feeling special did.

Bofinger enjoys an excellent reputation with American tourists, and getting a table between 8.30 and 10.30 p.m. during weekends can be an issue if booking on the day. The rooms are divided into four main areas: the front bar, a front room on the left, the back room and upstairs. For me, hands-down, the back room is the one. Ask for a seat along the banquette so you can face the room. And then look up at the amazing glass dome.

The menu is simple and very classical. I'd recommend the lobster salad, which reminds me of many three-star-chefs' salads, including a lobster and tomato salad I used to work on at Marco Pierre White's restaurant in London's Hyde Park Hotel. Foie-gras terrine is a classic here, as is the fish soup and, of course, the choucroute (though I'm not a big fan of this dish anywhere; I find it boring). Pigeon, simply roasted, is as good here as in any Paris bistro and so is the Red Mullet soup. Desserts are simple: try the soufflé or profiteroles. The wine list is medium-sized and a little on the commercial side, but there is plenty to choose from and enjoy. I would classify Bofinger as neither cheap nor expensive. Just keep your menu choices classic and simple.

Madeleine: A meal at Bofinger epitomises for me the delicious eccentricity of dining in Paris, capturing in perfect relief the sometimes bizarre, always enthralling, twilight world of France's restaurants. The food is lovely; the ambience, assisted by the glorious dome and profusion of gold paint and stained glass, is captivating. The diners? Well, they are something else. There is the couple in the corner studiously ignoring each other, both with faces that would have paid for a skilled surgeon's yacht. Each course is greeted with the same look of mild startlement. With coiffures to rival Napoléon's and Marie-Antoinette's, they are a study in New Age gentrification, interrupted only by fits of cooing over the tiny dog stashed in the lady's handbag when it emerges to sample a cold morsel straight from their plates.

To the right, a young bespectacled man arrives, weighty tome in hand, for a solo meal. A quick perusal of the menu and soon he is ploughing through a plate of rolls, a large bowl of snails and condiments, and a full charcuterie (designed for two), before attempting to tackle dessert—washed down with half bottles of white and then red. It is little wonder he was in a semi-comatose state when he departed, with satiated groans and much clutching of his distended girth.

And what dining experience would be complete without a tour group of Americans filleting the menu in search of anything vaguely American, then attempting to transcend the language barrier by repeating the same request in English, only louder. It's at these moments I scrape together what little French I have and pretend to be Gallic. Aah!

But the true joy in experiences such as Bofinger is just being there, another diner making up the numbers in the delightful culinary universe of Paris.

Benoît

Chef: Alain Souliac
20 rue Saint-Martin, 75004
01 42 72 25 76
benoit-paris.com
Michelin: ★
GaultMillau: 🍴🍴
Menu: 34€ (lunch)
À la carte: 55–100€

Now owned by Alain Ducasse, **Benoît** has long been one of the most-lauded Paris bistros. Paul Bocuse once called it his favourite restaurant in Paris—which made it even harder (and more expensive) to get into. People tend to be divided over the quality of the hearty Lyonnaise food, but everyone loves the Belle Époque interior (if not the grotty part of Paris in which it is situated). With Ducasse having taken control, it has entered a whole new era.

 LUXURY HOTEL

Villa Mazarin

Rating: 4★
6 rue des Archives, 75004
01 53 01 90 90
villamazarin.com
Rooms: 29
Single: 220–272€
Double: 220–360€

Villa Mazarin is a relaxed little hotel in the heart of the hustle and bustle of Le Marais. Housed in a Haussmanian building with a mansard roof, it is a perfect location from which to explore the historical heart of Paris.

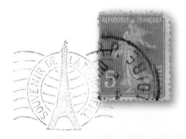

Jacques Garcia's reign as Paris's superstar designer-of-choice now extends over the Marais to the **Bourg Tibourg**, which was opened by a niece of Jean-Louis Costes (Hôtel Costes and others). It is centrally located, not far from the Centre Georges Pompidou and the Hôtel de Ville.

Garcia declared that the Bourg Tibourg 'has the ambition of taking guests on a journey not in space but in time'. Well, it is certainly a colourful journey through history, from 'Romantic and Baroque to Eastern and Neo-Venetian'. The rooms are stunning, though tiny (it is a three-star, remember). There is a beautiful interior garden.

Hôtel Bourg Tibourg

Rating: 3★
19 rue du Bourg-Tibourg, 75004
01 42 78 47 39
bourgtibourg.com
Rooms: 29
Single: 190€
Double: 250–370€
Suites: 1

Right in the middle of the Marais, the **Bretonnerie** is a very charming hotel. You feel a sense of calm and muted luxury as soon as you enter. The lobby-cum-seating area has rich red walls, impressive exposed beams and comfortable country-style chairs. The guest rooms at the front (some are duplexes) look out onto the rue Sainte-Croix-de-la-Bretonnerie, the location of several of Paris's top gay nightclubs. If you want less theatre, choose one of the rooms at the back or in the mansard attics. The owners and staff are all wonderful and there are myriad cute and cheap restaurants nearby. This is a genuine Marais experience.

Hôtel de la Bretonnerie

Rating: 3★
22 rue Sainte-Croix-de-la-Bretonnerie, 75004
01 48 87 77 63
bretonnerie.com
Rooms: 22
Single: 145–200€
Double: 145–200€
Suites: 7

Scott: Booked three rooms here. Sister Sue had a small but exquisitely decorated room (the prettiest we saw), whereas my attic room was much more spacious, if spartan. It had a limited but spectacular view over the Marais. I did, however, have to tie a cushion to one of the room's many crossbeams to save my head from being battered into submission. Stepfather David Helfgott had a duplex facing the street. As fans of *Shine* would know, David is not always fully attired, which meant his regular appearances leaning on the windowsill generated hours of appreciative comments from the perennially crowded street. One of the great boutique hotels of Paris, and remarkable value.

Caron de Beaumarchais

Rating: 3★
12 rue Vieille-du-Temple, 75004
01 42 72 34 12
carondebeaumarchais.com
Rooms: 19
Single: 145–185€
Double: 145–185€

The **Caron de Beaumarchais** became famous as the first reasonably priced boutique hotel in the Marias. It has a striking royal-blue exterior and large glass windows that allow you to see through to the Empire-style jewel-box interior. The 17th-century building features timber, polished stone and velvet, with Swedish-style (Gustavian) furniture. The guest rooms are beautifully decorated, though not large. Most look onto a delightful inner courtyard, ensuring a quiet night's sleep; the largest are at the front, overlooking the Rive Droite. The famous (and often scurrilous) playwright Pierre Augustin Caron de Beaumarchais lived nearby, at 47 Vieille-du-Temple.

Sue: I loved this hotel. My sixth-floor room, located at the front of the hotel and with a blue-and-white colour scheme, was light and the doors opening onto the tiny terrace made it feel airy. Breakfast on the terrace overlooking the street was a treat. The staff are really helpful, the Marais is a great location and this gem of a hotel is well-priced.

For Your Picnic

Cococook
30, rue Charlot, 75003
01 42 74 80 00
cococook.com
Cococook sells the freshest organic takeaway food. It is perfect for that favourite Parisian pastime: le pique-nique.

Shannon's Parisian Recipes

Chicken and Foie-gras Terrine

If you are not able to purchase foie gras, this recipe can be made with duck liver paté instead, which is available through most good providores. Alternatively, marinate whole duck livers in Calvados or Cognac—whatever you have in the cupboard—and layer them into the terrine to give a marbled effect.

500 g chicken thigh meat, diced

300 g chicken breast, minced

1 tablespoon finely chopped shallots

1 clove garlic, finely chopped

2 teaspoons salt

2 tablespoons finely chopped tarragon

200 g chorizo sausage, diced

2 tablespoons goose fat

15 slices flat pancetta or streaky bacon

150 g cooked foie gras, cut into strips 2 cm x 2 cm

freshly ground black pepper

Preheat the oven to 160ºC.

Combine the chicken meats, shallots, garlic, salt, tarragon, chorizo and goose fat in a large bowl, and mix by hand until well combined. Season with pepper.

Arrange the pancetta or bacon slices in a terrine dish mould of about 1-litre capacity, covering the bottom of the mould evenly with the ends of the slices overhanging over the sides. Place half the chicken mixture in the dish and pack down using your hands. Place the foie gras in a line along the centre of the chicken mix (leaving a border around the foie gras so it does not melt out the side). Place the remaining chicken mixture on top, then fold the pancetta over and press it down firmly. Cover with aluminium foil, put dish in a roasting tray and add water to reach halfway up the sides. Cook in preheated oven for 80 minutes, then remove and allow to cool. Place in the refrigerator with a heavy weight on top, and leave for 24 hours.

To unmould terrine, remove from mould, run a knife around the edge, easing it away from the sides, and turn out on to a chopping board. Slice terrine and serve with crusty bread.

Serves 10

Champs-Élysées, Concorde, Madeleine

8TH ARRONDISSEMENT

CHAMPS-ÉLYSÉES
FINE DINING (WITH LUXURY HOTEL)

Pierre Gagnaire gained fame and three stars at his restaurant in the industrial town of Saint-Étienne. After being forced into bankruptcy (Saint-Étienne was simply too far from anywhere), Gagnaire re-established himself in Paris in 1997. He instantly regained his three stars, Michelin referring to his 'unbridled creativity, akin to free-form jazz. Music maestro!' (Gagnaire is well known for his love of jazz.)

Gagnaire turns food into art; he makes it possible for young chefs to become excited about not just becoming a cook but an artist. He has inspired a legion of chefs who don't see a need to follow the old repertoire. This is a major factor in the modern food in today's top three-star restaurants, moving beyond the label (albeit an unfair one) of Nouvelle Cuisine. His artistry, skill and precision may not be apparent in every dish, but will be found over the entire meal.

Pierre Gagnaire
Chef: Pierre Gagnaire
6 rue Balzac, 75008
01 58 36 12 50
pierre-gagnaire.com
Michelin: ★★★
GaultMillau: 🍴🍴🍴🍴🍴
Menu: 105€ (lunch)
À la carte: approx. 300€

8ᵀᴴ

Shannon: In 2007, I had one of my most exciting experiences in Paris, eating at Pierre Gagnaire, which is situated in what feels like a basement area of the Hôtel Balzac, on the rue Balzac, a street running off the Champs-Élysées near the Arc de Triomphe. Before going there, I and friend Simon decided to have a drink at a bar. My wife Madeleine was four-and-a-half-months pregnant and decided to join us later at the restaurant. We were half an hour late getting to Pierre Gagnaire and Madeleine had already arrived. She wasn't drinking alcohol and had asked for an exotic fruit juice. (Being Madeleine, she hadn't wanted something off the shelf.) The waiter—the best she says she has ever experienced—instructed the barman to arrange a taste of every fresh fruit juice they had. Eight different nectars were presented in shot glasses on a wooden board; enough in total to fill a large glass and all complimentary. There were some really exotic concoctions there, like star fruit with cinnamon. Though I was late, she was completely happy: the waiters had made that experience for her.

Our waiter was just brilliant, a young African guy—disciplined, well-groomed, good-looking, gracious. You didn't realise he was even there because there was no ego attached. Each time Madeleine got up to go to the toilet, someone followed her. Each waiter had his or her own section, with invisible boundaries, and, once a waiter reached that border, a new one would meet Madeleine and escort her, opening every door along the way, helping her up the steps. It was as if they rehearsed this routine during the day.

There was some discussion about whether to go for the dégustation menu or à la carte. The à la carte really looked interesting; it was broken down into themes, such as 'Prawns', which constituted five miniature dishes in the one entrée. Among the mains was a lamb dish, also with several components: lamb smoked and grilled; with spices; poached. I was intrigued, but in the end we went for the dégustation menu. The wine match wasn't really sold to us, so we opted for half bottles from the list—there was a really good selection, not overly expensive. The meal started with very intricate canapés that looked and tasted amazing, including little beignets of petit pois, millefeuilles of pastry and seafood, and one shaped like a hat with apple-and-herb paper cut into a circle. They were no ordinary presentations, but miniature works of art, architectural design and vivid colour. From a chef's perspective, they were mind-blowing: I wanted to get straight back in the kitchen. Another incredible course was an egg dish. I cannot remember what was inside the beautifully cut and polished shell because I was too busy looking at the eggcup stuck on a 90-degree angle. Was this guy so good that he had designed a cup in two pieces and placed a magnet in one half? Amazing.

After that, there was grilled squid with a really smoky paprika flavour; the juices dripped by way of a perforated porcelain dish into a bowl of julienned red peppers flavoured with garlic-and-tomato-infused olive oil, which were exposed once the squid was finished. A bowl of langoustines (actually Norwegian prawns) with sautéed girolles was wonderfully flavoured, but so full of grit we couldn't eat it. We mentioned this to the waiter, who whisked it away and within

five minutes we had a new dish. That's all we wanted. For me, that isn't a negative memory but proof of how good the restaurant is: they handled it with grace and we moved on.

The only negative of the night was that we had booked for too late in the evening (8.30 p.m.), which meant we didn't finish till after midnight and were too tired to fully enjoy the beautifully constructed desserts. So, if you are going to go for the big experience, book early. One warning! It is expensive (though the lunch menu offers great value): the dégustation menu costs around 350€. But I am telling you, you will talk about it for years to come.

Hôtel Balzac

Rating: 5★
6 rue Balzac, 75008
01 44 35 18 00
hotelbalzac.com
Rooms: 57
Single: 420–500€
Double: 470–550€
Suites: 13

The **Balzac**, named after esteemed writer Honoré de Balzac (who once lived here), has for a long time been a hotel of choice for visitors to Paris—even before Pierre Gagnaire opened his three-star restaurant there. Though it's just a few steps from the Champs-Élysées, the area is surprisingly calm and free of the surging crowds. The hotel was extensively restored in 2007 by artist Anne-Marie Sabatier and looks even more stunning and colourful than before. The public rooms are very welcoming and luxurious, the guest rooms richly furnished with Murano lamps, heavenly beds and the latest in electrical equipment. The hotel avoids cutting-edge or ostentatious design in favour of the neoclassical. All rooms above the second floor have views of the Tour Eiffel.

Scott: I love this hotel. It may have 70 rooms, but it feels much smaller, genuinely cosy and intimate. The rooms are beautifully decorated, exceedingly comfortable and easy to live in. On the same street is a multi-screen cinema that shows quality films from around the world. So, with Pierre Gagnaire in the building and film culture just down the road, you can create your own Balzacian slice of paradise without venturing far.

Le Bristol

Chef: Éric Frechon
112 rue du faubourg
Saint-Honoré, 75008
01 53 43 43 00
lebristolparis.com
Michelin: ★★★
GaultMillau: ♟♟♟♟
Menu: 85 (lunch)/230€
À la carte: 175–275€

For years, the most persistent rumour in the days leading up to the release of the latest Michelin guide to France was that Éric Frechon's restaurant in the Hôtel Le Bristol had finally got three stars. While the wait continued (until finally satisfied in 2009), no one ever disputed that **Le Bristol** was one of the best, and most reasonably priced, of the great restaurants in Paris. It is also certainly one of the prettiest. In summer, it is set in a gorgeous garden; in winter, it moves to an oak-panelled room with tapestries and Baccarat crystal chandeliers.

Shannon: I have found the perfect way to appreciate a great restaurant experience. Arrive in Paris at 8 p.m. after a 6-hour train journey from San Sebastian via Biarritz and Bayonne, bored out of your brain and having not eaten for five of those hours, and sit down for dinner at 8.30 p.m. exactly. Having the weight taken off your shoulders about whether you were going to make it gets you right in the mood—especially for Éric Frechon's food!

A mystery I could not work out was how this head chef beat me. I had just arrived from the annual Les Grandes Tables du Monde congress, which is held in a different city every year. All 140 members meet to discuss issues and future ideas. Éric Frechon is one of those members.

Now, there are no direct flights from San Sebastian to Paris and I had explored all the possibilities, the quickest way being the train. But somehow he beat me. I suppose this is what makes chefs like Frechon so dedicated and why their discipline gets them a well-deserved three-star status.

Le Bristol is the only three-Michelin-starred establishment since Marc Veyrat closed to have a summer restaurant and a winter dining room.

My first thought sitting down there last October was: 'There is a lot of youthfulness in this room, for such a grande dame of the dining room, in the way of staff and energy.' Some people like to describe this room as 'Sarkozy's canteen' (the Élysée Palace is nearby). That's why a lot of the once-a-year French diners won't eat here! And this was told to me by a local.

Every table around me either speaks French or is French, a pretty good sign to me. There is not one American in the room.

The dining room is not as spectacular as, say, Restaurant le Meurice, but it is certainly a three-star dining room. It's certainly not bad for a 'canteen'!

The à la carte menu dominates here. All the dishes sound classical with a hint of the New World in them. Bacon-and-onion bread twists are the first item to arrive, quickly followed by a champagne trolley, with Krug Grand Cuvée the centrepiece of the trolley. This was followed by four stunning little canapés on a curved rectangular plate, starting with a porcelain shell replicating an egg with a rounded bottom that had a magnet attaching it to the plate. Inside this shell was a stunning warm foie gras custard topped with a perfectly weighted acidic sorrel foam. There was debate between Madeleine and I about whether this was the best flavour of the night. That is not to take away from all the other dishes. Other little tasters were a goat's cheese lollipop and lettuce jelly encasing a mint feta dressing.

We were then told we were having the five-course menu. The dishes were tasters from the à la carte. The first course to arrive was a poached Dublin Bay prawn tail cut into two perfect discs, wrapped in a very thin veil of jelly and topped with caviar, with a further large disc of caviar in the centre resting on a fromage blanc infused with yuzu juice (Japanese citrus) dotted with a herb oil.

It was followed by duck foie gras with smoked oyster and green-tea broth; scallops with potato gnocchi, white truffle and watercress juice; and a saddle of venison, roasted with juniper berries, beetroot perfumed with Port and puréed celeriac. After cheese, we had black figs poached in a spicy strawberry juice with ice cream and spéculoos biscuits, and some Nyangbo chocolate with a gold-gilded sorbet!

All delicious and very classical and, if this is what Sarkozy is having for lunch each day, then France will dominate the world for years to come.

Hôtel Le Bristol

Rating: 5★+
112 rue du faubourg
Saint-Honoré, 75008
01 53 43 43 00
hotel-bristol.com
Rooms: 166
Single: 770€
Double: 770–1370€
Suites: 47

Residing quietly on the great fashion and promenading street of rue du faubourg Saint-Honoré, **Le Bristol** is a model of reserved calm. It has an exquisite interior garden and arguably the finest swimming pool (created by Cäsar Pinnau, who designed yachts for Aristotle Onassis) of any luxury Paris hotel. In a hotel of this quality, it should not surprise that rooms start at the Superior level. They are a generous 30 m² and nicely, if conservatively, furnished. The Deluxe (45 m²), which have a separate seating area, are far more dynamic in their design. If you must, the Prestige (50 m²) is like having your own villa at Versailles. Given the presence of the three-star Le Bristol restaurant, you may never feel inclined to venture outside this hotel's comforting walls.

Shannon: What can I say about this hotel? It is archetypically English in its interior, versed in the school of high teas and 'Hail fellow, well met'. I simply cannot imagine Russian society of the 18th century coming here. It doesn't have a big enough foyer or high enough ceilings. I can stay here and simply not be noticed, only when I want to be.

I originally desired to stay here because of Éric Frechon's food and his emerging reputation over the past five years. When he won three Michelin stars in 2009, I knew had to come.

I have now stayed here on three separate occasions and each time the experience kept getting better. I can actually narrow it down to several moments and they all involved great staff.

One was the best welcome I have ever received in a hotel. It started when the doorman said, 'Welcome home, Mr Bennett', and continued when I was welcomed by three front-office staff who then proceeded to upgrade me. They were not aware I was writing up my stay in this book on Paris; they were just aware I was paying 800€ a night and wanted to make sure I was happy.

The Junior suites are generous in size. Request a room on the far left of the hotel on the top floor (seventh). All these rooms have some sort of a view to the Eiffel Tower. They have also been recently refurbished (as has the whole hotel).

The polarising effect a stay in a luxury hotel can have on a person is never to be underestimated. The cost is not the issue in most cases; it is whether one has the energy to use a hotel properly. This is the only way you can ever really test the full honours a hotel deserves.

My needs are sometimes complex when I am so far away from home. The hotel becomes my assistant. The staff needs to think for me at times—even function for me. I'm an owner-operator of a small business, so I like my costs to be inclusive and for it to be easy to make choices, like having the cost of the minibar and breakfast included. The rate is fine, but I want my money's worth.

Le Bristol gives you your money's worth, not with free Internet or minibar, but with its people. (Le Bristol should work on free breakfast and minibars in the future, though.)

In my mind, the Bristol is the best hotel in Paris. It's a big call I know, but I'm ready to stand by it and cop the flack from you if I'm wrong.

David: I have stayed in the penthouse suite of the Hôtel Le Bristol with my own rooftop garden and butler. I like the restaurant and probably it should have had three stars long before now, though I usually preferred to make the short walk to Lucas Carton (now Senderens).

Geoff: It's been a while since I stayed at the Bristol, but at the time the large rooms were complemented by ultra-smart service. A shirt with a button missing would be repaired, shoes shined and aspirins provided as soon as you indicated a slight hangover. Nothing seemed too trivial, nothing was unimportant, nothing required a fuss.

Le Cinq fell slightly from grace by losing a star, but there are gourmets everywhere who believe passionately that just-fallen restaurants are *the* places to go to as they pull out all stops to reverse their fortunes. Situated in the Hôtel Four Seasons George V, in the wealthiest heart of Paris, Le Cinq was restored architecturally to its former glory (or even surpassed it) in the late 1990s. The view over the hotel's garden and courtyard—where the restaurant partially moves in summer—is spectacular. In 2008 there was a changing of the guard in the kitchen as well, with Eric Briffard (formerly of Les Élysées) taking over. GaultMillau named him 'La Nouvelle Star' of that year.

Le Cinq

Chef: Eric Briffard
Hôtel Four Seasons
George V
31 avenue George V, 75008
01 49 52 71 54
fourseasons.com/paris/dining
Michelin: ★★
GaultMillau: ����
Menu: 78 (lunch)/160/230€
À la carte: 180–335€

8ᵀᴴ

The **George V** has long been a rival to the Hôtel de Crillon and Le Meurice, reigning over the Arc de Triomphe end of the Champs-Élysées just as the others do at the Concorde end. For some time, and especially after the dazzling renovation in 1999, the George V has been seen as the most luxurious, Le Meurice having tired and the Crillon refusing to buckle to new-fangled trends. That has now changed and all three are equally splendid. For those in the terrible position of having to decide between the three, the principal advantage of the George V is that it is far more in the heart of things. The Champs-Élysées is just a stroll away, as are the great shopping strips on the avenues George V and Montaigne; for the culturally inclined, the wonderful Théâtre de Champs-Élysées is also nearby.

This is a majestic hotel, full of marble, chandeliers and gilt, with a brilliant use of natural and artificial light—you at times feel as if you have wandered into a private art gallery or museum. The vast upper rooms have balconies or terraces, and there are flowers everywhere: trimmed in crystal vases, or growing freely in the sunny courtyard. Curiously for a luxury hotel, the starting-level rooms are named 'Moderate' (no photos of these demean the hotel's website). The illustrated rooms start at 50 m² and are sumptuously furnished. The swimming pool, with its trompe-l'œil vision of Versailles, is irresistibly seductive (even for those who can't swim).

Hôtel Four Seasons George V

Rating: 5★+
31 avenue George V, 75008
01 49 52 70 00
fourseasons.com/paris/
Rooms: 197
Single: 825–1095€
Double: 825–1095€
Suites: 48

Le Bar

31 avenue George V, 75008
Hôtel Four Seasons
George V
01 49 52 70 00
fourseasons.com/paris/

A traditional wood-lined bar in one of the great luxury hotels of Paris. There are nibbles and main meals (at a mere 45€ a plate).

Shannon: After not getting into the bar of the Plaza Athénée on the night I was going to Pierre Gagnaire, I walked with two friends to the Hôtel Four Seasons, which is much less fashionable but stunning nonetheless. We ended up in the smallish **Le Bar**, which has a clubby sort of feel. We sat at the bar, taking the last three available seats.

The bartender recommended some drinks; I had a Rusty Nail at about 26€. We turned our seats around and looked at the people: there were African politicians and businessmen, deals going on everywhere, money passing around. There were also a few women with a lot of 'opulence' around their necks, and with famous-label handbags, talking over champagne. 'Wow, élite Paris', we thought. 'And then we are going for dinner at Pierre Gagnaire!' We sat there for about an hour and it was all brilliant.

Restaurant Alain Ducasse au Plaza Athénée

Chef: Christophe Saintagne
25 avenue Montaigne, 75008
01 53 67 65 00
alain-ducasse.com
Michelin: ★★★
GaultMillau: ♙♙♙♙♙
Menu: 220/360€
À la carte: 195–310€

Alain Ducasse has the second-highest number of Michelin stars in the world (18 to Joël Robuchon's 26). His empire spans the globe and shows no signs of reducing its reach or its standards. In France, his three greatest restaurants are in Monte-Carlo (Restaurant Le Louis XV—Alain Ducasse) and Paris (at the Hôtel Plaza Athénée, and Le Jules Verne in the Tour Eiffel). The dining-room at the Plaza Athénée envelops you in luxury, its famed Regency décor recently modernised by Patrick Jouin. The two most iconic dishes (so far) are the *Caviar osciètre d'Iran, langoustines rafraîchies, nage réduite, bouillon parfumé* (at a mere 175€) and *Volaille de Bresse sauce Albufera, tartufi di Alba* (the same). There are 1001 wines to choose from.

Matt: I have eaten at Ducasse's restaurants a couple of times. My first meal in Paris, which was about 11 years ago, was when he took over the old Jamin in the Hôtel Parc and it was just amazing. Going there I felt like an absolute king. The service was just incredible, but it was the most expensive meal I have ever paid for. Even then it was about $1000 for two of us. I remember walking out with the menu and a loaf of bread and an ashtray. They gave me the menu because I was interested in what I ate, they gave me the ashtray because they knew I was going to steal one anyway and they gave me a loaf of bread because they knew I couldn't afford the dinner. That meal has always been the standout.

. . . .

Hôtel Plaza Athénée

Rating: 5★+
25 avenue Montaigne, 75008
01 53 67 66 65
plaza-athenee-paris.com
Rooms: 146
Single: 595–650€
Double: 825–1095€
Suites: 45

With abundant red flowers cascading from wrought-iron balconies, the elegant façade of the **Plaza Athénée** could be argued to be the most beautiful in Paris. The hotel stands in brand-label heaven (or hell, depending on your point of view) on the avenue Montaigne, where there seem to be more chauffeured cars than pedestrians. Inside, the décor is a mix of Louis XVI and Regency, though two floors are reserved for lovers of Art Déco. Like all great hotels these days, there is a 'pillow menu' (with options including wheat, horse-hair and de-stressing). Many of the rooms have views over the Tour Eiffel, the roofs of Montmartre or the avenue Montaigne; the others face the quiet and peaceful La Cour Jardin (a garden courtyard restaurant). A beauty-treatment centre, the Dior Institute, opened in 2008. The restaurant, Alain Ducasse au Plaza Athénée, has risen to culinary prominence (three stars) due to the fine work of the jet-setting Ducasse. The Bar du Plaza Athénée is universally famous, which is why it's almost impossible to get in.

Shannon: This is Paris's most exciting, most buzzy, most luxurious hotel. It has been featured in more films than any other hotel, and is in the best location. All walks of life walk to this spot on the avenue Montaigne; the surrounding streets represent Paris's grand history as well as its future.

Alain Ducasse is a great asset to the hotel as executive chef, personally supervising menus in each of the hotel's dining venues, as well as room service. La Cour Jardin is a fantastic place for a light lunch; I had a seafood salad that was reminiscent of the version Ducasse serves in his three-star restaurants. The rooms are surprisingly spacious, for Paris; even the smallest (the Superior) being at least 30 m².

Matt: The Plaza has the best breakfast in the world. It's incredibly expensive—about 200€ for a family—but it's just superb. You eat it in the hotel's second restaurant, Le Relais Plaza.

Le Bar du Plaza Athénée

25 avenue Montaigne, 75008
01 53 67 66 00
plaza-athenee-paris.com

It is difficult to avoid running into Philippe Starck designs, even when he doesn't do them. **Le Bar du Plaza Athénée** is famous for its pseudo-Starck glass bar created by next-generation designer Patrick Jouin, which lights up when you touch it. Over one or many of the stunning cocktails, you can discuss who does Starck better.

Shannon: We went down from the Champs-Élysées to the avenue Montaigne, hoping to get into the Bar du Plaza Athénée. When we arrived it was completely full, but the doorman graciously let us in to have a quick look around. This was on a Tuesday night, so you are better off going there during the day, or late in the afternoon. Order a drink that you have never had before, because it will blow you away; or have a famous one, because they will reinvent it for you. We went back the next day and it was exceptional.

Apicius is the name of both a Roman gourmet from the first century and a Roman cookbook published several hundred years later. Apicius is alleged to have created blood pudding (the Scots aren't happy about that), spiced duck with turnips (Alain Senderens named a duck dish after him) and bouillabaisse (with or without the saffron). Jean-Pierre Vigato's restaurant of the same name is in a Parisian townhouse in the middle of a park (the property is owned, incidentally, by filmmaker Luc Besson, who has his offices upstairs). Apicius has an atmosphere unlike any other major restaurant in Paris (and 55 000 bottles in its cellar).

Apicius

Chef: Jean-Pierre Vigato
20 rue d'Artois, 75008
01 43 80 19 66
restaurant-apicius.com
Michelin: ★★
GaultMillau: 🍴🍴🍴🍴
Menu: 150 (lunch)/
160/180€
À la carte: 110–190€

8TH

This is the newest Joël Robuchon restaurant in Paris and the second L'Atelier. (The other is in the 7th arrondissement.) It opened in the famous Publicisdrugstore on the Champs-Élysées and, in a sense, replaces La Table de Joël Robuchon in the 16th, which has closed.

L'Atelier de Joël Robuchon Étoile

Chef: Christophe Saintagne
133 avenue des Champs-Élysées, 75008
01 47 23 75 75
joel-robuchon.net
Menu: 150€
À la carte: 65–140€

This romantic dining-room, facing the back of the Grand Palais, has a roof that opens on summer evenings. Long held by the Lasserre family (René Lasserre was a legendary Paris restaurateur, who died in 2006), it changed hands in the late 1990s and its culinary reputation has consolidated. It is an old-fashioned place (in the best sense), with immaculate service and a magnificent setting. The velvet-lined lift that takes you there is the perfect apéritif en route to a charming evening and a menu offering modern twists on classic dishes (including several by Lasserre) by chef Christophe Moret.

Lasserre

Chef: Christophe Moret
17 avenue Franklin-D.-Roosevelt, 75008
01 43 59 53 43
restaurant-lasserre.com
Michelin: ★★
GaultMillau: not rated
Menu: 75 (lunch)/185€
À la carte: 145–245€

Taillevent

Chef: Alain Solivérès
15 rue Lamennais, 75008
01 44 95 15 01
taillevent.com
Michelin: ★★
GaultMillau:
Menu: 80/190€
À la carte: 130–225€

Taillevent has long been seen as the most discreet and haut-bourgeois restaurant in Paris, and the only one where the name of the owner, not the chef, appeared next to its three stars (now two) in Michelin. The argument was that the house style of food was more important than the individual contribution of any head chef. Since 1950, Taillevent has been ruled by the Vrinat family: André, Jean-Claude and now Valérie. Once the townhouse of the Duc de Morny (half-brother of Napoléon III), its austere surrounds have probably welcomed more world leaders and famous businessmen than any other restaurant in the City of Light. It is the favourite Parisian restaurant of the Australian-born composer and director of the Edinburgh Festival, Jonathan Mills.

BRASSERIES, BISTROS, NEIGHBOURHOOD RESTAURANTS

Le Bœuf sur le Toit

Chef: Patrick Proenca
34 rue du Colisée, 75008
01 53 93 65 55
boeufsurletoit.com
Menu: 56/75€
À la carte: 40–80€

Le Bœuf sur le Toit was a darling of the food guides until restaurant chain Groupe Flo took it over, refreshed the décor and improved the food. Now, none of them mention it. To anyone not driven by the restaurant politics of Paris (in which case you'd probably only eat in the 11th and 20th arrondissements), Le Bœuf remains a fun place to visit. The entry is dramatic, as you walk past an amazing display of crustaceans (a typical brasserie pleasure). The Art Nouveau salon is stunning. The staff are everything you want in a brasserie: hassled, efficient, curt and, just once in a while, inclined to a quick smile. The food is startlingly modern for so traditional a restaurant.

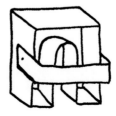

Scott: I have eaten here countless times (it has long been my uncle Pierre's favourite brasserie in Paris) and never been disappointed. The AAAAA-certified andouillette (a sausage made from pig intestines) is always a must: Le Bœuf's, which is of the highest grade and perfectly undercooked, comes with sautéed potatoes. (The AAAAA, or Association Amicale des Amateurs d'andouillette Genuine, was established to help maintain the quality and authenticity of the andouillette.) The nervous may think you have to shut down your sense of smell to enjoy an andouillette (you don't); it's the taste that is the challenge. But everyone save vegetarians should eat at least one andouillette in Paris before they depart this mortal coil. You can reward yourself with Gillardeau oysters to begin with and the rich desserts afterwards, such as the dramatic *Crème brûlée à la vanille bourbon 'flambée en salle'*.

....

A legendary restaurant on the Champs-Élysées, **Fouquet's** (you pronounce the 't') has long had a reputation for being where the stars of the French film industry hang out. But times have changed, and you are now more likely to meet tourists than stars. Once it lost its Michelin star, Fouquet's seems to have given up the effort of trying to remain a serious restaurant. But it is a dazzling space, majestically positioned on the calm (southern) side of Paris' most famous avenue, and sitting here can still generate a thrill. A *citron pressé* for breakfast, sitting outside with *The Herald Tribune* bought at the kiosk a few steps away, may be the best way to go.

Fouquet's

99 avenue Champs-Élysées, 75008
01 40 69 60 50
fouquets-barriere.com
GaultMillau: ♔
Menu: 78€
À la carte: 60–149€

Shannon: Fouquet's is one of the most stunningly beautiful restaurants in Paris, next to one of the most fashionable hotels in Paris (Fouquet's Barrière). They both have something in common: neither has staff who know how to smile and welcome someone who is about to spend good money in their establishment.

Fouquet's has several dining rooms with old feature ceilings, ornate lighting fixtures, a cute little central bar, where one can wait in an atmospheric environment for a table, and theatrical service, where chickens are broken down and smoked salmon sliced—well, once a upon a time.

I booked via the concierge at Fouquet's Barrière and I couldn't have received a worse table for one. With a half-full restaurant, I was plonked in the doorway sandwiched between two tables of six. One was a table of five Japanese and a local associate who was no doubt taking them to a restaurant to try and impress. The other table consisted of five bourgeois Parisians who wanted to be moved to a more prestigious table. They refused to be seated for least ten minutes and what I couldn't believe was that the staff would walk away and laugh about the situation.

I was sat down by a faceless guy in a suit who couldn't work out whether he wanted to speak to me in English or French. I said I would have a beer and Parmesan-and-puff-pastry twists arrived. I nibbled one, then rested it on a plain show plate, which was then whisked away. The waiter who removed the plate wiped the crumbs and the twist off the plate in a manner that suggested I was a bogan. His colleagues looked at me and laughed. To his surprise, I was looking at him and I was not amused.

Throughout the meal, he continued to have this arrogant smirk. Who were these people? This is not the France I loved.

The menu was dropped down, literally. Then the beer arrived—warm. Great!

I order a Sea Bream (Daurade) with a jus spiced with curry and celiac purée. I ordered the dish at precisely 7.48 p.m.; it arrived at precisely 7.57 p.m.!

I also ordered a glass of wine. Well, I didn't really order it: I was given it! I asked for the wines by the glass, but there weren't any listed, so they dropped down a glass of white. I had to yell out as he walked a way: 'Excuse me: what is the wine?' 'Sancerre', he replied, to which I replied I did not like Sauvignon Blanc. 'It is Sancerre!', he muttered. What a wanker! He then shrugged his shoulders, which I thought meant he was going to get someone else to help me, but, no, no one came.

Mind you, in all of this my beer was still three quarters full. I'm in a complete mental mess. But I must say, for a Daurade that has been held at temperature then flashed before serving, it wasn't bad.

It is really sad to see a great restaurant simply give itself over to the bad side of hospitality for the sake of a 'Get'em in get'em out' attitude. Avoid Fouquet's unless you wish to be treated like dining is a necessity rather than a privilege.

This glass-canopied restaurant on the roof of the Théâtre des Champs-Élysées is one of the most spectacular places to dine in Paris. The white interior is breathtaking, as is the view of Les Invalides. The modern food has its basis in the cuisine of the Languedoc. Heralded on its opening, it has never quite risen to the Michelin-starred heights expected of it. But the view will stop you from caring.

Maison Blanche

Chefs: Jacques and Laurent Pourcel
15 avenue Montaigne, 70008
01 47 23 55 99
maison-blanche.fr
GaultMillau: 🍴🍴
Menu: 55 (lunch)/69€
À la carte: 110–150€

8ᵀᴴ

This legendary restaurant makes you feel like you are in Saint-Tropez—if, indeed, that is what you want to feel while in Paris. It is strongly orientated to seafood, including the finest crustaceans. Try the *Daurade royale en croûte de sel*. A few years ago, this restaurant was lauded in all the guides (GaultMillau annually gave it 15/20), but it has fallen off the critical radar of late. It is outrageously expensive, but it is the stuff of legend. (See also the slightly cheaper Le Petit Marius.)

Marius et Janette

4 avenue George V, 75008
01 47 23 41 88
mariusetjanette.com
Menu: 48€ (lunch)
À la carte: 90–140€

Market

15 avenue Matignon, 75008
01 56 43 40 90
jean-georges.com
GaultMillau: 🍷🍷
Menu: 51€
À la carte: 45–105€

Jean-Georges Vongerichten is a superstar New York chef who ventured to Paris to try his luck in the city of love, life and food. Backed by two very successful men, millionaire filmmaker Luc Besson and billionaire François Pinault (head of luxury retail company PPR), Vongerichten is serving extremely modern fusion food in a chic restaurant just north of the Champs-Élysées. It has been universally praised and promoted, but one suspects Vongerichten would have expected a Michelin star by now.

Le Petit Marius

6 avenue George V, 75008
01 40 70 11 76
lepetitmarius.com
À la carte: 45–60€

Recalling Provence and especially Marseille, this seafood bistro is the simpler and cheaper sibling of Marius et Janette (but be prepared to pay more than you expect).

Scott: I go here with French film director Pierre Rissient. It is wonderful sitting outside on the avenue George V, eating a whole *loup de mer* cooked in a salt crust and drinking a Bandol rosé (surely the best in the world). *En croûte de sel* is a sensationally good way of cooking whole fish, provided you are sufficiently diligent about scraping away the rock salt (they leave you to do this yourself). The Breton sardines grilled with thyme, and the rock-fish soup with rouille and croûtons are also straightforward and delicious.

Books on Parisian Food and Restaurants

Chronological and only one book per author.

1. *The Food Lover's Guide to Paris* (Patricia Wells, 1984)
2. *Gourmet Guide to Paris* (Jacques-Louis Delpal, 1994)
3. *Gourmet Shops of Paris: An Epicurean Tour* (*Paris Gourmand: belles et bonnes boutiques de la ville*, Pierre Rival and Christian Sarramon, 2004)
4. *The Authentic Bistros of Paris* (François Thomazeau and Sylvain Ageorges, 2006, with photographs)
5. *Markets of Paris: Food, Antiques, Artisinal Crafts, Books & More* (Dixon and Ruthanne Long, 2007, illustrated edition)
6. *Taschen's Paris: Hotels, Restaurants & Shops* (Angelika Taschen, 2008)
7. *The Patisseries of Paris: Chocolatiers, Tea Salons, Ice Cream Parlors, and More* (Jamie Cahill and Alison Harris, 2008)
8. *Lunch in Paris: A Love Story, with Recipes* (Elizabeth Bard, 2010)

Alain Ducasse's reach is far and wide (though this very modern and trendy restaurant is close to one of his Parisian flagships, at the Hôtel Plaza Athénée). When it opened, it felt like a one-trick pony: the diner got to choose the protein … and then the sauce … and then the side-dish. Even though it was always packed, some diners must have convinced Ducasse to evolve his concept and now you can go for either the original **Spoon** menu ('Spoon Origins') or 'Spoon Now', where the chef does all the choosing for you. The decor also keeps getting redone. That's probably because it has never been quite right.

Spoon Paris
15 rue Marignan, 75008
01 40 76 34 44
spoon.tm.fr
GaultMillau: 🍴🍴🍴
Menu: 33€ (lunch)
À la carte: 46–66€

Hôtel Daniel

Rating: 4★+
8 rue Frédéric Bastiat,
75008
01 42 56 17 00
hoteldanielparis.com
Rooms: 26
Single: 350€
Double: 420–490€
Suites: 4

The **Hotel Daniel** is on the rue Frédéric Bastiat, a small street midway between the Champs-Élysées and the rue du faubourg Saint-Honoré. (Apicius is the local three-star restaurant.) Small, intimate and chic, it is a dazzlingly collage of East and West. There are traditional toile de Jouy fabrics mixed in with Chinese wallpaper, Lebanese ebony furniture and vases from Kazakhstan; the bathrooms are marble or Moroccan earthenware. The rue Frédéric Bastiat is a quiet and pretty street, but be careful which path you take to reach the Champs-Élysées if you wish to maintain a romantic mood: some streets, such as rue la Boétie (despite its marvellous cinema bookshop), have seen better days.

Hôtel Fouquet's Barrière

Rating: 5★
46 avenue George V, 75008
01 40 69 60 00
fouquets-barriere.com
Rooms: 86
Single: 730–950€
Double: 730–950€
Suites: 21

This is the newest trendy hotel in Paris and already 'the spot' for celebrities. It is behind the restaurant Fouquet's, which for decades was a principal hangout for film stars and showbiz personalities. The food has never been remarkable (rising to one star but now without), but that has never stopped the dining-rooms being packed. A brand was established and now it has been used to launch a hotel. This is a luxurious place, a mix of steel-grey minimalism and designer Jacques Garcia in full flight. Like the Hôtel Costes, it looks somewhat like one imagines an upmarket Parisian bordello would look like, if such things were still allowed in Paris. It is also rather expensive, but it does have a spa. Book early if you want to get in and merge with the super-cool.

Shannon: I'm absolutely stuffed, wrecked and I feel like Morgan Spurlock in Prada. I take back everything I have said in the France book about Scott on our trip from Monte-Carlo to Paris. He didn't really complain as much as I said about driving on a spare tyre from Maison Lameloise in Chagny to Paris. He didn't care at all.

If fact, after we limped into Paris, he finally learnt how to use the satellite-navigation system and my blood sugar levels dropped back to normal. I was starting to black out just as he got us to the door of the most boganville hotel in Paris. It is a place that Scott had wanted to review for a while, so he got me to book and pay the 740€, which included an upgrade to a Junior suite! Wow, now I'm excited, though still a bit sceptical.

To park our car out the front we really needed to be in a McLaren or an Audi R8 Spyder with the roof down to get noticed by the doorman. So Scott, who never swears, swore and cut in front of another driver and parked metres from the front door. Still no help!

We risked having our car towed away and went inside to be confronted by the most boring lot of grumpy faces behind a counter I have seen. Now I know why all the people who pay $5,000 a year so that they can have a wanky black card stay here. It makes sense now.

We have a Skype meeting planned with Eugenie, our *New York* book editor (we had to proofread the book while eating and driving around France, so please excuse any mistakes!). We hurry up to the room. I am thinking, 'Junior suite. Scott can start the meeting while I get sorted, then head off to the gym.' But the junior suite is just a normal room. It is very nice, though, and I must say better than the Murano Urban Resort!

I am introduced to my butler. You wouldn't believe this either! It's Romain from Syracuse in Melbourne. He worked literally 20 metres from Vue de monde. We know all the team from Syracuse; it's run by two great blokes, Paul and Charlie. This guy turns my thinking around. He goes though everything with me and I have a one-stop button for everything. It's like I have a cattle prod wrapped around his ankle and anything I need I just press the remote to his ankle bracelet. Now I have to work out what I'm going to use him for. Maybe he can go to the gym for me! But, on a serious note, the butler service is a wonderful and very efficient service.

The gym is fantastic. So is the pool and so are the two girls managing the pool.

Scott finally finishes the corrections on the New York book with Eugenie, the meeting I'm meant to be in, but the room is too bloody small. So, Scott goes down for a swim and his back seizes up, but he loves the pool and he loves the girls. We are having a ripper of a day. Scott finally heads off to his one of his French cousins' for an overnight stay and I settle in to watch a film. Going through the choices on the screen, which is projected through a two-way mirror (very nice), I chose *Iron Man 2*. It's a senseless film that I will love. I am about to press 'Confirm' when my hand seizes. 18€ for a film? Even though I try to force my fingers onto the okay button, I just cannot do it! Not after having fits at Madeleine for buying three different types of cereal for the kids and yelling we cannot afford them and then realising what a ridiculous thing to say. I'm really not happy here.

Breakfast the next day is lovely and is included in the room rate, so is the minibar with all non-alcoholic drinks, including the Barrière's own energy drink!

There is so much to like about this hotel. But the price, combined with the location just off the Champs-Élysées with all its budget-airline crowd and bogans, just doesn't cut it for me. I wouldn't mind as much if the people staying here didn't take themselves so seriously, but I suppose that may happen to you when you decide to accept that invitation for your titanium AMEX!

A lovely boutique hotel in the 8th arrondissement, just round the corner from the Champs-Élysées and avenue George V, the **François 1ᵉʳ** has been decorated by architect Pierre-Yves Rochon in a rich and luxurious 'country-house' style. The entrance and lobby will instantly win you over, as will the wood-lined bar and the comfortable salon with its distinctive chocolate-and-white-striped crockery (the pieces look like they have been made out of sugar). The Standard rooms are lovely and spacious, with abundant toile de Jouy and a calm use of colours; the Executive rooms have colour schemes that may well overwhelm. This is a very cosy home away from home.

Hôtel François 1ᵉʳ

Rating: 4★+
7 rue Magellan, 75008
01 47 23 44 04
the-paris-hotel.com
Rooms: 40
Single: 350–490€
Double: 350–490€
Suites: 2

8ᵀᴴ

Scott: This is a gorgeous hotel.

I had arrived in Paris exhausted after a two-week charge through France and too many three-star restaurants to remember, with Shannon at the wheel of our Audi A3—three wheels, that is; he shredded the fourth—to arrive at my much-beloved Hôtel Balzac.

However, when I tried to check in, I was told there was no room for me. A conference had been extended and the delegates wanted to stay longer. 'These are not people one says "no" to', the manger politely confided. 'But we have arranged a lovely room for you at a nearby hotel of exactly the same standard. They are waiting for you now. I will have someone take your bags, or would you like to relax first and have a drink as our guest?' I took up the offer and had a superb coffee and chocolates. How did they make the coffee so well? In France?

A little sad to be leaving the Balzac, I declined the kind offer of assistance, as the Hôtel François 1ᵉʳ was just a few hundred metres away across the Champs-Élysées.

At the François 1ᵉʳ, I was met by a man even more charming than the one at the Balzac—how was this possible?—who apologised for the discomfort I had been put through and assured me how happy the Hotel François 1ᵉʳ was to have me as its guest instead of the Balzac.

I looked around: everything was perfect and pristine and preciously French. The Balzac now seemed a distant regret.

My room was glorious. Some might say it was a trifle small for the price (370€), but it was more than large enough for me, and the quality of the furnishings and fittings were superb. I just loved my room. I didn't want to leave, which was just as well as my back seized up and I couldn't walk. Cars really need four wheels to go well. But my reduced mobility meant I really got to know my room. We bonded.

The public rooms, when I did venture out the next morning, I discovered to be just as superb, from the romantic breakfast cellar to the spacious and library-quiet sitting rooms.

When I left, the charming manager gave me a reassuring pat on the back as I hobbled off to the taxi and a plane home.

I had found the Parisian boutique hotel of my dreams.

. . . .

Hôtel Lancaster

Rating: 5★
7 rue de Berri, 75008
01 40 76 40 76
hotel-lancaster.fr
Rooms: 46
Single: 520–670€
Double: 520–670€
Suites: 11

Just a few steps from the Champs-Élysées, the **Lancaster** brims with history. (For film lovers, it was the Paris base of such actors as Dirk Bogarde, Marlene Dietrich and Lauren Bacall.) The walls are hung with paintings by Russian-born artist Boris Pastoukhoff, who famously paid for his board with artworks. The rooms, which face either the inner courtyard or the street, are discreetly elegant, the Art Déco bathrooms superb. Unlike many luxury hotels that rely on reproduction furniture, the Lancaster is plush with rare antiques, fabrics and porcelain. The Japanese-style Zen garden is small but filled with light. Standard rooms aren't enormous (26 m²) but they are gorgeous; the higher-grade rooms would surely satisfy any guest. A few years ago, the Lancaster invited Michel Troisgros, who has a three-star restaurant in Roanne, to oversee the hotel restaurant, La Table du Lancaster. It now has one star and is rumoured to be in line for more. For a luxury hotel, the Lancaster is unusually intimate and warmly enveloping. However, the rue Berri is not one of the prettiest streets in Paris, and the hotel looks a little unassuming (especially in overcast weather) from the outside.

The 8th arrondissement is leading the charge of boutique hotels charging four- and even five-star prices. Pershing Hall is the most famous (and hardest to get into); far more cutting-edge is **Le A**. Don't be fooled by the Haussmannian façade: this is a proudly modernist hotel. Designed by Frédéric Méchiche, the public rooms are a blaze of black and white. The guest rooms are duo-tone (fawn and white), with stripes on the floors or walls that are reminiscent of the Daniel Buren columns in the Palais Royal (a controversial legacy of President Mitterrand). The furniture is of Wenge timber.

Hôtel Le A

Rating: 4★
4 rue d'Artois, 75008
01 42 56 99 99
paris-hotel-a.com
Rooms: 25
Single: 189–499€
Double: 206–499€
Suites: 1

8ᵀᴴ

Pershing Hall

Rating: 4★
49 rue Pierre Charon, 75008
01 58 36 58 00
pershinghall.com
Rooms: 49
Single: 320–470€
Double: 320–470€
Suites: 6

Pershing Hall is the most expensive boutique hotel in Paris and easily the most sought-after. For the past decade or so, it has been a success bordering on a sensation. It has a luxury that belies its Michelin 3★ rating, and its hidden retractable-roof garden is the envy of Paris. The garden, which serves as a restaurant and drinks area, is alone worth the price of a stay. According to *Taschen's Paris*, 'tout Paris dines here'. The hotel interior, by designer Andrée Putman, is surprisingly muted, employing colours such as avocado and taupe: some people find the rooms a little understated, if not plain. The bathrooms have stand-alone baths; there is a small fitness centre and spa. Book well ahead because Pershing Hall is always full (especially of Americans, who have a knack for quickly discovering hotel gems).

Meliá Royal Alma Boutique Hotel

Rating: 4★
35 rue Jean-Goujon, 75008
01 53 93 63 00
solmelia.com
Rooms: 70
Single: 260–340€
Double: 260–340€
Suites: 9

This hotel no longer appears in Michelin or GaultMillau, yet it is a charming luxury hotel at remarkably reasonable prices. From the outside it looks uninspiring (a blank modern façade), but once inside you'll be enraptured. All the rooms are subtly yet sumptuously furnished and extremely comfortable. The rue Jean-Goujon is one of the most impressive streets in Paris, beautifully located in the triangle defined by the Seine, the rear of the Grand Palais and the avenue Montaigne. It is a pity the hotel's website is so unappealing. This lovely hotel deserves to be better presented.

Scott: My wife Alissa stayed here a few years ago and thought it easily the best hotel she had visited in Paris. Other people I have sent here have been equally impressed, refusing to return anywhere else. Its absence from Michelin and GaultMillau is inexplicable.

After undergoing extensive renovation work, **Le Royal Monceau** reopened its doors in October 2010. Designer Philippe Starck, under the creative direction of Alexandre Allard, has completely transformed the place and reinvented its spirit so as to make Le Royal Monceau the latest Parisian hotspot. Its newly opened Italian restaurant, Il Carpaccio, has already won the hearts of the *foodinistas*.

Le Royal Monceau

Rating: 5★+
37 avenue Hoche, 75008
01 42 99 88 00
leroyalmonceau.com
Rooms: 150
Single: 780–930€
Double: 780–930€
Suites: 64

A perfect hotel, from its stunning façade and window-boxes brimming with red flowers to a staircase decorated with stained glass, and guest rooms you won't ever want to leave. It is located in a residential part of the 8th, bordered by the Seine, the Grand Palais and the avenue Montaigne. It is quiet, supremely elegant and discreet, yet just a short walk to wherever you want to seek fun; many would say this is the best part of the Rive Gauche. The hotel's very pretty restaurant is in the lounge-library, but you may be tempted to wander further afield, given there are so many great restaurants nearby (such as Lasserre, Ledoyen and Alain Ducasse au Plaza Athénée).

Hôtel San Régis

Rating: 5★
12 rue Jean-Goujon, 75008
01 44 95 16 16
hotel-sanregis.fr
Rooms: 33
Single: 350–745€
Double: 465–745€
Suites: 11

Scott: I stayed in an apartment opposite the San Régis in 2007 and, much as I loved it, I spent some time wishing I were across the road. Few hotels are so picture-perfect from the street, or on so gorgeous a street. One year I confused the Meliá Royal Alma Boutique Hotel (which my wife loves) with the **San Régis** and sent a film producer requesting a good deal to the latter by mistake. She has never forgiven me the cost, but insists it is the finest hotel she has ever stayed in and that it ruined all her future trips to Paris.

L'Hôtel de Sers

Rating: 4★+
41 avenue Pierre 1ᵉʳ de
Serbie, 75008
01 53 23 75 75
hoteldesers.com
Rooms: 49
Single: 450–550€
Double: 480–680€
Suites: 3

If purple is your colour, Paris certainly looks after you. It is a design choice at countless hotels, including the **de Sers**. Described by their website as conveying a 'contemporary melancholy', the design combines old-world paintings with modern furnishings and, yes, purple carpet (the same colour as some exterior walls). As at the Murano Urban Resort, you can adjust the lighting in your room to suit your mood. The Panoramic suites are breathtaking and have few equals, even among five-star-deluxe hotels. There is a gym, hamman and spa, with a bath menu. The hotel is very well placed, just off the avenue George V: you can, for example, walk to the famous Le Bar at the Four Seasons George V in a few unhurried minutes.

Hôtel Le 123 Élysées

Rating: 4★
123 rue du faubourg Saint-
Honoré, 75008
01 53 89 01 23
astotel.com
Rooms: 41
Single: 199–420€
Double: 209–450€

The **123 Elysées** is another modernist affair, located north of the Champs-Élysées on the famous street known for its fashion designers and antique stores. Designed by Philippe Maidenberg, the hotel's interior is notable for its mix of fabrics and textures (leather, velvet, silk) in soft pastels against white walls and pale wooden floors. The guest rooms are mostly grey and white, without a patterned fabric or wallpaper to be seen; some rooms have modern four-poster beds. The hotel has an impressive staircase set against red brick walls, which is sometimes described as a 'London-style' staircase but is just as typical of modernised hotels in Eastern Europe.

Great DVD Shops

Virgin Megastore
52-60 avenue des Champs-Élysées, 75008
virginmegastore.fr

The best place to buy DVDs and CDs in Paris, even if it is an extremely frustrating exercise. Apart from a small 'Classics of French Cinema' section, all the French movies are bundled in with the Hollywood ones (with the latter filed under their French title, not the original), which makes searching for French movies rather arduous. Still, if you are prepared to put in the hours (and it does take hours), you will be able to build up a staggering collection of Godard, Bardot and Delon. But apart from the odd specials, prices are dear (especially for the NTSC-format imports).

FNAC
74 avenue des Champs-Élysées, 75008
fnac.com

FNAC is better organised than Virgin, but its range is far smaller. Still, it is only a short stroll away and visiting both is one of the joys of shopping in Paris. Like Virgin, it also has a fabulous collection of CDs.

 APARTMENTS

Paris Address
parisaddress.com

Scott: I have stayed in apartments in Paris on several occasions. Recently, I stayed in a gorgeous but small one on rue Jean-Goujon (opposite the Hôtel San Régis). It is perfectly located, provided you do not mind walking up to the Champs-Élysées to find a supermarket. The view from the terrace, over a private courtyard to the Tour Eiffel, was spectacular, especially when the tower was lit up at night. The furnishings were lovely, even if the second bed would be too small for anyone over the age of eight (I fled to a hotel to remove the cricks from my back). There was also full-on construction in the next-door flat. As usual, it is a case of 'renter beware'.

CONCORDE
FINE DINING (WITH LUXURY HOTEL)

....

Les Ambassadeurs

Chef: Christophe Hache
Hôtel de Crillon
10 place Concorde, 75008
01 44 71 16 16
crillon.com
Michelin: ★
GaultMillau: 🍴🍴🍴
Menu: 68 (weekday lunch)/140€
À la carte: 100–180€

Les Ambassadeurs is situated in the former Salon des Ambassadeurs in what was once the home of the dukes of Crillon (now the Hôtel de Crillon). It is a spectacular 18th-century room, golden light bouncing off the Siena marble walls and pillars, all delicately modernised by Sybille de Margerie. In the 1990s, the restaurant gained a considerable reputation under chef Christian Constant, who left to start his own restaurant, Le Violon d'Ingres. From 2004, the restaurant was under the inspired guidance of Jean-François Piège and many considered its mere two-star rating nothing short of a national scandal. Piège then left for Thoumieux, Les Ambassadeurs closing for refurbishment. It reopened in April 2010 under chef Christophe Hache, who has worked with Alain Senderens and Éric Frechon. The battle to regain multiple stars has begun.

Liz and Craig: This is a truly extraordinary dining space; the detail and decoration are decadent. Each table has so much room around it we felt as if we were dining alone—except, that is, for the hard-to-ignore neighbouring table, at which a very smartly dressed French couple were sitting with their small son (about eight years old, we thought). Dressed in a mini version of his father's suit, the boy sat calmly through the entire meal, choosing from the same menu as his parents, as if he were 48.

One dish that stands out in the memory was the *Coquilles St Jacques*, with generous discs of truffle leaning against the scallop structure. The scallops were perfect: just opaque but still transparent to the centre. We also had a dish of *homard bleu*: we found the texture rather challenging (we prefer our lobster a little more cooked). The pigeon with foie gras was superb. The servings were incredibly generous, particularly the foie gras, but it made the meal as a whole perhaps a little rich. The cheese trolley was to die for. It was nothing short of torture to have to limit our selection. Each cheese was in perfect condition.

The sommelier was brilliant. He first asked us to indicate what wines we were interested in and then discussed the dishes and the possibility of having a glass of wine with each. The wines he suggested were all within the price range of the ones we had mentioned.

We loved it.

Scott: In the early 1980s, I was staying at **Le Meurice**, but its stunning Grand Siècle dining-room had been turned into a conference room and all the hotel had to offer was a Texan Grill. So I headed west along the rue de Rivoli to the Hôtel de Crillon and Les Ambassadeurs. It was then a two-star, under the command of chef Jean-Paul Bonin. It was also one of the few quality places open on a Sunday evening.

The dining-room was quite breathtaking in its imperial beauty and was filled with the most elegantly attired patrons imaginable. It felt like attending a private soirée, where the sound level never rose above that of a babbling brook.

As my guests, I took my Versailles-based aunt Diane and her husband Pierre. Because Pierre wears the discreet thread of the Légion d'honneur in his lapel, the maître d' quite understandably concluded that Pierre was paying. So, he alone was trusted with the menu listing prices. When it came time to order dessert, however, I was accorded the honour of the prices. The staff, you see, had noticed that I selected the wine (a Bonne Mares), and quickly and silently corrected their false assumption. That is true service.

I do not recall all that much of the meal, which is strange in that I remember every detail of my visit to **La Tour d'Argent** three years earlier. What I do recall was an excellent *Daurade rôtie à l'ail doux, sauce vierge* (Sea Bream roasted with sweet garlic, with a sauce of uncooked tomatoes) and a dessert of 'sweet gnocchi' (tiny puffs of choux pastry filled with warm fruit creams). Having personally ordered the fine but unexciting sorbets, I sat there regretting a menu selection with more intensity than I have ever done before or since. The gnocchi were clouds of pure pleasure.

Hôtel de Crillon

Rating: 5★+
10 place de la Concorde,
75008
01 44 71 15 00
crillon.com
Rooms: 119
Single: 770€
Double: 770–1200€
Suites: 28

The grandest of all the top Parisian hotels, the **Hôtel de Crillon** stands majestically overlooking the place de la Concorde and the Obélisque de Luxor (where the guillotine stood during the French Revolution). For decades, the Crillon refused to modernise (air-conditioning was outlawed as vulgar), but in recent times it has subtly moved forwards: it was, for example, one of the first luxury hotels to dispense with the demeaning check-in desk, guests instead being shepherded to individual tables in the great lobby, each with a discreet slide-out computer. The Crillon is the epitome of elegance and style, and its one-star restaurant, Les Ambassadeurs, is one of the most ravishing dining spaces in Paris; fortunately, it is also where breakfast is served. An alternative to Les Ambassadeurs is the less expensive but still fine L'Obélisque. For the young at heart, underneath the Crillon (on the rue Boissy d'Anglas) is the ludicrously expensive Buddha Bar.

Liz and Craig: The biggest surprise of the Hôtel de Crillon was the incredibly welcoming and friendly staff. I had thought that in such a prestigious hotel we were at risk of being treated as nobodies, but the opposite was the case. Our room was beautifully decorated but, of course, small and the ceiling was disappointingly low for such a grand building (perhaps to make way for the recently installed air-conditioning). One imagines that, being such a grand building, its rooms would be airy. Contributing to a slightly confined feel was the fact the room looked into a courtyard. Only a couple of suites have views over the place de la Concorde. When we arrived, we asked naïvely if we could have a room overlooking the square, and were very tactfully told that only the best suites have such a view. Rather than making us feel silly, they sent a bottle of champagne to our room.

The bathroom was also a little disappointing in that it was dated (very late-1980s salmon-beige colours) and in need of a freshen-up. Breakfast in Les Ambassadeurs was, however, worth spending the night for, with the sun pouring in through the windows on the place de la Concorde; we were there in winter and the light on the gilded walls brought the room to life. The presentation of the breakfast was everything you'd expect from a hotel of this calibre and reputation (the homemade jams and brioche were amazing).

FINE DINING

Built in 1791, but completely redesigned in neoclassical style in 1842, **Ledoyen** is a striking building set in the Champs-Élysées gardens between the place de la Concorde and the Petit Palais. It is a fairytale setting, with the restaurant on the second floor affording remarkable and calming views. (Downstairs is the Pavillon Ledoyen, which is used for special events; the liveried staff you may see on arrival are not necessarily for you.) The restaurant is now at its culinary peak under the guidance of Breton chef Christian Le Squer. The only challenge about this restaurant is finding it: don't just study a map beforehand, take it with you.

Ledoyen
Chef: Christian Le Squer
carré Champs-Élysées,
75008
01 53 05 10 01
no website
Michelin: ★★★
GaultMillau: 👨👨👨👨
Menu: 88 (lunch)/199/299€
À la carte: 160–285€

Shannon: I really enjoyed Ledoyen. My expectations weren't huge: it was probably my third or fourth choice for a Friday lunch, but everywhere else was fully booked. Scott, Madeleine and I had a mutual friend with us in Paris, Simon, so we had to try and accommodate everyone's needs and what everyone would like to eat. We thought there was no better place than this, just off the Champs-Élysées in a lovely little park. It was the perfect setting, in a grand old building.

The booking was easily made on the day. When we arrived, the Pavillon Ledoyen was hosting a press call for models for some Parisian fashion shows, which was a pleasant surprise! You enter the Napoléon III dining-room up a grand staircase, and every seat has a view over the Champs-Élysées, which is perfect. Tables are well spaced and the atmosphere is pretty glamorous; there is plenty of conversation going on; it is not stuffy in any way. The service is very experienced, with older waiters, but don't be intimidated by that, because it is what great French dining is about. This restaurant deservedly has three stars.

Simon had arrived 15 minutes before us, and asked for a pot of chamomile tea. He says he's never had tea service like it.

Ledoyen has a great-value lunch menu (three courses, with two offerings per course), which I think is important, especially in Paris. From memory, we started with langoustines. The main courses were a lamb dish, *Canon d'agneau*, and Tuna with a tomato coulis. I was staggered by the presentation of the fairly humble food and by all the extras: the little *amuse-bouches*, a wonderful cleansing course, an exceptional pre-dessert, amazing petits fours with the coffee. The execution was sensational: everything was perfectly cut; there was no slapping something on the plate. Just be aware that in France Tuna is usually served rare. That's something Madeleine had to come to terms with! I think it's very important to remember that eating in France is about the execution of perfection, and eating the way the chef intends. You will have to mention if you'd prefer something cooked more, especially meat and oily fish.

I enjoyed watching the customers, especially one older gentleman accompanied by his lovely young mistress, both immaculately dressed; neither of them spoke a word to the other throughout the meal. Those sorts of moments remind me that I'm really in Paris.

Shannon's Favourite Parisian Treats

Caviar

The best caviar comes from the Caspian Sea. Due to over-harvesting, wild Russian caviar is banned in many countries, but not France. There are several varieties farmed across Europe, including in France and Italy. Farmed caviar is very popular in Paris and the company Prunier has a long tradition of producing quality caviar; it is by no means a cheap or lesser alternative.

Kaspia

Since 1927

17 place de la Madeleine, 75008

01 40 17 95 71

lamaisonkaspia.com

The shop, beneath the restaurant of the same name, is a veritable Aladdin's cave. It has the traditional Caspian range—from Beluga down to Sevruga—along with farmed caviars, including Baccari (from a hybrid sturgeon) and Baéri (from Russian sturgeon bred in France and Italy). There is also a range of smoked Salmon, Swordfish, Tuna, Marlin and, best of all, Sturgeon (farmed in France), as well as other luxury foods. Accompanying the food are its own vodkas and champagne. There is a restaurant (Kaspia) upstairs.

Scott: This has long been one of my favourite shops in the world. The Russian ladies with their Soviet-style lack of charm make buying anything quite a challenge, but their products are always well worth it.

Another joy is the vodka: Kaspia used to be one of the few places in the world you could get decent Russian and Polish vodka,

including Stolichnaya Cristal, which was for decades the best premium vodka. (Fabergé now wins hands down. Don't listen to all the hype about Russian Standard; it isn't in the same league.) Today, sadly, Kaspia seems to concentrate on its own brands. So, if you are not happy with what you can find to drink with your precious caviar, head off to Hédiard or Nicolas (both a few metres away). Do make sure the vodka you decide on is really cold and viscous. Cold vodka and quality caviar go straight onto the list of the World's Greatest Culinary Pairings, alongside tarragon and chicken, macaroni and truffle, and wine and dear friends.

Petrossian

Since 1920

18 boulevard de Latour-Mauborg, 75007

01 44 11 32 22

petrossian.fr

The Petrossian family has run this caviar boutique throughout its life. It has a slightly more upmarket image than Kaspia, probably because its restaurant, Le 144, has at times risen to culinary greatness. (A few years ago, Le 144 had two stars and was destined for three; with the departure of Philippe Conticini, things went rather quiet, though hopes are held for Rougui Dia, whose food GaultMillau rates with two toques.) Regardless, Petrossian is still one of the two top places in Paris for caviar. Like Kaspia, it also specialises in a stunning array of smoked fish and crustaceans (such as scallops).

Bar L'Éclaireur

10 rue Boissy d'Anglais,
75008
01 53 43 09 99
Menu: 10–30€

Luxury fashion and interior-design store L'Éclaireur operates an über-chic bar and restaurant behind its shop in the arcade Galerie Royale. It's a great place (with a great atmosphere) to take a break from power-shopping with an alfresco lunch, even in cool weather since there are outdoor heating lamps. The shop sells items ranging from handbags to cool glasses and trays. It is 'now' Paris, but with respect for the past.

Shannon: Behind the Hôtel de Crillon, this place has great coffee with little surprises, such as *pain d'épices*.

MADELEINE
FINE DINING

Senderens

Chef: Alain Senderens
9 place de la Madeleine,
75008
01 42 65 22 90
senderens.fr
Michelin: ★★
GaultMillau: ♕♕♕
Menu: 110/150€
(wine included)
À la carte: 75–110€

Alain Senderens is from the South-West. He came to Paris at 21 as *chef rôtisseur* at La Tour d'Argent. After then working at renowned restaurant Lucas Carton, and in a few luxury hotels, Senderens opened his own restaurant, L'Archestrate, in 1968, in rue de l'Exposition, later moving to the rue de la Varenne (in the building now occupied by L'Arpège). He gained his third Michelin star in 1978. He returned to Lucas Carton as owner-chef in 1985, where he pioneered the matching of wine with each course of a meal. This infuriated snobby critics, who claimed he had turned his restaurant into a wine bar. A few years ago, Senderens created a new scandal by returning his three stars to Michelin, saying he was tired of the limitations imposed on three-star chefs (all that foie gras and truffles) and wanted to cook simpler, more affordable food; he also changed the restaurant name to **Senderens**. Michelin retaliated by giving him two stars. Senderens' passionate belief in not interfering with the purity of quality ingredients was revolutionary in the 1990s, when Nouvelle Cuisine had a tendency to over-fiddle and include too many disparate ingredients (a flaw that haunts diners to this day).

Shannon: Senderens was for me a surprise. I had had no intention of actually dining there, but I loved the area it was located in—you walk up the rue Royale to the place de la Madeleine. This is the best part of Paris when it comes to shops, architecture, history; it is a beautiful area with big wide streets.

Walking around the area I saw the restaurant and wandered in to have a look. (It's actually quite difficult to spot, as the signage is discreet and you don't notice a lot of people coming in and out. It always looks closed!)

I thought the restaurant was going to be very stuffy and 'old-world', but it was in fact very modern and inspired by Philippe Starck's work, with touches of beautifully restored history throughout; there are no tablecloths, which gives it a bistro feel. Also a surprise to me was the lunch menu, which was terrific value. I had a tempura of langoustine, which was sensational, followed by chicken with mushrooms for a main. The food is very well executed and the portions perfect. It has a great wine list and I really loved the wines that were served with each course. I also had a great dessert: a taste of four crèmes brûlées. They were the most perfect ones you could imagine.

The restaurant is divided into several rooms. I walked out of our two-hour lunch totally satisfied: the cooking was very modern; it's a credit to a historic chef like Senderens (he's now 72) to be producing such food at his age. I think the restaurant's blend of interior design, style of service and cuisine is exactly 'in sync' with modern Paris. I loved it: great buzz, great atmosphere. There were loads of business people and very few tourists, which I like: it makes me feel I am not just following the herd from restaurant to restaurant. I am sure that anyone who goes there will be pleasantly surprised.

David: I recently had lunch at Senderens with a close friend who is very close to Michelin. We had a superb 'Passage'. The restaurant was full on all floors; it was cheap as chips and is one of the bargains of Paris lunchtime. I had eaten here when it was Lucas Carton probably 20 times but never since the latest incarnation. Of course, the décor, wine, food and service are all very different to before. I like it a lot, but I am not sure that the whole package is worth two stars, even though the food alone deserves it.

Scott: I went to Senderens in the days when it was still the three-star restaurant known as Lucas Carton. It was in 1997. My wife Alissa and I arrived at the magnificent Art Déco restaurant (as architecturally perfect as any in Paris) and, from the first moment, it was magic. Alissa is generally uncomfortable about three-star formality, but this restaurant was filled with a soothing elegance and charm. She felt immediately at ease.

For Alain Senderens, matching wine and food was not just a case of complementing his signature dishes (such as duck with Roman spices, or lobster with Madagascan vanilla bean, surely the best lobster dish ever): he often spent months creating a dish to match a new wine he had discovered. This was just as likely to be a peasant variety wine from an unknown region as a grand cru (his preferring little-known wines caused great derision at the time).

My first course was two large zucchini flowers stuffed with crab, and two with *homard*; a white Gevrey-Chambertin was the perfect match. My main of roasted Bresse chicken was served in two parts, the second (a leg given additional grilling) with a 1949 Volnay. The understanding was that a glass would be refilled if you were still eating. In the case of the Volnay, this was exceedingly generous as a glass of it cost twice as much as the chicken.

As an example of Senderens' simplifying philosophy, take my dessert. It was a baked peach with vanilla ice-cream. That's it. The peach, not unexpectedly, was sublime (and ever so slightly al dente); as was the ice-cream, which was churned to order. Senderens was a pioneer in making ice-cream a fresh (and refreshing) experience. Sadly, I cannot remember the wine match.

The most dramatic example of his wine-and-food matching, though, was Alissa's cheese course. There were four cheeses matched with four wines, three of which were white, including an 80-year-old Banyuls (a fortified wine from the Pyrénées). At the end of this simple and extraordinary meal, Alissa mentioned how much she had liked the Banyuls. A moment later, our waiter returned with a bottle of it and two glasses: this warm and most generous gesture would have transformed a bad meal into a pleasant experience; in our case, it just made a perfect meal even more memorable.

If you have the strength of will to walk past the shop downstairs, which sells caviar, smoked fish and vodka, upstairs is a delightfully eccentric restaurant.

Kaspia

17 place de la Madeleine,
75008
01 42 65 66 21
lamaisonkaspia.com
Menu: 69/109/189€
À la carte: 45–235€

8ᵗʰ

Liz and Craig: After walking through the beautiful streets of Paris on a cold day, we decided to have a late lunch at **Kaspia**. We were not properly dressed for the visit and the looks from the welcoming committee made sure we knew that. We sat down as the lunch crowd was just finishing up, a mixture of perfectly tailored 'suits' and immaculately dressed older people.

We ordered the world's most expensive baked potato, which was scooped out, mashed and then refilled, topped with crème fraîche and Sevruga caviar. It was unbelievably good. With this we ordered shots of the best vodka in the house. The first was poured at the table, reasonably short of the brim, but, after the waiter observed how much we enjoyed the experience, the subsequent shots were filled to the top. As we warmed up to the lunch, thanks to the vodka, so did the staff's attitude and attention; suddenly we had become very important diners! We think they enjoyed our enthusiasm for the lunch as much as we enjoyed the lunch. Such was the experience, in the shop we bought a set of shot glasses and mother-of-pearl spoons: we have replicated the potato dish at a number of subsequent dinner parties, but using Salmon roe instead of Sevruga!

Hôtel Bedford

17 rue de l'Arcade, 75008
01 44 94 77 77
hotel-bedford.com
Rooms: 135
Single: 172–354€
Double: 206–354€

This discreetly elegant hotel, nicely positioned a short walk away from place de la Madeleine, was built in 1860, though it is perhaps more famous for its 1900 Belle Époque dinning room. With a remarkable glass-domed ceiling, this spectacular space is now a notable restaurant after having been a breakfast room—but what a breakfast room!—for too long. The guest rooms are subtly toned, spacious for the price and restful, as indeed are the public rooms—this is a hotel of restraint. Too few people stay near Madeleine: here is your chance!

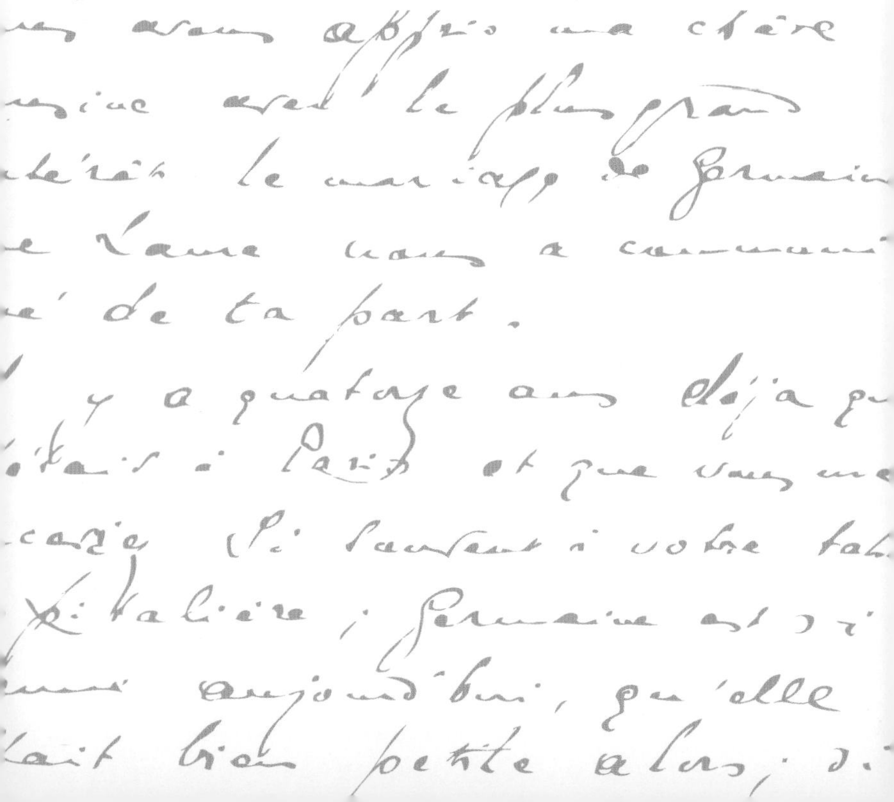

Shannon's Favourite Parisian Treats

Truffles

French cuisine simply could not exist without the humble truffle.

Maison de la Truffe

Since 1932
19 place de la Madeleine, 75008
01 42 65 53 22
Also at:
14 rue Marbeuf, 75008
maison-de-la-truffe.com

One of the most gorgeous and eccentric food stores in Paris, this is, not surprisingly, a temple to the truffle. You can buy fresh truffles from all around the world, in season; when they are not, you can find them preserved in all manner of ways. They are also mixed in with various other ingredients. If hunger strikes, you can go to the restaurant and eat *Œuf poché truffé en gelée* (truffled poached egg), thinly sliced truffle with champagne-smoked Salmon and boiled potatoes or *Foie gras d'oie truffé en millefeuille* (millefeuille of goose foie gras and toast). Goose foie gras is getting increasingly hard to find these days, so make the most of it. But how can anyone go past a truffled white sausage (*boudin blanc*) with a Périgord black-truffle purée?

Shannon's Favourite Parisian Treats

Food Stores

Entering one of the great Parisian speciality stores, you feel like a child visiting Disneyland for the first time. They truly are magic kingdoms.

Fauchon

Since 1886
24–26 place de la Madeleine, 75008
01 70 39 38 00
fauchon.com

Fauchon was once revered as the epitome of a Parisian food emporium, but its aura appears to have slipped a tad. Its prepared foods don't look quite as inviting as before (all that dull aspic), the tea-room now uses teabags instead of loose tea and the name has become more an exercise in branding than something that truly excites. Still, it is only a short walk from the great place de la Madeleine trio of Kaspia, Hédiard and La Maison de Truffe, so why not drop in and check it out for yourself. But be aware there are now two Fauchon shops opposite each other; they have a rather supermarket feel.

La Grande Épicerie (at Le Bon Marché)

24-24 place de la Madeleine, 75008
01 70 39 38 00
lagrandeepicerie.fr

Le Bon Marché combines three main activities: a fine grocery store known as La Grande Épicerie; department stores Le Bon Marché Rive Gauche (the only one in Paris to offer a genuine cultural dimension) and the Franck & Fils store on the rue Passy, acquired in 1994; and real estate. La Grande Épicerie (owned by Hédiard) has a mindboggling array of foodstuffs and wine, both French and from around the globe. It is the perfect place to buy absolutely everything you could need to stock your apartment or to take on a picnic. Equally, grab a hamper so you don't starve on a plane or train trip.

Hédiard

Since 1854
21 place de la Madeleine, 75008
01 43 12 88 88
Also at:
31 avenue Georges V, 75008
Printemps Haussmann,
115 rue de Provence, 75009
Terminal Eurostar, Gare du Nord, 75010
Gare de Lyon, place Louis Armand, 75012
70 avenue Paul Doumer, 75016
106 boulevard de Courcelles, 75017
hediard.com

Of all the (purely) gourmet food stores in Paris, Hédiard reigns supreme. At the place de la Madeleine shop, the fruit and vegetable area is a masterpiece of pristine produce, lovingly presented. The wine and spirits selection is also remarkable for the quality and range packed into a small area. The deli section has intricately presented food but without the tizziness other stores resort to. In total, there are 6000 gourmet items on sale. Yes, traditionally there has been a Soviet feel to the way you get served, but why argue with tradition? Hédiard is brilliantly located, next door to the Maison de la Truffe and two doors from Kaspia. Nowhere else in the world has three stores of such iconic standing nestling side by side.

Scott: One day I went to the fruit section here and bought a pear that cost $17 (and this is quite a few years ago). It was individually numbered, with the name of the Normandy orchard printed on a label stuck on with red wax. Biting into the pear on the street, I wanted to let out a scream of joy. I have never had a piece of fruit to equal it—it was as sublime an eating experience as the plate of herb-scented peas at Bras or Senderens' lobster with Madagascan vanilla. The price, ultimately, was irrelevant.

I also love Hédiard for its Armagnac selection, which includes a bottling from almost every year of the 20th century. As my sister adores Armagnac, this is where I go to get a bottle from her birth year (given the price, this tends to be once a decade).

Shannon's Parisian Recipes

Chocolate Soufflé

Soufflés are utterly delicious, and it is worth travelling to Paris just to eat one! It is very easy to notice the disaster of a failed soufflé, but sometimes appearances can be deceptive: a souffle that looks perfect may not be perfectly cooked inside, or the flavour balance may not be correct. Far too many people replace the skill of making a soufflé with adding too much sugar. I find modern soufflés, all around the world, way too sweet.

A soufflé should be very light and always be served with a sauce or ice-cream. The waiter should serve it at the table, make an incision in the soufflé and pour in the sauce, or drop in a quenelle of ice-cream (this then starts to melt and becomes sauce-like). My favourite flavours are chocolate and pistachio, but soufflés also reflect the seasons, so in late summer try one of the berry flavours or try stone fruits in winter (when a prune and Armagnac soufflé is a classic).

CRÈME PÂTISSIÈRE

325 ml milk
6 egg yolks
80 g caster sugar
25 g cocoa powder, sifted
50 g cornflour, sifted
25 g plain flour, sifted
80 g good-quality couverture, roughly chopped

To make the crème pâtissière, place the milk in a heavy-based saucepan over medium heat, bring to the boil and then set aside. Beat the egg yolks and sugar with an electric mixer. Add the cocoa powder and the flours, and continue beating until mixture is pale and thick. Pour one-third of the hot milk over the egg mix and whisk until smooth. Pour this mixture back into the remaining milk, place over low heat and whisk continuously until the custard begins to thicken and coats the back of the spoon. Remove from the heat as soon as it comes to the boil, place in a mixer bowl and beat on high speed, gradually adding the dark chocolate. Whisk until the chocolate has melted and the mixture is thick and smooth. Reserve in the fridge until required.

SOUFFLÉ MIX

40 g softened butter
50 g grated couverture
140 g egg whites
90 g caster sugar
extra cocoa powder to serve

Preheat the oven to 180°C.

Now prepare the soufflés. Butter four small copper pans and coat the insides with the grated chocolate. Beat the egg whites with an electric mixer until soft peaks have formed, then gradually add the sugar, continuing to beat until mixture is stiff and shiny. Remove crème pâtissière from fridge, take 6 tablespoons and smooth out in a separate bowl and add a tablespoon of the meringue. Fold it in gently and, once well incorporated, gently fold in the rest. Spoon the mix into the copper pans and place in preheated oven for 6–8 minutes.

CHOCOLATE SAUCE

300 ml cream
100 g couverture

To make the chocolate sauce, place cream in a small saucepan over medium heat and bring just to the boil. Remove from heat, pour over the chocolate and leave to soften for 1 minute. Whisk together until combined.

Dust cooked soufflés with the cocoa powder and serve with the chocolate sauce.

Serves 4

LOANO
MILLESIMO
DEGO
MONDOVI
ROVEREDO
BASSANO
S'GEORGES

MANTOUE
TAGLIAMENTO
SEDIMAN
MONT THABOR
CHEBREISSE
BASSIGNANO
SAN GIULIANO
DIETIKON
MUTTA THAL
GENES

LE VAR
MONTEBELLO
LE MINCIO
CALDIERO
CASTEL FRANCO
RAGUSE
GAETE

Opéra

RESTAURANT (WITH LUXURY HOTEL)

This is an extremely glamorous and famous restaurant in the Intercontinental Paris–Le Grand, with million-dollar views of the Opéra Garnier. Opened in May 1862, it has been attracting the Parisian hoi polloi (and American tourists) ever since.

Café de la Paix

Chef: Christophe Raoux
5 place de l'Opéra, 75009
01 40 07 36 36
cafedelapaix.fr
GaultMillau: 🍽️🍽️
Menu: 46 (lunch)/85€
À la carte: 60–135€

One of the most famous of Paris's luxury hotels, the **Paris–Le Grand** is on the rue Scribe, around the corner from the Opéra Garnier. That makes it a little adrift of the main hubbub (except for opera lovers), even if it is a relatively short walk west to the place de la Madeleine or south to the Louvre. It has long been a favourite of Americans (American Express is on the same street and many airlines have their main offices nearby). French New Wave director Jean-Luc Godard loved the hotel so much he shot his 1985 film *Détective* there. Standard rooms (45 m²) are rather dull; the dearer and better ones are in the flamboyant style of Napoléon III. The wallpaper and fabrics are predictably exquisite.

Intercontinental Paris–Le Grand

Rating: 5★+
2 rue Scribe, 75009
01 40 07 32 32
intercontinental.com
Rooms: 442
Single: 335–580€
Double: 335–580€
Suites: 28

BISTRO

This is a famous bastion of old-fashioned seafood dishes.

Charlot, Roi des Coquillages

12 place de Clichy, 75009
01 53 20 48 00
charlot-paris.com
Michelin: not listed
GaultMillau: 🍽️
Menu: 27 (lunch)/64€
(wine included)
À la carte: 40–80€

Shannon: Charlot is the only Parisian establishment to have signed up to the official bouillabaisse charter (which specifies the components of an authenthic bouillabaisse). Located in the historic area of Pigalle, the bistro is a lovely old space with food that is generally nothing to write home about except for the two-course bouillabaisse. First up is the soup, served with slices of baguette topped with cheese and grilled, plus extra cheese and a rouille. The second course is the fish that was cooked in the soup, classic species used being Weever, Scorpion Fish, Angler Fish and Bluemouth.

 HOTEL

Hôtel Amour

Rating: 3★
8 rue Navarin, 75009
01 48 78 31 80
hotelamourparis.fr
Rooms: 20
Single: 100€
Double: 150–280€

Located in a beautiful, quiet residential pocket of the 9th arrondissement close to Montmartre, this quirky place has become a darling of the international fashion and music world. The décor varies greatly from room to room. There is a beautiful boulangerie at the end of the street and excellent food shops right around the corner.

Shannon's Parisian Recipes

Crème Caramel

Ancient Romans discovered the binding properties of eggs, and utilised them in omelettes and sweet puddings. Custard dates back to the Middle Ages and versions of crème caramel, or custard tarts, can be found throughout Europe and parts of Asia. This is the simplest and most skilful French dessert there is.

CUSTARD
4 eggs
2 egg yolks
80 g caster sugar
2 cups milk

To prepare the custard, combine the eggs, egg yolks and caster sugar in a mixing bowl. (Do not over-beat, as this will create air bubbles.) Warm the milk in a saucepan and pour over the egg mixture, whisking constantly. Pour mixture through a fine sieve and set aside.

Preheat the oven to 100°C.

CARAMEL
300 g caster sugar
100 ml water

To make the caramel, combine the sugar and half of the water in a heavy-based saucepan and cook over medium heat for 3–4 minutes or until a light golden colour. Test with a sugar thermometer (the temperature should be 128–132°C). Very carefully stir in the remaining water and boil for 2 minutes. (If you don't have a thermometer, remove pan from heat as soon as caramel starts to turn golden, as the residual heat will bring it to the desired medium-gold colour.)

Place a teaspoonful of the caramel in the bottom of six dariole moulds and put aside for 20 minutes to set (use heat from the bottom of the oven if it has this option). Pour the custard over the caramel until each mould is three-quarters full. Place the moulds in a baking tray and pour boiling water into the tray to come halfway up the sides of the moulds. Bake in preheated oven for 45 minutes or until set. Place in the refrigerator for at least 30 minutes or until ready to serve (they are best served within 24 hours).

To turn out custards, place each mould in warm water, then gently invert onto a small serving plate.

Makes 6

Gare de l'Est,
Gare du Nord

10TH ARRONDISSEMENT

BRASSERIES

Jean-Paul Bucher's Groupe Flo caused a lot of controversy by buying up many of Paris's historic brasseries. People were concerned the restaurants' souls would be lost, but in fact Groupe Flo has restored these restaurants to their pristine best and guaranteed a decent standard of cuisine. Some of the atmosphere of shabby old Paris has gone, but one can only applaud the group for having saved these icons from the scrap-heap of history. The group's namesake brasserie is this hidden gem in a cobblestone court behind the rue du faubourg Saint-Denis (take a map): it is like entering an Alsatian tavern from the time of the Three Musketeers (the bistro actually dates from 1855, but one can dream).

Brasserie Flo

7 cour Petites-Écuries, 75010
01 47 70 13 59
floparis.com
Menu: 19 (lunch)/23/28€
À la carte: 35–80€

10TH

Harry: Getting to **Brasserie Flo** was like a turbulent lightning-struck plane trip I once had: scary, but after I got to my destination the experience there was so well worth it that nothing was going to stop me from going again. I had called my friend Christopher for a restaurant recommendation. An Australian doctor who has worked for Médicins Sans Frontières in some of the most horrific war zones, Chris was living in Paris and arguably knows more of the city than many Parisians do, especially the northern and eastern sectors.

Without any hesitation he gave me his tip, and I thought how great it was to know a local: none of that overly hyped guidebook stuff for me. He instructed me to walk along rue Saint-Denis, which was an absolute war zone if ever I saw one: known as 'Prostitute Central', to me it was like a French version of the Wild West. I was certain I heard gunshots as I saw a guy trying to break free of a prostitute's aggressive arm lock—only to have the police pull up next to him to see why he was harassing her. I began to wonder where Chris had sent me, and slightly on edge I walked towards the lane leading to the Brasserie Flo: there it was, like an oasis, and well worth the bumpy ride. The setting and service were excellent, and the food absolutely amazing. We had a wonderful shells-themed meal of oysters and snails, with a bottle of something glorious recommended by the waiter, and ended with some kind of Bombe Alaska.

I went to Flo again, this time with Chris, for a mountain of oysters. I was more relaxed with Saint-Denis this time, especially with my war-weathered guide beside me.

Scott: Impossibly dark, moody and irresistible, this is a place that could only exist in France. The food is far more varied than you might expect, ranging from sole meunière with steamed chat potatoes to a 'tartare' of avocadoes and mint, accompanied by a brunoise of vegetables.

. . . .

Terminus Nord
Chef: Pascal Boulogne
23 rue de Dunkerque,
75010
01 42 85 05 15
terminusnord.com
Menu: 31€
À la carte: 29–69€

This is a traditional brasserie opposite the Gare du Nord. If the food doesn't seduce you (*Fruits de mer, Bouillabaisse marseillaise*), the exquisite mix of arts Déco and Nouveau certainly will.

Shannon: I love this area near the Gare du Nord.

A hard-core bar in the Saint-Denis district, with delicious bistro snacks (charcuterie, cheese).

Chez Jeannette
47 rue du faubourg
Saint-Denis, 75010
01 47 70 30 89
chezjeannette.com

Harry: On the way to Brasserie Flo, my friend Chris and I stepped into this bar, a must-see place that is like something out of a classic film. Chris ordered two demis of 1766 beer. Don't let the toothless barman put you off, and take time to admire the magnificent neon signage over the bar.

Owned by the same people as the wildly popular Café Charbon, this stunning Belle Époque building houses a bar, a restaurant and an exhibition space (up the grand staircase). If Charbon made the 11th arrondissement cool, then **Delaville** seems to be doing the same for the 10th. There is a DJ from Thursday to Saturday.

Delaville Café
34 boulevard Bonne-
Nouvelle, 75010
01 48 24 48 09

10ᵀᴴ

50 Films Set in Paris

Chronological and only one full-length feature per director.

1. *Les Misérables* (Raymond Bernard, 1934)
2. *Les Enfants du Paradis* (Marcel Carné, 1945)
3. *Madame de …* (Max Ophüls, 1953)
4. *French CanCan* (Jean Renoir, 1954)
6. *Du Rififi Chez les Hommes* (Rififi, Jules Dassin, 1955)
7. *Bob le Flambeur* (Jean-Pierre Melville, 1956)
8. *Le Ballon Rouge* (Albert Lamorisse, 1956)
9. *Une Parisienne* (Michel Boisrond, 1957)
10. *Love in the Afternoon* (Billy Wilder, 1957)
11. *Gigi* (Vincente Minnelli, 1958)
12. *Paris Nous Appartient* (*Paris Belongs to Us*, Jacques Rivette, 1960)
13. *Les Bonnes Femmes* (Claude Chabrol, 1960)
14. *Chronique d'un Été* (Paris 1960) (*Chronicle of a Summer*, Edgar Morin and Jean Rouch, 1961)
15. *Cléo de 5 à 7* (Agnès Varda, 1962)
16. *Le Procès* (*The Trial*, Orson Welles, 1962)
17. *Charade* (Stanley Donen, 1963)
18. *Paris vu par Chabrol Douchet Godard Pollet Rohmer Rouch* (1965)
19. *What's New Pussycat* (Clive Donner, 1965)
20. *Masculin Féminine: 15 faits précis* (*Masculin Feminine: 15 Precise Facts*, Jean-Luc Godard, 1966)
21. *Play Time* (Jacques Tati, 1967)
22. *Baisers Volés* (*Stolen Kisses*, François Truffaut, 1968)
23. *Quatre Nuits d'un Rêveur* (*Four Nights of a Dreamer*, Robert Bresson, 1971)
24. *Ultimo Tango a Parigi* (*Last Tango in Paris*, Bernardo Bertolucci, 1972)
25. *La Maman et la Putain* (*The Mother and the Whore*, Jean Eustache, 1973)
26. *C'était un Rendez-vous* (*Rendezvous*, Claude Lelouch, 1976)
27. *Danton* (Andrzej Wajda, 1983)
28. *Les Nuits de la Pleine Lune* (*Full Moon in Paris*, Eric Rohmer, 1984)
29. *Police* (Maurice Pialat, 1985)
30. *Cérémonie d'Amour* (*Love Rites*, Walerian Borowczyk, 1987)
31. *Frantic* (Roman Polanski, 1988)
32. *Un Monde sans Pitié* (*A World Without Pity*, Eric Rochant, 1989)
33. *I Want to Go Home* (Alain Resnais, 1989)
34. *Trois Couleurs: Bleu* (*Three Colours: Blue*, Krzysztof Kieslowksi, 1993)
35. *Nelly & Monsieur Arnaud* (Claude Sautet, 1995)
36. *French Kiss* (Lawrence Kasdan, 1995)
37. *Le Fabuleux Destin d'Amélie Poulain* (Jean-Pierre Jeunet, 2001)
38. *Le Divorce* (James Ivory, 2003)
39. *Clean* (Olivier Assayas, 2004)
40. *Before Sunset* (Richard Linklater, 2004)
41. *Angel-A* (Luc Besson, 2005)
42. *Paris Je T'aime: petites romances de quartiers …* (various, 2006)
43. *Dans Paris* (Christophe Honoré, 2006)
44. *Ne le dis à Personne* (*Tell No One*, Guillaume Canet, 2006)
45. *Ratatouille* (Brad Bird and Jan Pinkava, 2007)
46. *Le Voyage du Ballon Rouge* (Hsiao-hsien Hou, 2007)
47. *Paris* (Cédric Klapisch, 2008)
48. *Le Concert* (Radu Mihaileanu, 2009)
49. *Gainsbourg, Vie Héroïque* (Joann Sfar, 2010)
50. *Inception* (Christopher Nolan, 2010)

Shannon's Parisian Recipes

Crêpes Suzettes

....

This is the essence of a great bistro dish. There is much theatre involved in the traditional manner of serving it, which is for it to be flamed at the table by an experienced waiter and ladled with care onto the diners' plates. The fresh, zesty flavour of the orange in the sauce is a great complement to the sweetness of the crêpe and the mandatory vanilla ice-cream.

CRÊPES
125 g plain flour
80 g ground almonds
2 eggs
1 teaspoon salt
25 g vanilla sugar
200 ml milk
2½ tablespoons rum
2 tablespoons melted butter
100 g diced butter

For the crêpes, combine the flour, ground almonds, eggs, salt, sugar and milk in a large mixing bowl. Beat until the batter is smooth and has the consistency of single cream (a little more milk may be needed to achieve this). Add the rum and the melted butter, and set batter aside for 2–3 hours in the refrigerator.

To cook the crêpes, heat 1 tablespoon of the diced butter in a non-stick frying pan over low-to-medium heat. Spoon a ladleful of the batter into the centre of the pan and tilt to spread it evenly over the base of the pan. After 2–3 minutes, when underside of crêpe is golden-brown, flip gently and cook for a further 1–2 minutes, or until second side is golden. The more crêpes you make, the better you will get at it! Fold each cooked crêpe into quarters and set aside in a warm place.

SAUCE
200 ml freshly squeezed orange juice
100 ml Grand Marnier
2 tablespoons soft brown sugar
2 Seville oranges, segmented
2 cups vanilla ice-cream

To serve, arrange 2–3 crêpes in the centre of each plate. Make the sauce by combining the orange juice, Grand Marnier and brown sugar in a saucepan and bringing to the boil. Add the orange segments at the last second, pour the sauce over the crêpes and serve with a scoop of vanilla ice-cream.

Serves 6

République

BISTROS

Regularly highlighted in seemingly every food magazine in the world, and the undisputed pin-up of all the New Wave Parisian bistros, **Le Chateaubriand** (which opened in 2006) is the coolest restaurant in Paris. Expect to queue with all the gorgeous twenty-somethings who frequent the 11th. (Aizpitarte has also now opened Le Dauphin at 131 avenue Parmentier; 01 55 28 78 88.)

Le Chateaubriand

Chef: Iñaki Aizpitarte
129 avenue Parmentier, 75011
01 43 57 45 95
no website
Michelin: no stars
GaultMillau: 🍴🍴
Menu: 14/19/50€

Shannon: Le Chateaubriand was an interesting experience, as I had heard so much about it in the previous 12 months. Oh, I thought, another fancy place some journo has talked about because it is a bit different, and everyone has got on the bandwagon. But if you are really into Parisian bistros, you are going to love this one—or hate it. Being young and excited about the direction Paris is taking generally, I really liked it. There is little formality; it is in an old building, in an area I would never visit if Le Chateaubriand were not there, and it gives you an insight into Paris.

I took the Métro there, which is easy but time-consuming, on a Friday afternoon. I was with a friend of mine, Ute, who used to work at the Melbourne Food and Wine Festival but has moved to Paris and is rediscovering herself there. She had been to Le Chateaubriand several times and we had a little bit of special treatment because she knows the owners. There were three young waiters (white shirts, long hair, jeans, unshaven) prancing around, serving a hip, young clientele in a daggy old restaurant that has been a bistro for a very long time. It has a very similar feel to Restaurant le Meurice, in that it presents history in such a way as to appear modern; even the old Basque glassware is so rarely seen it looks modern.

The lunch menu was only 14€ (it is now 19€), for which you got a choice of five entrées, four or five mains, and a choice of desserts, as well as a couple of daily specials. We ordered what was simply described as a 'salad of leaves', but they were varieties I'd never seen before, grown in the restaurant's garden—you would never find them at a market. We ordered beef tartare, thinking it was pretty traditional, but when it came out the beef was diced into one-cm pieces, which I had never seen before. Apparently it is a really old recipe, featuring Tabasco; there are no gherkins and no egg, so we didn't know whether to be excited or disappointed. When we ate it, the verdict was, 'This is really cool.' That's what this place is about: bistro food that's different, that has integrity. I had a little carafe of house Riesling (not from any particular region) for 5€ and it was great.

It took us a while to leave, as we got talking to people (the bartenders were curious to know where we came from); in one visit you get to know them and you want to go back. There were people arriving who every Friday come for a glass of wine and a little beef tartare on a baguette. We came away agreeing that if those guys are happy to run this one restaurant, and want to run it for a long time, they are likely to change Parisian dining. I would definitely go back: apart from anything else, it shows you the continuing evolution of the Parisian bistro.

Trying to book by phone from Australia was a bit of a saga. When I tried to book, I found no one spoke very good English and the background music was very loud. When I told them the nights I had available, they weren't sure they would be open and suggested I call back later. However, they only answer the phone for two hours a day and, when I mentioned this would mean waiting until 3 a.m. in Australia to make the call, they said, 'Well, call us when you get out of a club or bar!' They don't mean anything by this sort of attitude: they just wanted to open a bistro in a place where the rent was affordable, and put their great ideas into practice. They're not after international stardom and they don't want or need all the attention—they are full anyway. Bryan, my maître d', ate there for dinner and he loved it. He, too, felt there was great integrity, really good produce, and an unusual reinvention of dishes. But definitely book!

Adam: Headed up by Basque chef Iñaki Aizpitarte, this is a hot 'bistronomique'. We had the miso soup with foie gras and a wonderful set-menu lunch. Excellent value and a fabulous décor.

....

With Le Chateaubriand, this is one of the hottest bistros in one of the trendiest arrondissements. The menu has a retro 1950s feel, with such classics as chicken braised in *vin jaune* (a yellow wine from the Jura) and veal kidneys in mustard sauce. It is noisy and crowded, and with waiters who present a challenge. There are 400 labels in its cellar.

Le Bistrot Paul Bert

18 rue Paul-Bert, 75011
01 43 72 24 01
no website
GaultMillau: ♔♔
Menu: 17 (weekday lunch)/32€
À la carte: 40–80€

....

11ᵀᴴ

In the 11th, where everything is said to be happening, there is also **Le Villaret**, one of the rare restaurants to gain GaultMillau's *Coup de cœur*. Before GaultMillau, the infallible Patricia Wells had long sung its praises. In this atmospheric bistro, with its classic zinc bar, always go for the market specials, which are prepared with a modern twist. In the great bistro tradition, its wine list is strong on Burgundy and Côtes-du-Rhône.

Le Villaret

13 rue Ternaux, 75011
01 43 57 75 56
no website
GaultMillau: ♔♔'
Menu: 25 (lunch)/50€
À la carte: 35–55€

Sarah's Paris

Angélina
226 rue de Rivoli, 75001
01 42 60 82 00
groupe-bertrand.com
Best known for their beautiful
marrons glacés.

Il Était une Oie dans le Sud Ouest
8 rue Gustave Flaubert, 75017
01 43 80 18 30
il-etait-une-oie.fr
Please do try it if you love foie gras.

Le Relais de l'Entrecôte
15 rue Marbeuf, 75008
01 49 52 07 17
relaisentrecote.fr
The best steak and *pommes allumettes*.

 MARKET

Marché Richard-Lenoir
boulevard Richard-Lenoir,
Thursday and Sunday
morning

In the heart of the 11th arrondissement, here is a buzzing street market with lots of interesting stalls, including North African. Regulars prefer Sundays.

 BARS

Café Charbon
109 rue Oberkampf, 75011
01 43 57 55 13

Regarded as the leader in the revitalisation of the Oberkampf neighbourhood, **Café Charbon** has a striking Belle Époque interior and a terrace from which to watch the parade of trendy Parisian youth. Many will be heading to the live-music Nouveau Casino next door. If you prefer less hectic times, go for breakfast.

Modern, stylish and colourful hotel ideally situated in a quiet street behind Républic. Walk to the Canal St Martin and Upper Marais neighbourhoods. The best boulangerie and chocolaterie are less than ten minutes away. What more could you want?

Le General Hotel

Rating: 3★
5–7 rue Rampon, 75011
01 47 00 41 57
legeneralhotel.com
Rooms: 41
Single: 157–177€
Double: 172–252€

11TH

Shannon's Favourite Parisian Treats

Kitchenware shops

Merci
111 boulevard Beaumarchais, 75003
01 42 77 00 33
merci-merci.com
Fresh kitchenware and home decorating ideas can be found in the basement of this trendy concept store. Drop in around lunchtime to indulge in the delicious offerings of La Cantine Merci.

Shannon: The Merci store in the 3rd arrondissement, not far from the Murano Urban Resort, is now the new 'IT' store in Paris. I am embarrassed to say that it is the new hip place to shop, because it is actually so good. The entrance of the store is through a small internal courtyard, where there is a very unique installation of a small car that changes monthly.

This modern version of a one-stop department store promotes using the store as a place of community interaction, with a small café and second-hand bookstore where light lunches are served.

There is a light and airy basement kitchen restaurant similar to a bouchon Lyonnais. Bowls of salads, vegetables, braises and meats are served by waiting staff from the buffet style set-up.

Cool furniture, practical modern kitchen accessories, and men and women's fashion are the feature attractions.

One feature I think would attract Scott to Merci is the movie of the month. It could be a Brigitte Bardot that never made it to the big screen or a quirky Cannes film from the 1970s re-digitised. Each month the feature film has a little flyer that can be torn away and given to friends.

This is my new favourite store for homewares.

E. Dellherin
18 and 20 rue Coquillière, 75001
51 rue Jean-Jacques Rousseau, 75001
01 42 36 53 13
e-dehillerin.fr
Iconic kitchenware specialist.

Mora
13 rue Montmartre, 75001
01 45 08 19 24
mora.fr
Another brilliant kitchen supply shop with the largest range of pâtisserie selections.

Shannon's Parisian Recipes
Duck-leg Confit with Pommes Sautées

....

Duck-leg confit has been lost in translation around the world, which is why you have to eat it when you are in Paris; the perfect version has the skin still intact. Be prepared, it is salty! That is because it has been salted for at least six hours before being cooked gently in its own fat, in a very slow oven, for at least five hours. It is left in the fat for at least a week, which is when the flavour really develops. A confit develops like a terrine, set in its own fat; no air can get in. In a good confit, the meat will be a red-pink colour from this ageing.

The duck leg is finished in the pan 'à la minute', just before coming to the table, and should be crispy and well seasoned; it is often served with *pommes sautées*—very small potatoes (traditionally Ratte) sliced and roasted in the fat rendered when making foie-gras; the dish is finished with fresh herbs and some curly endive or frisée lettuce (or oakleaf in honour of Stephanie Alexander and Alain Chapel). If you're lucky, you may get some of the sauce! (However, I don't actually think a good confit actually needs sauce, as it should have enough flavour of its own.) It should be very moist, but too many chefs remove the cooked duck leg from the fat: resting it in the fat keeps all the moisture in. Chefs are so busy these days, especially in large establishments, that they don't work far enough in advance—a really good backstreet bistro will give you a taste of real confit, which may have been sitting in a sealed jar for several months.

CONFIT
4 duck legs
100 g sea salt
2 tablespoons eight-spice powder (see page 173)
3 sprigs thyme
1 bay leaf
1 kg duck fat

MADEIRA JUS
500 ml Madeira
500 ml white wine
5 shallots, sliced
1 clove garlic, minced
2 sprigs thyme
1 bay leaf
5 peppercorns
500 ml veal or beef stock

SAUTÉ POTATOES
25 ml duck fat or foie-gras fat
500 g Kipfler potatoes, cooked and sliced
100 g sliced pancetta, cut into lardons
1 knob of butter
1 tablespoons chopped shallots
1 teaspoon minced garlic
salt and pepper
1 teaspoon chopped parsley

TO ASSEMBLE
1 tablespoon olive oil
25 g unsalted butter
15 ml duck fat
100 g yellow frisée, picked and washed
5 ml truffle oil
1 teaspoon sherry vinegar

To prepare the confit, season each duck leg with salt, eight-spice powder, thyme and bay leaf, and leave for 12 hours.

Preheat the oven to 100°C.

Rinse and pat dry the duck pieces. Place a rack in a deep oven tray, and place the duck legs on top, stretching the skin to cover the whole leg. Cover with the duck fat and cook in preheated oven for 6–8 hours (when ready, the meat should be nearly falling off the bone). Once cooked, carefully drain duck pieces on the rack and leave to chill in the fridge.

To make the jus, bring the Madeira, white wine, shallots, garlic, thyme, bay leaf and peppercorns to the boil in a heavy-based pan, and reduce by half. Add the veal stock and reduce again until the sauce coats the back of a spoon. Strain through muslin and set aside.

To cook the potatoes, heat the duck fat in a hot frying-pan, add the potatoes and sauté until coloured on each side. Add the pancetta and cook until crispy. Add the butter, shallots and garlic, season with salt and pepper and add the chopped parsley, then keep warm.

Preheat oven to 180°C.

To serve the confit, heat the oil in a frying-pan, place the duck legs skin-side down in the pan and cook in preheated oven until the skin is crisp and golden. Place some of the potatoes in the centre of each plate, and place a duck leg on top. Warm the jus in a small pan, whisk in the butter until the sauce becomes shiny and then add the duck fat (the sauce should have a 'split' effect). Pour sauce over the duck leg.

Season the frisée with truffle oil and sherry vinegar, and place on top of the duck leg.

Serves 4

Gare de Lyon

12TH ARRONDISSEMENT

RESTAURANT

This restaurant has been used as the location of so many French films it is hard to know how to begin listing them (Luc Besson's *Nikita* and Jérôme Salle's *Anthony Zimmer* are but two). The reason is that **Le Train Bleu** is one of the world's most outrageously theatrical places. Rightly accorded 'historical monument' status by writer André Malraux when he was Minister of State for Cultural Affairs, the restaurant features gilding, parquet flooring, 42 paintings, wood panelling and leather banquettes that may take your breath away. Some people complain that the food is not what it was or could be, but no other restaurant can quite equal the thrill of this space.

Le Train Bleu
Gare de Lyon
place Louis Armand, 75012
01 43 43 09 06
le-train-bleu.com
GaultMillau: ☁
Menu: 54/68/97€
À la carte: 60–95€

BAR

This tiny wine bar is close to the famous street market, Marché d'Aligre. It has a wide and reasonably priced range of wines by the glass, and several rare beers on tap (including Pietra, Saint-Omer, Jenlain), and you can fill up your empty wine bottles from the many barrels. There are cold snacks (pâtés, sausages) to help stave off hunger.

Le Baron Rouge
1 rue Théophile Roussel, 75012
01 43 43 14 32

Harry: My favourite bar in Paris. It is a great place to stop in after the Saturday street market, for a glass of wine and a *saucisson sec*.

Great Paris Parks

Parc des Buttes-Chaumont
rue Botzaris, Manin, 75019

This fairytale park is straight out of Disneyland (or Las Vegas), with its fake Roman temple, artificial waterfalls and a lake with its own island. Constructed on the site of a former rubbish dump by Baron Haussmann in 1867, it should be kitsch but somehow manages to charm. Some of *Gigi* was filmed here.

Jardin du Luxembourg
boulevard Saint-Michel, 75014

Possibly the park most commonly associated with inner Paris, the site of a thousand film shoots and a million life stories. It is where students congregate, where people escape the bustle of Saint-Germain, where lovers meet by one of the fountains. At 22.5 hectares, it is one of the city's largest green spaces, blessed with statuary and lush lawns (where you can't walk), shady trees and a riot of colourful annuals.

Jardin des Tuileries
rue de Rivoli, 75001

The Tuileries Gardens are where the great Palais des Tuileries once stood, before being destroyed by arsonists on 23 May 1871. It caused enormous controversy in its day, but few would argue with the transformation of the charred remains into a radiant open park today. Bordered by the place de la Concorde, the Louvre, the River Seine and the freeway known as the rue de Rivoli, it is a refuge of calm that offers extraordinary views of the Louvre (if you can ignore the pyramids) and, through the Arc de Triomphe du Carrousel, up the Champs-Élysées to the majestic Arc de Triomphe.

Parc Monceau
58 boulevard de Courcelles, 75008

The most bourgeois park in Paris, this small but perfect retreat from city life is surrounded by magnificent apartment buildings belonging to the wealthy. In some ways it feels like a private park, but don't be put off: instead, calmly enjoy one of Paris's unexplored treasures. It has an enchanting lake (modelled on Roman pools) with a beautiful colonnade at the end. There are several spectacular trees, included a maple and two glorious plane trees.

Parc de Bagatelle
Bois de Boulogne, Route de Sèvres à Neuilly, 75016

Part of the Bois de Boulogne, the Parc de Bagatelle is a magical place, a mixture of forest, parkland, sculptured gardens and, best of all, an exquisite rose garden (with more than 9000 plants). There is even a small 18th-century château, built by the Comte d'Artois, which for a while housed the famed Wallace Collection of artworks, whose owners lived here in the mid-19th century. One can take a rest at the delightful café.

Shannon's Favourite Parisian Treats

Foie Gras and Confits

Shannon: Despite opposition in various parts of the world to the production of foie gras, the industry thrives in France (and especially Périgord, which, it is worth noting, for those whose are concerned about the human-health angle, has the lowest heart-attack rate in Europe). Tinned foie gras and confit are perfect for picnics in a Paris park, with a good baguette, some good French butter and some cornichons. What more could you want?

Tinned duck confit is of very good quality. Goose foie gras is very popular in parts of France; preserved gizzards are also delicious. You don't see tinned duck confit much outside France. (When we think 'tinned food', we think: No, thanks!) Foie gras is so plentiful in France that it is used in tinned rillettes, pâté and terrines, so they are very good products.

Rillettes are basically confit trimmings that are ground up and mixed to a paste, often flavoured with shallot, salt and spices, and then packed into tins. It is delicious on a baguette! I recommend Rougié as a most reliable brand.

Comptoir de la Gastronomie

Since 1894
34 rue Montmartre, 75001
01 42 33 31 32
comptoir-gastronomie.com

This shrine to foie gras, opened in 1894, is packed with countryside goodies, from chocolate cake, smoked Salmon and caviar to fine wine. It is the perfect place to stock up for a picnic. If you are overcome by the myriad aromas and sights and feel the need to eat straight away, there is a restaurant where you can sample wild Baltic or Norwegian Salmon, a foie-gras carpaccio with honey and Guérande sea salt, or the house cassoulet.

Dubernet Foie Gras

2 rue Augereau, 75007
01 45 55 50 71

Dubernet is widely regarded (see, for example, *chowhound.com*) as the best place in Paris for foie gras, pâtés and hams. Specialising in food from France's South-West, it has vacuum-packed pre-cooked dishes including *blanquette de veau*.

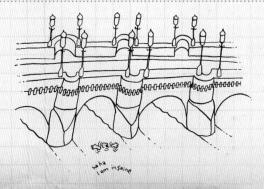

ha ha
I am inSeine

Shannon's Parisian Recipes

Croque Monsieur

....

This renowned toasted sandwich is thought by some people to have been first produced in Paris, at the turn of the 20th century, by builders who left their ham-and-cheese sandwiches on a radiator during winter to warm them up: after the butter and cheese melted, they became particularly appetising. I'm not sure if that explanation is folklore or fact, but one thing is certain: you must always make these sandwiches with a Swiss cheese such as Emmental or Gruyère; also, they should be crunchy, and buttered on the outside before serving. I like to add a fondue of tomatoes, which makes the dish a Croque Provençal. Another popular variation is the Croque Madame, which is topped with an egg and béchamel sauce.

It's very easy to make; if you've ever fried an egg for breakfast, you can do this croque.

CHEESE MIX

40 g unsalted butter

50 g plain flour

250 ml cider

200 g mature cheddar, grated

1 tablespoons Dijon mustard

1 teaspoon Worcestershire sauce

2 egg yolks

salt and pepper

TO ASSEMBLE

50 g unsalted butter, at room temperature

16 slices white sourdough bread

8 slices ham

250 g emmental or gruyère cheese, grated

salt and pepper

Melt the butter in a heavy-based pan, add the flour and stir with a wooden spoon until mixture comes together. Continue to stir over medium heat for another minute. Swap the wooden spoon for a whisk, slowly pour in the cider and whisk to form a thin velouté sauce, then continue whisking over a medium heat for a further 3 minutes until the flour is cooked. Remove from the heat and whisk in the cheese, then add the Worcestershire sauce and egg yolks. Season to taste.

To assemble, first butter the sourdough slices on both sides. Spread some cheese sauce on one side of each bread, place the ham on top and season with salt and pepper. Put the grated cheese on eight of the slices, then top with the remaining slices. Place in a sandwich press and toast until golden-brown.

Serves 8

Étoile, Trocadéro, Bois de Boulogne

ÉTOILE AND TROCADÉRO
FINE DINING

....

For the past few years, Pascal Barbot has been the hottest young chef in Paris. After opening **Astrance** in 2000 with sommelier Christophe Rohat, Barbot was declared Cuisinier de l'Année for 2005 by GaultMillau, which also rocketed his rating from 17 to 19/20. Rarely has a chef so quickly assumed such prominence. Not that Barbot hadn't trained hard, under Tony Bilson in Sydney and Alain Passard at L'Arpège, among others. His restaurant, just near the Trocadéro, is tiny, seating just 26 people in two simple rooms; you need to book a long time in advance (as they don't have a website or email, you'll just have to ring). The restaurant name, incidentally, comes from the Latin *aster* and refers to the star-like flower.

Astrance
Chef: Pascal Barbot
4 rue Beethoven, 75016
01 40 50 84 40
No website
Phone bookings only
Michelin: ★★★
GaultMillau: 🍽🍽🍽🍽
Menu: 70 (lunch)/120/190€

Shannon: Here is another restaurant that has been talked about in foodie circles for a number of years, especially on the website *gastroville.com*, where they rave about it. I think giving this restaurant three stars has done it a disservice: it doesn't need three stars—the prices and the dining-room (with very unassuming décor) are two-star.

The food has great integrity, but on the night we went there was only one (set) menu. I enjoyed a poached langoustine in broth, with nasturtium flowers: the freshness of the langoustine was evident, which was great. The slice of mushroom-and-foie-gras gâteau (layers of fresh white mushrooms and poached foie gras) was nice, but not extraordinary—something you wouldn't mind having in your local bistro or deli. A dessert of little creams served in eggshells was really nice. And there was fresh fruit to finish the meal, which I thought lovely and original.

I can't really remember any dishes that were mind-blowing. I felt that Barbot was inspired by Michel Bras in the simplicity of his dishes and the presentation, but the restaurant doesn't have the atmosphere to carry that sort of food. The wine matching was interesting and the wines were good, but they matched each wine with two courses, which I felt was a cop-out; I simply don't get that philosophy.

When Barbot was declared Chef of the Year by GaultMillau, Michelin abandoned its usual cautious approach and quickly followed suit. Perhaps it should have held out a little longer. But my experience wouldn't deter me from going back, because I would like to see the evolution of the food.

Le Cristal Room Baccarat

Chefs: Guy Martin,
David Angelot
11 place des États-Unis,
70016
01 40 22 11 10
baccarat.fr
GaultMillau: 🍽️🍽️🍽️
Menu: 55 (lunch)/149€
(wine included)
À la carte: 70–92€

Easily the most over-the-top dining space in Paris, **Le Cristal Room Baccarat** is, as its name might suggest, in the building occupied by specialist glassware manufacturer Baccarat. The mansion was built by the grandfather of the Vicomtesse de Noailles, who lived there during the 20th century. Designed by Philippe Starck, the restaurant has been lauded by *Wallpaper** and all the usual suspects, but may overwhelm some. The food is luxurious (oyster ravioli, foie gras from the Landes, roast *homard* with vanilla sauce, caramel soufflé) and expensive, but does not carry a star.

 BISTRO

Oscar

6 rue Chaillot, 75016
01 47 20 26 92
Menu: 22€
À la carte: 40–50€

A charming neighbourhood bistro in a very charming (and upmarket) neighbourhood. The food used to have Michelin's prized Bib Gourmand, but it was removed a few years ago, despite the prices remaining unchanged and Michelin still being rhapsodic about the quality of the food. A mystery.

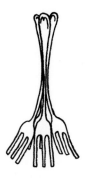

Also known as the Marché du Pont d'Alma, this fabulous market has fish delivered fresh from Normandy and Brittany, along with a choice of affordable *vins de pays*, and the usual meats, cheese, fruit and vegetables.

Marché avenue de Président Wilson
Wednesday and Sunday till 2.30 p.m.

Shannon: This is the best market in Paris. (You might recognise it from the Paris episode of *MasterChef* in Series 2.) It operates on the avenue de Président Wilson just behind the Tour Eiffel every Saturday and Wednesday, from 7.30 a.m. until around 1 p.m. All manner of fruit and vegetables are available when in season. It really shows the foodie tourist what Parisians are craving right now.

Local greengrocer legend and supplier to the best restaurants in the city, Joël Thiebault, has a stall here, mainly specialising in herbs and tomatoes, as well as heirloom varieties of root vegetables. Great fresh seafood—from oysters and scallops to Turbot—is available, as well as pre-made salads and terrines. Try the pre-cooked beetroots that you will see at each stall. As you know, Parisians are busy and have limited kitchen space, so when corners can be cut without compromising quality they will be the first to take it up, and pre-cooked beetroot is the new hit of 2011.

On a recent visit, I purchased some sel de Guérande from the only salt store at the market. It was flavoured with onion, garlic, oregano and parsley. As I smelt the salt, all I could think about was roast lamb. After being handed the two packets of flavoured salt, the storeowner kissed the bags and said goodbye in French to his babies! How good is that?

Before leaving, make sure you have a few of the roast potatoes that have been sitting at the bottom of the numerous chicken rôtisseries dotted around the stalls. They are the best you will ever taste. There is something magical about baby new potatoes roasted in chicken fat at 8 a.m. in the morning!

16ᵀᴴ

Hôtel Bassano

Rating: 4★
15 rue Bassano, 75116
01 47 23 78 23
hotel-bassano.com
Rooms: 33
Single: 175–295€
Double: 215–345€
Suites: 1

The **Bassano** is a modern and minimalist affair, with fabric-covered cubes and art-object chairs throughout the lobby. The floor is of dark wood, the walls slate-grey and white, the furniture mostly incandescent-blue. It is definitely a design statement, cool edging towards cold. The guest rooms, while similarly minimalist, are more welcoming: the clean lines and variants of pale blue and grey make the spaces both eye-catching and restful. The Superior Doubles are much more spacious (18–22 m²) than the Standard (15 m²). Just off the avenue Marceau, five minutes' walk south of the Champs-Élysées, this hotel is perfectly located.

Radisson Blu Le Dokhan's Hotel

Rating: 4★
117 rue Lauriston, 75116
01 53 65 66 99
dokhans.com
Rooms: 45
Single: 210–450€
Double: 210–450€

This delightful hotel is close to the place du Trocadéro, just off the avenue Kléber. It has a Haussmannian façade, with an extremely cute corner entrance that makes one happy just to be allowed through. (Some observers find the hotel reminiscent of the Flatiron Building in New York, albeit much smaller.) The semicircular lobby is adorned with Matisse and Picasso drawings, the small sitting-room exquisitely decorated in the neoclassical style; the walls of the public rooms house temporary art exhibitions. The guest rooms are a triumph of hand-painted, black-and-white wallpaper and elegant fabrics; some offer superb views of the Tour Eiffel. There is a spa and fitness centre, and you can eat seasonally on the summer terrace. **Le Dokhan's** has a champagne bar with a remarkable selection of rare marques and vintages.

Hôtel Raphael

Rating: 5★+
17 rue Kléber, 75116
01 53 64 32 00
raphael-hotel.com
Rooms: 83
Single: 335–505€
Double: 335–505€
Suites: 37

This Belle Époque hotel of one's dreams is on the rue Kléber, just south of the Arc de Triomphe. With its many artworks (you are greeted by a Raffaelo, but look for the Turner) and luscious wood panelling, the hotel oozes old-world comfort and charm. The guest rooms are ravishing and spacious (even the smallest, the Classic, is 30 m² but go for the Boudoir Deluxe: you'll never want to leave). However, the hotel's pièce de résistance is arguably the casual restaurant Les Jardins Plein Ciel on the seventh floor; the views of Paris from this terrace are utterly breathtaking. The Raphael also has a beautiful, if sparse and formal, restaurant, but it really deserves to have one that is Michelin-starred. Yet, with so many other great restaurants nearby, why complain?

Described as the only château-hotel in Paris, **Saint James** is a large townhouse built in 1892 and, as Michelin thoughtfully tells us, is 'on the site of the first Parisian aerodrome for hot-air balloons'. It only became a hotel in 1992, after years as a private school and then as a London-style 'gentlemen's' club (whose members still have rights in the hotel). In many ways it has the air of a small château, with its imposing stone façade and commanding interior staircase; it also has an unusually large garden, creating the ambience of a luxurious retreat. The dining-room, the former home of Joël Robuchon's Atelier and then Alain Ducasse, is for guests and club members only. This is a top Parisian address, though the rooms could be a little more lavishly furnished.

Saint James Paris

Rating: 5★
43 avenue Bugeaud, 75116
01 44 05 81 81
saint-james-paris.com
Rooms: 38
Single: 300–560€
Double: 300–560€
Suites: 10

Between the Maison de Radio France (headquarters of the French public broadcasters) and the place du Trocadéro (and very close to Astrance) is a very bold design statement. On the outside it looks like a classic Haussmann-style building; inside, **Sezz** is a burst of vibrant colour, contemporary design and grey Portuguese stone. It is on just about everybody's 'hippest hotel' list, from *Condé Nast Traveller* to *Times Online* and *tripadviser.com*. The guest rooms follow the current trend of placing the bed in the middle of the room. However, instead of an annoying sink behind your head (as in so many groovy Vienna and Prague hotels), there is a desk and chair. But there's no dividing wall, so make sure your partner doesn't like to do their emailing at the crack of dawn, or you'll wake to the sound of typing a few centimetres from your head. You can, though, overcome any such stresses by ordering a massage in your room.

Sezz

Rating: 4★
6 avenue Frémiet, 75016
01 56 75 26 26
hotelsezz.com
Rooms: 20
Single: 285–570€
Double: 335–570€
Suites: 6

Hôtel Square

Rating: 4★
3 rue de Boulainvilliers,
75016
01 44 14 91 90
hotelsquare.com
Rooms: 20
Single: 300–560€
Double: 300–560€
Suites: 2

Hôtel Square is an incredibly trendy hotel in the 16th, adjacent to the Maison de Radio France and close to the equally cool Sezz. The minimalist design is cutting-edge, with subtle influences from far-away places. (The restaurant is called Zébra Square, reflecting design patterns found elsewhere in the hotel.) Needless to say it is also full of curves. The rooms are vast and a striking visual feature is the room number woven into the carpet at the door. The hotel is somewhat off the tourist beat, but it is only a short stroll to the Seine, and the Palais de Chaillot at Trocadéro is about 800 metres away. Note, though, that the nearest Métro station (Mirabeau) is not exactly on a central line. This is the perfect modern boutique hotel if you want to stay in Paris but in discreet semi-obscurity.

 OTHER HOTEL

Le Kléber

Rating: 3★
7 rue de Belloy, 75116
01 47 23 80 22
kleberhotel.com
Rooms: 23
Single: 80–299€
Double: 90–299€
Suites: 1

Feeling a little like an upmarket antique store (the owners are passionate collectors), this unusual hotel has a veritable cornucopia of styles. The guest rooms have parquet floors, while the furniture and décor ranges from Oriental to Commedia dell'Arte; some rooms have a jacuzzi. Unlike most small hotels, **Le Kléber** has its own restaurant, in a gorgeous bare-brick room, with hanging drapes. The hotel is especially well located, just a short walk south of the Arc de Triomphe.

BOIS DE BOULOGNE

FINE DINING

. . . .

One of the most picturesque scenes in Luis Buñuel's *Belle de Jour* is when Séverine (Catherine Deneuve) is picked up in a carriage in front of a stunning restaurant terrace. It is **La Grande Cascade** and it has been a favoured film location for decades; it is now also an acclaimed restaurant in its own right and has long fought with Le Pré Catelan for supremacy of the park. Chef Frédéric Robert, who arrived after stints at Le Grand Véfour and Lucas Carton (now Senderens), has only one star at present but is predicted to improve on that. This reminder of Paris's Belle Époque (red velvet is everywhere) is true luxury in the woods.

La Grande Cascade

Chef: Frédéric Robert
Allée de Longchamp, 75016
01 45 27 33 51
grandecascade.com
Michelin: ★
GaultMillau: ☺☺☺☺
Menu: 85/135/185€
À la carte: 140–195€

David: I have never had a good meal at La Grande Cascade, even though it is a handsome setting (ditto for Ledoyen).

. . . .

Le Pré Catelan is the most highly rated of the restaurants in the Bois de Boulogne; chef Frédéric Anton has won the French government's exalted rating of Meilleur Ouvrier de France (best artisan in France). The restaurant is located in a Napoléon III building (formerly the emperor's pleasure pavilion) deep in the woods, and on arrival you feel you have travelled long and far, even though it is but a short taxi ride. (Don't try the buses either to here or to La Grande Cascade unless you are brave. And don't follow any chickens you see on the road, as they are a signal to punters that a young lady working the woods is available for paid assignations.)

Le Pré Catelan

Chef: Frédéric Anton
Route de Suresnes, 75016
01 44 14 41 14
restaurant-precatelan.fr
Michelin: ★★★
Menu: 85 (weekday lunch)/
180/230€
À la carte: 190–245€

16ᵀᴴ

Shannon's Favourite Parisian Treats

The Perfect Picnic

Shannon: The perfect picnic is something you would not really associate with Paris—or myself, really, because I have only ever made up a picnic once and it was not for me but for a good friend. It was a complete disaster, mainly due to the fact that I completely forgot his girlfriend was a vegan: in my frustration at having forgotten, I really let him have it about my thoughts on vegetarians and their hypocritical ways, particularly vegans who one week have milk in their coffee because soy is not available, and who eat chocolate. I did feel bad about the situation, though.

I met up with the couple a few months later, and after five minutes of chatting she said, out of the blue, that she had been secretly eating meat for the past few weeks. She had started having cravings for it after the picnic and had just found out she was expecting. Anyway, this couple have a lovely son together and I feel in many ways some responsibility for his having had a healthy gestation, which I don't believe being a vegan gives you. I always have to have the last word!

Here, then, is my idea of the perfect picnic lunch to enjoy in any number of beautiful Parisian parks.

The Menu

- Bread (a quarter of it pre-sliced) from the wonderful baker Poilâne)
- Foie gras terrine (Le Bon Marché)
- Gazpacho soup x 2 (Le Bon Marché)
- Spinach and smoked Salmon salad with a small tin of caviar (optional; Bon Marché, Kaspia or Petrossian). This is just a suggestion, but I recommend some sort of salad with a touch of class to it. Cold truffled macaroni is another favourite, as is crayfish salad from Bon Marché)
- Duck ballotine, plus green leaves with hazelnut dressing (Comptoir de la Gastronomie, or Bon Marché)
- Cheese with baguette (Boulangerie Kayser, Le Moulin de la Vierge, Paul). I'd recommend a cheese like semi-soft Morbier or a small aged Crottin (goat's cheese: Androuët, Barthelemy)
- Ginger crème pot. Most patisseries have take-away glass vessels. They are very cost-effective and don't feel like take-away
- Truffled Brie (Petrossian)
- Trifle for dessert (Pain de Sucre)
- Miniature pistachio cupcakes for dessert (Pain de Sucre)
- 2 bottles Charles Heidsieck champagne (Nicolas)
- Evian water

The best places to buy a complete picnic are Le Bon Marché, Petrossian, Fauchon and Hédiard (place de Madeleine) or even small places like Pain de Sucre.

Note: If you're travelling on one of those budget airlines, why not splurge on the food side of things and buy a little hamper from somewhere like Caviar House. Even nicely made sandwiches are the go, such as rillettes in a nice baguette. I love them for this purpose.

Shannon's Parisian Recipes

French Onion Soup

This is something I am very passionate about. Traditional onion soup is very simple, made with caramelised onion and using a very good beef stock, and served with croûtons topped with Emmental or Gruyère cheese. You can't beat that kind of soup, especially in the European winter months. Another great variation is to add beer or cider—approximately 100 ml alcohol per 300 ml serve—to the soup just before it is ready, then simmer it for a further minute to evaporate the alcohol before serving. The beer or cider adds an extra dimension to the soup.

50 g duck fat

2 kg brown onions, thinly sliced

2 tablespoons minced garlic

2 sprigs thyme

50 ml white wine

1 litre veal stock

20 ml sherry vinegar

4 pieces puff pastry (2 cm x 2 cm), approximately 5 mm thick

2 egg yolks, lightly beaten, for glazing

200 g grated Gruyère or Emmental cheese

In a heavy-based pan over a low heat, melt the duck fat. Add the onions, garlic and thyme, and cook slowly until the onions are soft and golden. Continue cooking until they begin to caramelise, then add the white wine and reduce by half. Add the stock and cook again until the liquid is reduced by one-third. Add the sherry vinegar, remove pan from the heat, and check seasoning.

Place the soup in four oven-proof serving bowls and leave to chill in the fridge. Roll the pastry into rough circles slightly larger than the serving bowls, drape one over each bowl and firmly press the edges down past the rim, ensuring it is sealed but allowing for the pastry to shrink during cooking. Brush the pastry with the beaten egg yolks, then return bowls to fridge for at least 30 minutes prior to baking.

Preheat the oven to 180°C. Place bowls in oven and bake for 12 minutes, then sprinkle the pastry with grated cheese and put back in the oven for 2 minutes or until the cheese is melted. Serve immediately.

Serves 4

Ternes

17ᵀᴴ ARRONDISSEMENT

It seemed the day would never come when Michelin would give Guy Savoy a third star. And this despite his regularly receiving the highest accolade of 19/20 from GaultMillau (excluding, that is, the silly 20/20 for Marc Veyrat). A very modern art-filled restaurant not far from Étoile, **Guy Savoy** is free of the hype that other places generate: quietly and professionally he has gone about his perfectionist ways, delighting a very solid base of loyal customers. His *Soupe d'artichaut à la truffe noir* (artichoke and black-truffle soup), accompanied by a layered brioche with mushrooms and truffle butter, is seen as defining his approach of using modern techniques to achieve utter simplicity. On his website, Savoy writes: 'The restaurant is the last civilised place on Earth. No one can be indifferent to its calming effect ...'

Restaurant Guy Savoy

Chef: Guy Savoy
18 rue Troyon, 75017
01 43 80 40 61
guysavoy.com
Michelin: ★★★
GaultMillau: 🍴🍴🍴🍴🍴
Menu: 275/345/480€
À la carte: 150–300€

Shannon: All day I had been thinking, 'I am not really looking forward to eating here tonight.' Scott had been desperate for me to dine here, as it was the only three-star in central Paris that between us we had not eaten at. I thought of Guy Savoy and his signature dish of Artichoke Soup with Black Truffles. Why bother? It sounds like I could make it at home.

To get myself in the mood, and also to educate my better half on why she has suddenly put on 3 kilos and is about to put on another kilo tonight, I look to the restaurant website for inspiration and help.

When a chef has the courage and stupidity (we call it passion in the industry) to actually make a 7-minute film about his life and restaurant, captured in cinema quality, you start to realise maybe the soup might have some twist to it. After you shake your head in amazement at the film, which starts with the team buying girolles in a 1940s truck and driving it down rue de Rivoli, you find the current menus. The blood starts to turn into adrenaline and now I'm looking forward to experiencing Savoy's food.

Something extraordinary had happened to me that afternoon. It was the first time a restaurant website has actually done its job on me. I was truly blown away and informed. Through its graphics and smart presentation, it had sold me the dégustation menu. There were actually four dégustation menus on when I dined in late October. One was the Menu Autour de la Truffe, the game menu (four choices of main courses), the Menu Prestige and the Menu Noir et Blanc (later replaced with the Menu Couleurs!). Though the Black and White looked great, I choose the Menu Prestige, which had the most dishes from the à la carte menu. I always think this is the best way to see a chef's work in one visit.

With restaurants in Las Vegas, Singapore and his flagship three-Michelin-starred restaurant in Paris, plus three other brasseries and a private club, you would expect Guy Savoy to be a little incapacitated and not on the floor of his dining room. I certainly was, so it was a real surprise to be greeted by him, just as every other table was in the three separate dining areas.

The restaurant is in a very small and quaint but opulent side street not far from the Arc de Triomphe. There is no bar as such to have a pre-dinner drink, so you are seated immediately. The welcome is warm and friendly, but the room we were placed in was at the end, to the right of the building, and was an afterthought in many ways. I had cold sweaty flashes back to the cellar at L'Arpège.

The dinner starts with two rounds of mini club sandwiches on sticks that are basically foie gras terrine and toast. A Champagne trolley comes and goes with a great selection of vintage and non-vintage cuvées from various producers. If I ever see vintage rose on offer, I take it, and on this occasion Billecart Rose 2002 was on offer and I gladly accepted.

The first dish to arrive after a small little soup and game spring roll was Whiting, barely cooked and topped with Bordeaux caviar. Next to it was the most sublime langoustine tartare with lemon jelly—very classic but timeless.

At this stage, the two young sommeliers looking after our table convinced me to try a Sancerre made in the style of Didier Dageneau. It was very flinty with a gunpowder nose and lemon palate—everything sav blanc drinkers probably hate and I love. It is amazing how great wine makers can unlock this terrible grape and turn it into a masterpiece. It was a 2008 Domaine Vacheron.

At this stage, we had our own bread waiter, who had immediately deduced Madeleine's ability to consume her own weight in great bread. Over the entire length of a great three-star meal, we were served a slice of different bread with each course. I struggled after the lobster to keep up.

The next course was a masterpiece: a simple roast lobster with avocado, finished with the sauce made from the corail (egg roe) blended into a lobster stock that had also been infused with mushrooms. The dish needed bread!

Next came the artichoke soup. It looked simple enough, a grey-coloured soup presented in a very simple bowl with three slices of cooked black truffle floating in the top. Served on the side was a brioche filled with mushrooms and accompanied with whipped truffle butter. Then came the taste. I deserved to be sent back to Australia by cargo ship in confined quarters for my sinful thoughts that this artichoke soup might be boring. The texture was velvety without the use of my pet hate—unnecessary cream in soups and sauces—with a meaty taste like a white lamb stock. By this time, we were served a 2006 Meursault Terres Blanches from Pierre Morey.

Dishes kept coming and going, and all three-star. The main course we left in the hands of the maître d', who chose for us a combination of wood pigeon, pheasant and wild duck, sealed with bread and baked in a cast-iron pot. It was brought to the table, presented and then carved in front of us. We don't get game like this in Australia, I explained to the maître d'. The closest we get is kangaroo or hare.

A 1999 Château Leoville Poyferré from Saint Julian was a match that had been well analysed.

The cheese trolley, as usual, was a sign of pure indulgence and excess. But, hey, what the heck! I threw my arms in the air and told our waiting team, who were all great fun, that 'Whatever you choose, four small tastes.' I was beyond needing anything more and did not want to spoil the evening with overindulgence, but I immediately felt I had more room and a hell of lot better when I looked over to Madeleine. It was as if I was a mere mortal compared to this country girl from Kyneton who weighs only 52 kilos!

The dessert trolley—or, should I say, the mini ice-cream van—created another 'Yes I can, no I can't' moment. The trolley was full of mini desserts, cakes and ice-creams. In the end, I had no choice. I was given all sorts of sweet treats, including a black pepper toffee mouse with chocolate sorbet, bourbon vanilla frozen cream with apple purée, the most amazing hazelnut marshmallows and all sorts of macarons, plus salted caramel ice cream with mini caramel tarts ... I didn't know where to stop.

Three hours later, I think it was over, but I cannot even remember paying the bill. I was in the state of delirium that I want to be in every time I visit a restaurant in Paris.

Bigarrade is one of the hottest restaurants in Paris and a rising star of the Michelin pantheon, despite its limited menu du marché. Normally, restaurants with two-star ratings need to offer a substantial number of à la carte choices and spend more attention on the bourgeois ambiance in the dinning room; Bigarrade just has a few simple prix fixe menus. Some have seen Bigarrade's surprise elevation as proof that tastes and review standards are changing, part of a *nouvelle bistronomique* movement, with less-formal settings and market-fresh produce. After a small cube of focacia with olive oil, you might have deep-fried *moscardini* (octopus), herring row with a rocket and clam granita, raw scallops with celery and apple, and langoustine with a shallot compote. Irrespective of one's view of what should constitute a classic French restaurant, everyone agrees chef Christophe Pelé is offering some of the most exciting food in Paris at incredibly reasonable prices.

Bigarrade

Chef: Christophe Pelé
106 rue Nollet, 75017
01 42 26 01 02
bigarrade.fr
Michelin: ★★
GaultMillau: ☜☜
Menu: 35 (lunch)/45/65

One of the most famous restaurants in the South of France in the late 1970s and early 1980s was La Bonne Auberge (Antibes). The owner-chef was Jo Rostang, father of Michel. The latter moved to Paris in 1978 and opened Chez Denis. It later became **Michel Rostang** and won two stars (1980), which it has held ever since. A pioneer of 'second' restaurants, Rostang opened several *bouchons lyonnais* (restaurants specialising in traditional Lyonnaise cooking), including l'Absinthe (where daughter Caroline rules) and Jarrasse. But it is his namesake restaurant that is Rostang's greatest achievement—a beautiful space, with darkly lacquered wood and hundreds of Robj porcelain figurines. It is classical cooking with discreet modern influences.

Michel Rostang

Chef: Michel Rostang
20 rue Rennequin, 75017
01 47 63 40 77
michelrostang.com
Michelin: ★★
GaultMillau: ☜☜☜☜
Menu: 76 (lunch)/169/185€
À la carte: 140–200€

Steve's Paris

L'Espadon

Hôtel Ritz Paris
15 place Vendôme, 75001
01 43 16 30 30
ritzparis.com

L'Espadon is magnificently decorated and opulent in the extreme. We opted for the dégustation menu, but selected our own wines: a Grand Cru Chablis and a Grand Cru Ruchottes-Chambertin.

Each dish was brilliant and transcended the previous: crab, langoustine, foie gras. The only criticism was that the lamb wasn't as tender as it could have been, but it was oh-so flavoursome. We had too much cheese, which was fantastic.

A highlight was being seated next to a table of three: Anna Winter, her Paris editor and Karl Lagerfeld.

Restaurant le Meurice

Le Meurice
228 rue de Rivoli, 75001
01 44 58 10 55
meuricehotel.fr

If it's possible to be more opulent than L'Espadon, then here you have it. Everything—cutlery, crockery, glassware, decanters—was outstanding.

Again, we opted for the dégustation: brilliant, but no cheese course!

The highlight was the foie gras—real goose liver—and my partner Paula was gobsmacked. Waiters were like the 'teeming hordes' and maybe just a little intrusive, especially in their haste.

The wine list is outstanding.

L'Atelier de Joël Robuchon

5 rue de Montalembert, 75007
01 42 22 56 56
joel-robuchon.net

The concept—sitting at a bar on stools, supposedly so you can view the kitchen; we couldn't—didn't work for me. The staff had difficulty reaching over and serving.

The food is very good but not in the league of L'Espadon or Restaurant Le Meurice and the wine list is inadequate.

Our friends joined us. It was raining and they put their umbrellas in the tub at reception as requested. When we were leaving, their brollies were nowhere to be found!

Restaurant Guy Savoy

18 rue Troyon, 75017
01 43 80 40 61
guysavoy.com

We were greeted on arrival by the great man himself and shown through to a smallish room of only six tables. It became obvious that this was the English-speaking room!

Unlike other establishments of this ilk, the décor was understated, but the banter between the diners transcended tables. We befriended two couples from the US, one of which were engaged on the night—he popped the question, flashed the rock, she said, 'Yes'.

We opted for the 'smaller' dégustation menu, but at 235€ each we expected something special.

It was all good and included caviar, crab and langoustine, all delightfully prepared and served—even the foie gras. Notwithstanding, we felt we had had better elsewhere.

Glassware and decanters disappointed, as did the cutlery. However, the carte de vin was impressive and we indulged in a 1999 Domaine Dujac Morey St Denis 1er Cru. Magnificent.

Shannon's Parisian Recipes

Garlic Snails with Caper Butter and Parsley Crust

I'm including here a recipe for preparing and cooking your own snails, but the quality of tinned snails from France is so good that you don't need to be concerned about using them. If you are using tinned snails, you can buy shells separately to serve them in, or you can use the specially made dishes that have little hollows for the snails.

There are two main types of farmed snails: *petit gris* and Bourgogne. Ordinary garden snails can be eaten, but they need to be carefully purged for a fortnight beforehand. If you have a lot of basil or dill in the garden, this will flavour the snails if you feed them exclusively on these plants for a few days before cooking. Purge the snails by feeding them cornmeal for about two weeks, which ensures that any toxins or impurities are cleared out of their bodies. Stop feeding the snails two days before cooking them: clean under running water to remove any dirt or debris.

Place snails in a bucket or large bowl, add 100 g of salt to every 500 g of live snails, and leave for 2 hours. Bring a large pot of water to boil. Add 1 roughly chopped carrot, 1 chopped onion, a sprig of thyme, a stick of celery and a leek, followed by a bay leaf and 2 cloves garlic, and any opened white wine you have to hand (about 1–2 cups). Drop in the snails and simmer for about 15 minutes. Skim off the murky foam that gathers on the surface; when no more forms, the snails will be fully cooked. Remove snails and take off any shells that are still attached (they often separate during the boiling process, but you may need to remove a few yourself).

24 snails, meat removed from shells, and shells and meat reserved separately

CAPER BUTTER

10 g anchovies, chopped

15 g lilliput (baby) capers

1 tablespoon Dijon mustard

1 tablespoon chopped tarragon

1 tablespoon chopped parsley

2 tablespoons chopped basil

juice of ½ lemon

1 tablespoon finely chopped garlic

salt and pepper

100 g butter at room temperature, diced

PARSLEY CRUST

50 g dried breadcrumbs

½ bunch parsley, washed and dried

1 sprig thyme

salt and pepper

75 g grated Gruyère cheese

50 g butter, softened

To make the caper butter, combine all the ingredients with the butter, place on a piece of cling wrap and roll into a sausage shape. Refrigerate until required.

For the parsley crust, place the breadcrumbs, herbs, salt and pepper in a blender and blend on high until the breadcrumbs are green. Add the cheese and blend again, then add the butter in small quantities, pulsing between each addition. Season to taste, remove from blender and roll between two sheets of baking paper to form a layer approximately 2 mm thick. Place on a tray and refrigerate until required.

To Serve

Preheat the oven to 180ºC.

Stuff each of the snail shells halfway to the top with caper butter. Place the snail meat in the shell and cover with more caper butter. Cover the opening with parsley crust (cut to size) and place in an egg carton (or on rock salt in an ovenproof tray) to stabilise the shell and avoid the butter leaking out. Place the snails in preheated oven for 3 minutes (or until the butter starts bubbling). Place under the grill until the crust is crispy, and serve immediately.

Serves 4

Montmartre

18TH ARRONDISSEMENT

RESTAURANTS

Antoine Heerah, the Mauritian chef-owner, very success-fully mixes spices from his island home country with tradi-tional French flavours and ingredients. It is one of those very rare Parisian restaurants that is open seven days for lunch and dinner.

Chamarré Montmartre

Chef: Antoine Heerah
52 rue Lamarck, 75018
01 42 55 05 42
chamarre-montmartre.com
GaultMillau: 👕👕👕
Menu: 25 (lunch)/52/115€
À la carte: approx. 60€

Sébastien Guénard, formerly at Alain Ducasse's Aux Lyonnais, has teamed up with the former sommelier from La Tour d'Argent, serving home-style food at amazing value for money in this very popular neighbourhood bistro. Bookings are essential.

Miroir

Chef: Sébastien Guénard
94 rue des Martyrs, 75018
01 46 06 50 73
no website
GaultMillau: 👕👕👕
Menu: 32€

Guided Tours

Unique Taste Experiences

Ute Biefang
uteinparis.com
06 19 89 74 29

Shannon: Ute Biefang is a mate from Melbourne, who now lives in Paris. She offers guided gastronomic tours individually designed to reflect personal interests. Experience the best of hidden Paris—as I do—with a unique emphasis on culinary and cultural discoveries.

18ᵀᴴ

La Table d'Eugène

Chef: Geoffroy Maillard
18 rue Eugène Sue, 75018
01 42 55 61 64
no website
Menu: 18€ (lunch)/35€

A tiny gem of a restaurant with creative cuisine up in the northern part of the 18th.

 CAFÉ

La Fourmi Café

74 rue des Martyrs, 75018
01 42 64 70 35

A Pigalle legend, **La Fourmi** ('the ant') is always packed. An eclectic mix of retro, industrial and classic design, it has a groovy zinc bar and a fabulous clientele. With a chandelier made out of empty wine bottles, deliberately mismatched chairs and 1970s hippie feel, it is one of the places for singles to practise their skills and discover what is happening in town.

 LUXURY HOTEL AND BAR

Kube

Rating: 4★
1-5 passage Ruelle, 75018
01 42 05 20 00
muranoresort.com
Rooms: 41
Single: 250€
Double: 300–900€

Behind a historic façade on a quiet street, this high-tech designer hotel has featured in all the trendy magazines and guidebooks.

Ute: This is the second gem from the Murano Resort group. It is slightly more avant-garde than its relative in the Marais, and features futuristic cubist design. It is home to the very popular Ice Kube bar.

Ice Kube

The bar is made entirely of ice—some 25 tonnes of it—as are the glasses. The only vodka served here, though, is France's Grey Goose.

Shannon's Parisian Recipes

Macarons

Macarons should be the same size, very shiny, crisp and yet chewy in the centre. Delicacy is the key: it is very hard to make a good macaron—another reason to go to Paris. They should also be reasonably thin, with a rim that looks as if it has slightly lifted (this lets you know that it has been cooked at the correct temperature). The filling should be made with a butter cream (butter whipped with sugar and a flavouring), as this won't send the macaron soggy, whereas custard will.

180 g almond meal
350 g icing sugar
190 g egg whites
90 g caster sugar

Preheat oven to 150°C.

Mix the almond meal and icing sugar in a food processor, then sieve into a bowl. Whisk the egg whites to a soft peak, add the caster sugar and continue to mix until firm and glossy. Carefully mix one-third of the dry mixture into the meringue, without beating out too much air. Fold in the remaining dry ingredients.

Place mixture in a piping bag and pipe onto a baking tray lined with silicon paper. Bake in preheated oven (on half fan if you have this option) for 12–15 minutes.

Flavours

- For *chocolate*, add 30 g Dutch cocoa powder for each 20 g of icing sugar
- For *beetroot*, add 20 g beetroot powder for each 20 g icing sugar
- For *orange*, add freeze-dried orange powder to taste (approximately 1 teaspoon)

18™

Belleville

20TH ARRONDISSEMENT

CAFÉ

One reason for the rise of the 20th arrondissement as a must-see district is bistros like **Café Noir**, which has a massive reputation among New Age foodies (as opposed to conservative restaurant guides). The food is classic bistro, but with subtle Asian influences (expect cardamom with your duck breasts and honey, or Chinese cabbage with scallops). The super-trendy La Flèche d'Or club is nearby.

Café Noir
15 rue Saint-Blaise, 75020
01 40 09 75 80
Menu: 19€
À la carte: 35–60€

BAR

A popular wine bar with Basque cheeses and charcuterie on offer. The décor is funky, with lots of dog images. The name apparently comes from a remark in a novel by US author John Fante.

Mon Chien Stupide
1 rue Boyer, 75020
01 46 36 25 49

HOTEL

East of Père Lachaise cemetery is this collaboration between architect Richard Castro and designer Philippe Starck. *Time Out* voted it the boldest and best new hotel in town in 2009; whether you warm to it or not is a question of taste. Do you, in fact, want a lampshade shaped like a Wookie mask right next to your head? (Upgrade the room and you get Superman.) The Luxe rooms look like padded prison cells, with very low ceilings, but the Deluxe have slightly more colour and life. All rooms and bathrooms, though, are small. Still, for a single room as low as 79€ a night (and a double 89€), this place is a steal—especially with Alain Senderens now running the main restaurant. There is also an in-house Mama Pizzeria.

Mama Shelter
Rating: 3★
109 rue de Bagnolet, 75020
01 43 48 48 48
mamashelter.com
Rooms: 169
Single: 79–219€
Double: 89–219€
Suites: 1

20TH

188

Ute: This is the current 'it' hotel that has everyone talking since its opening in October 2008. It is located in the *quartier* behind Père Lachaise, in a part of Paris not usually frequented by tourists. It was built on the grounds of an old garage and its creators are the Trigano family (co-founders of Club Med) and French philosopher Cyril Aouizerate. The Philippe Starck interiors offer an eclectic and electric ambience, which includes 60-cm iMacs in each room.

Facts on the French Fry

Shannon: Belgians fiercely hold that it was one of their own who first 'frenched' a fry. Expert opinion on this matter is divided. Whatever the case, by the 1830s deep-fried potatoes had become a popular taste sensation in both France and Belgium, spreading quickly to other parts of mainland Europe.

The first place in Paris to do this was by the bridge Pont Neuf and thick-cut fries in France are still known as *pommes de terre Pont Neuf*. These fries are served stacked up on top of each other to resemble the nine pillars of the bridge.

Sometimes limp, sometimes greasy, sometimes too dark on the outside and not cooked enough on the inside, the path to total fry perfection constantly eluded every cook and chef around the world.

Eventually it was discovered that potatoes that had been waiting for longer periods in storage cooked up better than those placed immediately into the fryer. 'Curing' potatoes for exactly three weeks prior to frying them became standard practice, allowing for enough of the spud sugars to be converted into starches. Without this waiting period, the sugars in the potato make them turn brown too quickly.

What fat to use is also a matter of great debate. Horse fat seems to be the best, not only because of its unique but subtle flavour, but also because of its viscosity at high temperature. My favourite for flavour is most definitely goose fat.

Shannon's Parisian Recipes

Perfect French Fries

. . . .

Pommes de terre frites (or simply *frites*), as French fries are formally known, are arguably the world's most popular snack.

4 large Sebago potatoes
1 litre vegetable oil
sea salt

Wash potatoes, cut into 1-cm slices and then cut these into 1-cm strips. Rinse under cold running until the water runs clear, then drain. Place in a large saucepan of water with a tablespoon of salt, bring to the boil and simmer for 2 minutes. Strain.

Place oil in a large saucepan (it should only come one-third of the way up the sides) and heat to 180°C. Watch the oil carefully (do not leave it unattended): it should not reach smoking point. To test the temperature, drop a chip into the pot: if the chip disappears in a stream of bubbles, the oil is ready.

Cook the fries in batches, a quarter at a time, until golden. Drain on a tray lined with absorbent paper. If they lose their crispiness, before serving, bring the oil back to 180°C and cook the fries until crisp again (about 1 minute). Drain again on absorbent paper, season well with salt, and serve.

Serves 4

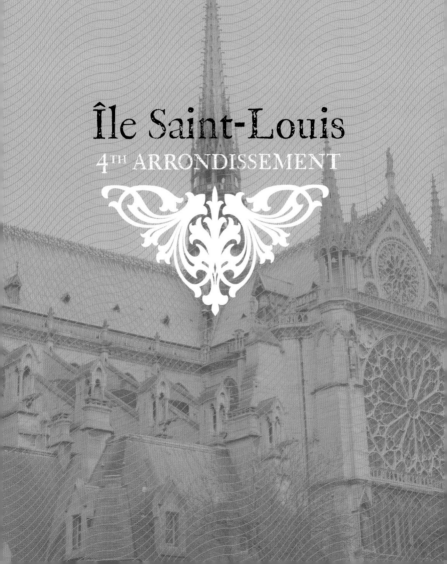

Île Saint-Louis

4TH ARRONDISSEMENT

Brasserie de l'Île St-Louis

55 quai de Bourbon, 75004
01 43 54 02 59
no website
GaultMillau: ☂☂
À la carte: 30–50€

This is a fun place to sit and eat, with fabulous views across the Seine. It serves old-fashioned food (*Frisée aux lardons, Foie de veau à l'anglaise*) in chic surroundings.

Mon Vieil Ami

69 rue Saint-Louis-en-l'Île, 75004
01 40 46 01 35
mon-vieil-ami.com
GaultMillau: ☂☂
Menu: 41€
À la carte: 32–55€

In the culinarily erratic 4th arrondissement, one pretty and interesting place is **Mon Vieil Ami**, owned and operated by Antoine Westermann, former chef at Buerehiesel in Strasbourg (his son Eric runs the brasserie Drouant). It gives vegetables 'pride of place'.

LUXURY HOTEL

Hôtel Jeu de Paume

Rating: 4★
54 rue Saint-Louis-en-l'Île, 75004
01 43 26 14 18
jeudepaumehotel.com
Rooms: 27
Single: 185–360€
Double: 285–360€
Suites: 3

A former Royal Tennis court, the **Jeu de Paume** is a modern hotel in a very old shell. The public rooms and apartments (which require a minimum stay of five nights) are stunning, everything you ever dreamed a Parisian hotel could be. The regular guest rooms are simply pleasant, with a slightly Mediterranean feel and rattan furniture. The large, well-vegetated, paved courtyard is a welcome respite on this sometimes-airless island. The hotel has been in the hands of the original owners since it opened in 1988.

OTHER HOTELS

Hôtel des Deux-Îles

Rating: 3★
59 rue Saint-Louis-en-l'Île, 75004
01 43 26 13 35
deuxiles-paris-hotel.com
Rooms: 17
Single: 169€
Double: 205€

This and the Lutèce have the same owners. Both are charming three-star hotels on one of the most romantic streets in the world. The bedrooms aren't large but are nicely presented, with patterned wallpaper and flat-screen televisions. The fresh and modern bathrooms have Portuguese *azulejos* (traditional glazed ceramic) tiles above the bath.

In an imposing 17th-century building, the **Lutèce** is arguably more elegant than its sister, the Hôtel des Deux Îles, the bedrooms more striking: some have mansard roofs and most highlight exposed beams. The small rue Saint-Louis-en-l'Île can be noisy, especially when the garbage trucks empty the bins before dawn. Ask for a room at the back if you want quiet—but then you have to give up a perfectly gorgeous view.

Hôtel de Lutèce

Rating: 3★
65 rue Saint-Louis-en-l'Île, 75004
01 43 26 23 52
paris-hotel-lutece.com
Rooms: 23
Single: 165€
Double: 205€

APARTMENTS

Stephanie: I had a very happy renting experience through *guestapartment.com*, which specialises in rentals on the Île Saint Louis. They have very helpful young men.

Guest Apartment Services

guestapartment.com

Steve Feletti's French Oyster Primer

Like Shannon and Mr Jarnet (see "What Paris Mean to Me", p. 1), it was language study that led me down a wobbly path to France. My French teacher in junior high, Miss Millthorpe, was a bit of a small-town bombshell. In a dry, dusty western wheat town, she was a standout.

She was 1960s slim, pencil skirt, high heels, flame red rimmed glasses, sleeveless tops—how Française was that, especially for a hot pubescent teenager.

Despite her venal attractions, I experienced a deep gender crisis—not of the flesh, but of the noun. After three short months of confused gender, I fled to Commerce and Business Principles.

By university, however, my language guilt was too much to bear. I copped a great tip down at the student bar: Indonesian, it seemed, was log-falling–off easy.

Bahasa led me to Hindi, which led to Urdu, which led to Arabic, which led to flogging the nation's wheat in obscure overseas destinations. France is a sworn enemy for Aussie wheatfloggers—think wheat subsidies. It wasn't until the Tokyo days, hawking wheat into the world's most sophisticated food market that I overcame my grain prejudice, and began to see France as the only other worthy food culture. Not long after, I fell naïvely into oysters, thinking an oyster lease would be a great place to go fishing. And oysters plugged my destiny with France because, as with most things foodish, it is the holy grail of oysters.

Why France?

France should be the role model for every oyster-producing nation. Production there is around 130,000 tonnes; ours is around 10,000 tonnes. Sixty million citizens and eighty million tourists consume most of that figure and not one oyster is sold pre-shucked and tap-rinsed. Get it?

Oysters in Paris

Everywhere you look in Paris you will find 'les huîtres'. It's a safe bet that on any street corner in Paris you are never more than 500 metres from an oyster outlet. And, with unstated aplomb, the French always look after them, open them cleanly and serve them professionally. I have yet to find a place that 'cooks' oysters and, if I did, I'd probably move along. The main difference is with the dressings, but the universal dip is champagne vinegar and eschallots.

If you really need a specific Paris oyster address, the one most quoted in the centre of Paris is:

L'Écume St-Honoré
6 rue du Marché St-Honoré, 75001
01 42 61 93 87

However, on my last visit to L' Écume St-Honoré, I raised both eyebrows at the sight of some gaping Belons displayed in the shop front baskets. Upon my placing an order, the same gapers were about to be served up. I blew the whistle and they were replaced. They didn't like my taking photos either.

The two species you will encounter in Paris are: the Pacifics, *crassostrea gigas* (la creuse), and the flats *ostrea edulis* (les plats), commonly known as the Belon. In southern cities, these are known as la gravettes. There are many other smoke-and-mirrors names that we'll come to later, but these are the two species.

The history of oyster production in France is pockmarked by successive blights over the past century and a half. The once proud and prolific Belon was decimated by bonamiasis and today is difficult to find in any strength. The specimens I saw during my last visit from Paris to Montpellier were decidedly inferior to those five years ago—and clearly inferior to the Belon's DNA cousin, the Australian angasi.

How to Decipher an Oyster Menu

I collect French oyster menus. It's a fetish. They are very formulaic once you understand the French penchant for gilding the oyster: if it's simple, make it complicated with a spider web of calibration—a bit like wine appellation.

Oyster appellation revolves around the species, the provenance, the finishing method, the size, and one famous family dynasty.

I have five menus in front of me. The first difference is by provenance: Bouzigues (Mediterranean), Marennes d'Oléron (mid-West Atlantic Coast), Isigny (Normandy), Arcachon (Atlantic near Bordeaux), Quiberon (lower Brittany), Cancale (Normandy) and Bretagne (central Brittany and ancestral home of the Belon). All of them except the last will be Pacific gigas. Each of these regions has a distinct role in the broader national industry.

The second level of calibration is of size and finish (affinage). Don't worry too much about No. 3, G2, Calibre 4, No. 2, 00 and Pied Cheval ('horse's hoof'—not the Australian translation). Then comes more smoke and mirrors: La Spéciales, Les hulîtres Pousse en Claire, Les Fines de Claires and la hulître verte.

Let's start with the Fines de Claires. This simply means 'finished in the ponds'. These are special finishing ponds (formerly salt-maker's ponds) around the Marennes-Oléron basin.

However, the appellations then flow into mind-boggling names for specific stocking rates in the ponds, ranging from say fifty oysters per square metre down to one per square metre. These earn a higher ranking and price.

Huître Verte, The Green Oyster

On top of that we find the huître verte (green oyster), a deliberate attempt by otherwise honest oyster growers to produce green-coloured oysters. This is executed by inculcating in a series of small ponds, a blue algæ (naviculæ blu). The gigas oysters are then lodged in the ponds in varying densities. They start to filter the blue algæ, which turns the oyster flesh green over time. These oysters earn a ranking based on time spent in the blue algæ pond, together with relative stocking density. Believe it or not, the guys at Marennes have lodged a patent application with the EU administration to claim their IP rights to the green oyster process. Sorry, it tastes no different and looks disgusting.

Pousse en Clair essentially means 'blossomed in the ponds'. I believe it means what we natives in NSW carefully articulate as 'chuckin' an edge', indicating a growth spurt.

So, as an example, we have Fines de Claire vertes Label Rouge No 3 (en saison), which translates as finished in the ponds (at Marennes), the green Pacific oyster of medium size #3, Blue Ribbon quality.

Label Rouge or Blue Ribbon is the tick of approval found in oyster products, cheese products, poultry and lentils. Being a wantonly naughty boy, I have 'borrowed' it myself for one of my own trademarked products, partly out of whimsy and part tribute to the French industry. I am expecting a call from the French trade office any day now.

Gillardeau Dynasty

Let me be brief. There are Gillardeau oysters, daylight and then the rest. They are shipped with meticulous care all over the nation. Thierry Gillardeau is the fifth-generation farmer, holds an MA in Economics and has grown the family business 300 percent in six years. To manage the risk of the current disease blight, he acquired farms in Ireland. He brings in product from all over Europe and finishes it at family headquarters, at Bourcefranc le Chapus at the foot of the Chapus Bridge linking the mainland to the Île d'Oléron.

I will risk everything here and declare you will never have a substandard Gillardeau oyster anywhere in France. He, like me, remains trenchantly selective about who he sells to.

Oyster ATM

Yes, believe it or not, Thierry innovated the oyster ATM in 2010, in an otherwise-forlorn paddock just off the Chapus Bridge road a half-kilometre from head office. When we drove past, there was a police car pulled up outside. Suspecting trouble, Thierry phoned a manager. 'No worries, they're just loading up the police car while on duty.'

Affinage, the gentle art of Finishing

In France, a large sector of the oyster industry does nothing but finish oysters. They're called 'affineurs'. Their function is to basically achieve what a feedlot does for cattle or sheep, by manipulating a range of variables on hand. There is a French saying: Oysters without finish are like wine without oaking.

The Oyster Vatican: La Cité de l'Huître, Marennes

Should your oyster perversity know no bounds, then there is really only one French destination you must see before departing this world. Unfortunately, it's not in Paris but along a narrow canal (le canal de la Cayenne) lined with oyster craft and adjacent to a pretty town called Marennes on the central Atlantic coast. The largest nearby city is La Rochelle. You take the local train to Rochefort, then a bus or cab to Marennes. Lucky, there are terrific restaurants along the way.

This oyster exposition centre is incredible. Five mock oyster cabins are perched around a wooden deck walkway with a huge central reception and restaurant area. A wall of flat screens rotates through oyster-information programmes. Each cabin utilises multilingual, virtual-reality technology to present chapters in oyster history. You can even play with remote-controlled toy oyster punts in the pond under the complex.

La Cité de l'Huître
Chenal de la Cayenne, Marennes
05 46 36 78 98
cite-huitre.com

Pearls Along France's Oyster Trails

Rochefort sur Mer, near Marennes-Oléron
Les Quatres Saisons
76 rue Edouard Grimaux, 17300
05 46 83 95 12

Marennes
La Grillardière
4 place Chasseloup Laubat, 17320
05 46 85 42 78
Yes, try the oysters!

Gujan-Mestras (Arcachon basin)
La Guérinière
Chef: Thierry Renou
18 cours de Verdun, 33470
05 56 66 08 78
lagueriniere.com
Unbelievable Paris quality in an eye-blink village. Chef Thierry Renou is a Maître Cuisinier de France. There is also an oyster museum nearby.

Montpellier (Étang de Thau— think oysters on ropes)
Les Vignes
2 rue Bonnier d'Alco, 34000
04 67 60 48 42
lesvignesrestaurant.com

Cellier & Morel, "Cabiron"
de l'alguillerie, Montpellier, 3400
04 67 66 46 36
celliermorel.com

Bouzigues
Les Jardins de la Mer
Avenue Louis Tudesq, 34140
04 67 78 33 23
On the waterfront of the Étang de Thau, this restaurant is famous for chargrilling the day's catch over coals of local grapevine roots.

Paris: my personal favourite
Au Petit Riche
25 rue le Peletier, 75009
01 47 70 68 68
restaurant-aupetitriche.com
Loire specialties, with a comprehensive oyster list and veal as I had never seen it before in my life.

Shannon's Parisian Recipes

Pear Tarte Tatin

There are countless stories about the invention of the famous tarte tatin, all centred on the Hôtel Tatin in Lamotte-Beuvron (south of Orléans). This hotel–restaurant was run by two sisters, Stéphanie and Caroline Tatin (usually known as 'les demoiselles Tatin'). According to one story, in 1898 Stéphanie was browning apples in butter and sugar for a traditional apple pie, when she realised they were overcooked and slightly burnt. She threw a sheet of pastry on top to hide her sins and then placed the pan in the oven. When she took it out and upturned it, there was a glistening, perfectly caramelised tart. A legendary dish had been born. There are other versions of the story, but this one sounds just right to me.

Tarte tatin should be served for at least two, as it is difficult to make singly. It is best made in the morning and reheated just before serving, to allow the caramel (with the vanilla and spices it carries) further time to permeate the fruit.

90 g sugar

90 g butter

1 vanilla bean, split in half lengthways

2 pears, peeled, halved and cored, and studded with cloves

1 square puff pastry, rolled to a circle slightly larger than the pan you will use to cook the tart

EIGHT-SPICE POWDER

4 g juniper

6 g star anise

3 g white peppercorns

4 g cinnamon sticks

4 g cloves

2 saffron threads

2 cardamom pods

5 g pink salt

First prepare the eight-spice powder: toast the spices (except the pink salt) over medium heat, allow to cool and then blend to a powder with the salt. Set aside.

Preheat the oven to 190°C.

Evenly spread the sugar over the base of a medium-sized sauté pan. Cut the butter into four squares, place on the sugar, sprinkle with several pinches of the eight-spice mix, and lay vanilla-bean halves in the shape of a cross. Place pears core-side down, with the narrower ends pointing inwards. Lay the pastry over the pan, tucking edges firmly underneath the pears, and chill for 10 minutes.

Score pastry in the centre and over the middle of each pear. Place pan over medium heat on the stove-top until sugar and butter begin to caramelise. Baste the pastry with the caramel, put pan in preheated oven and bake for 10 minutes. Baste the pastry again, then bake for a further 10 minutes. Remove from the oven and turn tart out onto a chopping board. Cut in half and serve with a generous amount of cream, ice-cream or vanilla crème anglaise (custard).

Serves 2

4TH

Rive Gauche
LEFT BANK

Panthéon

FINE DINING

La Tour d'Argent stands proudly at the corner of the quai Tournelle and rue de Cardinal Lemoine, beside the Seine, overlooking most of Paris. The restaurant claims a history of more than 400 years; you can sense this in the downstairs Petit Musée de la Table, a museum dedicated to the glory of the restaurant. Here you are seduced into believing you are joining Kaiser Wilhelm I of Prussia, Tsar Alexandre II of Russia and his son (later Alexandre III), along with the Prussian prince Otto von Bismarck, at the historic Three Emperors Dinner held at the Café Anglais on 7 June 1867.

La Tour d'Argent reached its zenith in the 1980s under Claude Terrail, who died in 2006. His last years saw a decline from three Michelin stars to one, leading many (including chef Paul Bocuse) to publicly denounce Michelin's appalling manners. Why could it not have waited until Terrail had passed away before massacring the restaurant's reputation?

The restaurant's magnificent wine cellar (which diners are sometimes permitted to visit) contains more than 500 000 bottles.

La Tour d'Argent
15 quai Tournelle, 75005
01 43 54 23 31
tourdargent.com
Michelin: ★
GaultMillau: 🍴🍴🍴
Menu: 65 (lunch)/ 160/180€
À la carte: 130–305€

Shannon: La Tour d'Argent, in a lovely old building, is one of the oldest still-operating restaurants in the world, and is located where restaurants have stood since 1582. The entrance acts as a museum to the glory of the restaurant and informs you who has eaten there in the past. It has a really interesting display from the Three Emperors Dinner: it includes quite a few pieces from the Café Anglais, including an original menu and the original table setting. It looks sensational, so definitely allow yourself 20 minutes there (it gets quite crowded after lunch, so go beforehand). You then take a lift up three or four floors into the dining-room, which pays homage to the 1970s (décor, service, everything)— it is very retro and I love it. The restaurant only has one Michelin star at the moment, but it used to have three and they haven't changed anything since those glory days. The menu is quite expansive and it has a lot of duck dishes, which I recommend for the main course.

The smoking policy has changed since the new anti-smoking laws came into effect, but when Madeleine and I dined in the restaurant in 2007 we were sat next to an old couple who obviously dine there on a regular basis and who chain-smoked throughout the meal. Madeleine was pregnant and we asked to be moved on several occasions, but because the restaurant was full there wasn't a table available until much later. We were then moved to the famous corner table overlooking Nôtre Dame.

The entrées were lovely. I had a prawn bisque with delicious poached prawns in it. I was going to have the famous *Canard à la presse* (pressed duck, invented at La Tour d'Argent in the 19th century), which Scott had told me about, but it is very heavy so I decided on the *Caneton Mazarine à l'orange*. It is also served in two courses, but with a much lighter sauce. I was a little disappointed in the end that I didn't go for the pressed duck, but my dish was excellent: it was cooked to perfection, the meat of the leg falling off the bone. For dessert I had a really wonderful strawberry soufflé, which you can't go past.

Madeleine wasn't drinking, so I had a half-bottle of wine, of which they have plenty. The wine list is one of the best tributes to French vineyards you can get your hands on. The wines aren't cheap—nothing in this restaurant is going to be a bargain—but they are definitely worth it. Go for lunch and take your time: it's a great place for watching all sorts of people: tourists, old Parisians and, most of all, the waiters!

The views are amazing, looking out over the river. It is such a great part of Paris and a restaurant that I hope never disappears. It costs upwards of $300 per person to eat here, and you could probably go to a two- or three-star for that price. But if you are planning on making several trips to Paris, I definitely recommend reserving one of your lunches for Tour d'Argent. I don't think there is any better example of the grand old days of Paris. Do go there with the right expectations, though: you are going to have great classic French cooking, served in the great classic French manner, and you won't be disappointed.

Madeleine: Paris is a riot of olfactory stimuli. Where else do premier pâtisseries, magnificent gardens and medieval plumbing intersect so intimately? From the sublime to the malodorous, it is all there for your nasal delectation. But nowhere is the whiff of history quite so potent as at La Tour d'Argent. It is there in the quaint antiquities on display as you enter, the ancient elevator, the famous wine cellar, the studied aloofness of the liveried wait-staff, the weight of its reputation and its solemn dignity: everything that is quintessentially *parisien*. What I didn't expect was the double-barrelled blast of stale cigarette smoke we copped from the two diners adjacent. This divine elderly couple, decked out in 1940s-style glamour, enjoying what was clearly a regular *déjeuner* outing, proceeded to puff away before, after and during each course. Shannon shrugged it off as French whimsy.

Scott: La Tour d'Argent was one of my first three-star experiences. It was in the late 1970s and I had driven to Paris after the annual Cannes Film Festival. I decided to splurge and take my aunt Diane, her French husband, Pierre, and Sylvie, a filmmaking friend from Australia. I had asked my aunt to invite Pierre but somehow this didn't happen and I wrongly believed Pierre did not want to come. In turn, Pierre felt slighted, precipitating an unease that existed in the family for several years, until I discovered the problem and took Pierre and Diane to Les Ambassadeurs. So, my happy recollections of La Tour d'Argent are inextricably mixed with uncomfortable memories about a minor family rift. Restaurant experiences are not only about food.

We arrived, walking past the shrine dedicated to the Three Emperors Dinner at the Café Anglais, having no idea I would make a film decades later about a recreation of that famous meal by a precocious young Melbourne chef named Shannon Bennett.

We took the lift and entered the spectacular dining-room. This was still the 1970s, so the retro décor that so struck Shannon still looked modern. We were escorted to a table on a rise towards the back; not the best spot, but with a good view of all the diners and, beyond them, through the floor-to-ceiling glass windows, the whole of Paris.

The room felt as if it were full of Americans and Japanese, but it couldn't have been because the French had introduced a rule whereby only 25 per cent of places at a three-star restaurant could be allocated to foreigners. Parisians were feeling swamped by currency-rich tourists, unable to get into their own restaurants. I noticed that many diners were all drinking famous labels—Château Latour, Palmer (very much in vogue then), Mouton and Lafitte Rothschild—but vintages that were only three or so years old. This seemed extraordinary in the restaurant with the largest collection of fine wine in the world, and with vintages going back to the 19th century. People find it hard to believe now, but back then there was minimal mark-up on old wines and a 1955 Latour, for instance, was only about 20 per cent dearer than a 1975. Surely that should not have made the decision difficult.

As was the tradition then (indeed, still is), ladies were given menus without prices. With unerring accuracy, Sylvie headed straight for the truffled scrambled eggs, which was ten times the price of anything else. Being a young man of limited means, I wondered if this was going to be my last meal ever in a grand establishment.

Instead of the eggs, Diane and I had the famous, ethereal *Quenelles de brochet 'André Terrail'* (Pike dumplings), complemented by a superb Chassagne-Montrachet from 1973. When I ordered the 1949 Château Beychevelle to go with the *Caneton Tour d'Argent*, also known as *Canard à la presse*, the sommelier looked at our table with unmistakable enthusiasm. He walked across and whispered to owner Claude Terrail, and in an instant the wine glasses were gone and replaced with finer ones. Monsieur Terrail came across and chatted with us most charmingly.

The duck is pure theatre. The whole roasted duck is brought out first, on a silver platter. A waiter cuts off the legs, which go back to the kitchen for further cooking, and he then slices off the breast before placing the carcass in a highly polished copper press. After the blood and cooking juices are extracted, they are carefully made into a sauce in front of you, with beef consommé, old Madeira and Cognac. The duck breast and sauce, enriched with the blood, was divine. The legs came out later after additional grilling, served with a simple green salad.

It was all one needs after the richness of the breast. The only unsettling note came at the end of the meal when Diane and I were each given an old photograph of a duck farm in Challans with the number of the duck we had just eaten printed on it. That's far too Disneyland for me.

For dessert, we ordered the crystallised-violet soufflé, a magnificent creation I have never seen since on any restaurant menu. Once, I tried to recreate it at home—a mistake. To match it, I chose an 1899 Château Rabaud-Sigalas (only later would the vineyard be renamed Sigalas-Rabaud). The sommelier dashed off to confer once more with Claude Terrail, who returned and graciously explained that such a wine could not be drunk at so ordinary a table and perhaps we would like to move to the famous table in the corner bay window, overlooking the Seine and Nôtre Dame. This special treatment had nothing to do with wealth or class or fame (we could claim none of these), but was simply because we had shown an interest in the world's greatest wine list and gone beyond the obvious and most recent. (Times have, of course, changed, with wine buffs having far greater interest in back vintages—and discovering prices to match.)

The moment the wine arrived remains the most magical moment of my restaurant-going life. Two black-tie waiters carried the bottle ever so gently, holding it near the horizontal so as not to disturb the residual sugar. Monsieur Terrail explained that the label had been washed away in a flood many decades ago, but that I might just be able to just see the name Rabaud-Sigalas printed on the cork inside the neck. At this point, I cared nothing for provenance or verification: never has a wine looked so inviting. The cork came out in a hundred pieces, but the wine was indeed sublime and the equal of the many Château d'Yquems I have been fortunate enough to taste since. It cost $25.

I later discussed the wine with uncle Pierre, who explained that the French considered sauternes to be a horrible English invention and no self-respecting French house ever cellared them. As I had given Pierre a bottle of Sauternes a year or so earlier, I realised I had unintentionally added to the faux pas of his not being invited to dinner with yet another one. In France, one must keep on one's toes.

Marco Pierre White's Top 10 French Dishes of All Time

Soupe aux truffes V.G.E. (Paul Bocuse)

Loup de mer en croûte (Bocuse)

Poularde de Bresse en vessie
   (Fernand Point)

Canard à la presse (Tour d'Argent)

Gratin de queues d'écrivisses (Point)

Escalope de saumon à l'oseille
   (Jean and Pierre Troisgros)

Pigeonneau en croûte de sel (Roger Vergé)

Pied de cochon aux morilles
   (Charles Barrier)

Gâteau marjolaine (François Bise)

Croustade aux pommes (Pierre Koffmann)

Shannon's Favourite Parisian Treats

Fromageries

There are more different cheeses in France than there are days of the year, and visiting one of the many *fromageries* (or *crèmeries*—dairies) is one of the great joys of being in Paris.

Androuët

Since 1909
134 rue Mouffetard, 75005
01 45 87 85 05
Also at:
37 rue de Verneuil, 75007
93 rue de Cambronne, 75015
1 rue Bois le Vent, 75016
23 rue de la Terrasse, 75017
androuet.com

For decades, Androuët was the most famous cheese supplier in Paris. But, as the number of stores increased (now six), its name became a little diminished in comparison to such smaller concerns as Barthélemy and Marie Anne Cantin. No matter: this is still a fine place to get your fromage, with more than 200 different types available and all cured in the store's own cellars.

Barthélemy

51 rue de Grenelle, 75007
01 42 22 82 84
no website

A master *fromage affineur* (ager of cheese), Barthélemy has its tiny and iconic shop on the corner of boulevard Raspail and rue de Grenelle. Barthélemy has been described as the 'high priest of cheese' in Paris.

Shannon: The best cheese shop in Paris, without a doubt. Only seasonal cheese is sold here, and only what is at its best will be passed on to a very loyal and local clientele.

Fromagerie Quatrehomme

62 rue de Sèvres, 75007
01 47 34 33 45
Also at:
9 rue Poteau, 75018
no website

Marie Quatrehomme is the supplier of the cheese served in the three-star Restaurant le Meurice. She is particularly known for her Beaufort, chèvres and Saint-Marcellin.

Marie Anne Cantin

Since 1950
12 rue de Champ de Mars, 75007
01 45 50 43 94
cantin.fr

Official supplier of cheese to the French president and parliament, Marie Anne Cantin runs a bold and New Age *crèmerie*. She even has the audacity to place alongside her French masterpieces several cheeses from Spain, Greece and Portugal. She also runs several shops in Japan. With an encyclopædic knowledge, she will happily discuss with devoted customers her recipes (including milk and Roquefort soup, and canapés of goat cheese with paprika, cumin, tarragon, chives and chervil). Don't forget to buy some of her demi-sel butter.

Craig: Off Rue Cler, with its wonderful market and cafés, is Marie Anne Cantin, a cheese store from heaven. On one occasion when my wife Liz was six months pregnant, she went into Cantin and spoke to the cheesemaker. She optimistically thought that, if the cheesemaker said that French women could eat soft French cheeses when pregnant, then it would be good enough for her. She was most disappointed when the cheesemaker said, 'Non, non, non', and pointed to the hard cheeses.

Brasserie Balzar

49 rue des Écoles, 75005
01 43 54 13 67
brasseriebalzar.com
À la carte: 35–65€

Brasserie Balzar, established in the 1930s, is an institution. There is so much history attached to it that the website rightly promotes the place with this story: 'Paris, 1947. Western Europe is threatened by a Soviet invasion. Albert Camus and Jean-Paul Sartre are lunching at Balzar. "What will you do if the Soviets attack?" asks Sartre. "I'll join the Resistance. Like Malraux. What about you?" "I will not shoot against the proletariat," replied Sartre. History has not recorded what they were eating.' What you can eat today are classic brasserie dishes in a beautiful glass-fronted space overlooking the rue des Écoles. If you sit there long enough, you may see another May 1968 protest develop in the street.

Marty

20 avenue des Gobelins, 75005
01 43 31 39 51
marty-restaurant.com
Menu: 36€
À la carte: 35–45€

A charming Art Déco restaurant, opened in 1913 by Étienne Marty. Étienne's granddaughter, Geneviève Péricouche, runs it today.

Matt: We had lunch at **Marty** and ate simple things like a tomato and buffalo mozzarella salad, and an entrecôte steak with Paris butter. It was great.

Moissonnier

28 rue Fossés-St-Bernard, 75005
01 43 29 87 65
Menu: 37€
À la carte: 30–65€

A typical bistro, across the road from the Institut du Monde Arabe (one of the great modern buildings of Paris, designed by Jean Nouvel), with jugs of Beaujolais and hearty Lyonnaise-style food.

This bistro has soothing café-au-lait-coloured walls, some bare stonework and plenty of space between the tables. It is especially pleasant at lunchtime, with light flooding in. The day's menu is written up on strategically placed chalkboards, visible from any table. Why don't more bistros follow their example?

Restaurant Itinéraires

5 rue de Pontoise, 75005
01 46 33 60 11
GaultMillau: 🍴🍴
Menu: 41€
À la carte: 32–55€

 MARKET

On one of the most ancient streets of Paris, this market is always a pleasure to walk through, even if nothing tempts you on the stalls or in the speciality stores.

Marché rue Mouffetard

Tuesday to Sunday morning

Le Piano Vache

8 rue Laplace, 75005
01 46 33 75 03
lepianovache.com

This Rive Gauche dive (in the best sense of the word) might remind you of the places Jo (Audrey Hepburn) visits in *Funny Face*, in search of the genuine bohemian experience. It is a preferred film location of director Cédric Klapisch and singer Patrick Bruel.

 LUXURY HOTELS

Hôtel Les Rives de Nôtre-Dame

Rating: 4★
15 quai Saint-Michel, 75005
01 43 54 81 16
paris-hotel-rivesnotredame.com
Rooms: 10
Single: 134–320€
Double: 134–320€

This little-known gem is on the quai Saint-Michel right beside the Seine. All its rooms have astonishing views over the river and Nôtre Dame. They are furnished simply with outdoor-style metal-and-cushion furniture, but the rooms are large, filled with light, and completely soundproofed; the spacious penthouse is a long attic room. If you get restless, walk down to the river and visit *les bouquinistes* (the famous riverside booksellers), who sell everything from cheap paperbacks and magazines to (increasingly rarely) hard-to-find first editions.

Villa Panthéon

Rating: 4★
41 rue des Écoles, 75005
01 53 10 95 95
villa-pantheon.com
Rooms: 59
Single: 160–380€
Double: 195–450€

Most lovers of the Rive Gauche head to the 6th and 7th arrondissements, due to the paucity of quality hotels in the 5th. The **Villa Panthéon** is a four-star exception. On the fairly major rue des Écoles (which runs parallel to the boulevard Saint-Germain), this well-soundproofed hotel has an English-club feel, with wooden floors and leather chesterfields. The public rooms have the subdued lighting one expects from a respectable gentlemen's abode. The guest rooms are altogether brighter, with vibrant striped wallpaper.

This ultra-modern boutique hotel has small rooms that are boldly coloured with Chinese lacquer. It is a long way from the centre of the Rive Gauche, a few steps from boulevard de Port Royal. In 2009, *Time Out* listed it with Le Bellechasse and Mama Shelter as 'Best Newcomer'. The hotel is non-smoking throughout.

The Five Hotel
Rating: 3★
3 rue Flatters, 75005
01 43 31 74 21
thefivehotel.com
Rooms: 23
Single: 89–202€
Double: 116–342€
Suites: 1

One of the most charming hotels in the 5th, the **Hotel des Grands Hommes** sits proudly on its street, next to the Hotel du Panthéon. An 18th-century building, it is famous for being the abode of the father of surrealism, André Breton. The Empire-style décor is very inviting, especially in the Deluxe rooms, which have private terraces with stunning views over Paris from the majestic dome of the Panthéon north to Sacré-Cœur. The staircase is a masterpiece, so on at least one occasion do bypass the lift. There is an enormous range in prices, making it possible for anyone to stay and enjoy its enveloping atmosphere. The Jardin du Luxembourg is handily nearby.

Hotel des Grands Hommes
Rating: 3★
17 place du Panthéon, 75005
01 46 34 19 60
hoteldesgrandshommes.com
Rooms: 31
Single: 80–310€
Double: 90–430€

Located directly opposite the Panthéon, this 18th-century building (completed in 1789) is a riot of pinks and reds, set off beautifully with white linen and flowers. There is a vaulted breakfast room (de rigueur, surely, for a romantic Parisian hotel) and an elegant sitting-room off the lobby. The Louis XVI-style rooms offer views over the Temple de la Renommée dome. The staircase is a gem (as is the one in the neighbouring Hotel des Grands Hommes; go next door and compare).

Hotel du Panthéon
Rating: 3★
19 place du Panthéon, 75005
01 43 54 32 95
hoteldupantheon.com
Rooms: 36
Single: 90–270€
Double: 100–270€

5ᵗʰ

Shannon's Favourite Parisian Treats

Tea

The French have taken the art of drinking tea to an unparalleled level, though you need to be a millionaire to indulge the passion fully. The price of some rare teas may bring on a faint that only stronger liquids can banish.

The gourmet food stores Hédiard and Ladurée both have tea-rooms and sell tea: Hédiard has a fine range of rare and delicious blends; Ladurée has a smaller but also delicious selection, mostly of scented teas.

La Maison des Trois Thés
1 rue Saint Médiard, 75005
01 43 36 93 84
troisthes.com

Run by Madame Tseng Yu Hi, this is the most expensive and mysterious tea shop in Paris (you ring a bell to be let in). Inside it looks like a film set from Jean-Jacques Annaud *L'Amant*, with its low light levels, dark polished wood and ornate tea canisters. The daughter of tea planters in Fujian (home of Oolong), Tseng Yu Hi is one of the world's leading tea experts; to guarantee supply, she has her own plantations in China and Taiwan. Her shop is particularly strong in aged fermented teas (*pu-ers*), which are valued more than grand-cru Bordeaux for their complexity of flavour and ability to mature over time.

Mariage Frères
Since 1854
30 rue du Bourg-Tibourg, 75004
01 42 72 28 11
Also at:
13 rue des Grands-Augustins, 75006
260 rue du faubourg Saint-Honoré, 75008
17 place de la Madeleine, 75008
mariagefreres.com

Mariage Frères, the most internationally known name in Parisian tea shops, was started in 1854 by the Cottin family. It was taken over in the mid-1980s by a Thai national and a Dutchman, a move that has given the brand great impetus, even if at the risk of over-commercialising the name. There are now four outlets in Paris, all with museums, restaurants and tea-rooms (the one in the 6th is the prettiest). The teas come from all around the world, but Mariage Frères loves to put its own twist on scented teas: Green Maté from Latin America, for example, has 'a mild hint of honey and vanilla, fruit and flowers from Tibet, plus a profusion of berries'. Exceptional teas come at exceptional prices.

Le Palais des Thés
64 rue Vieille-du-Temple, 75003
01 48 87 80 60
Also at:
61 rue du Cherche-Midi, 75006
25 rue Raymond-Losserand, 75014
21 rue de l'Annonciation, 75016
36 rue de Lévis, 75017
palaisdesthes.com

Le Palais des Thés started as a community project, when 50 tea-lovers joined together to ensure they could get access to the finest and freshest teas. There are now five shops in Paris and several in the regions, and the range of teas is extraordinary, imported from nearly 30 countries. Naturally, most come from China (50 varieties) and India (28). There is a wonderful selection of truly rare teas, including China's New Season green teas (around 27€ for 100 g).

Shannon's Parisian Recipes

Scallops Baked in Bread

This dish is a great way to introduce children to seafood. It is a very traditional peasant way of making a complete meal from only a few ingredients, and makes a great dinner-party recipe as the bread and scallop can be prepared well in advance, allowing you time to enjoy the company of friends rather than be stressed in the kitchen.

219

DOUGH

300 g plain flour, sifted

15 g olive oil

½ tablespoon fresh yeast

6 g salt

½ teaspoon sugar

380 ml water

SCALLOPS

12 large live scallops in their shells, roes removed

salt and freshly ground pepper

300 ml fish stock

1 clove garlic, crushed

½ bulb fennel, finely chopped

½ carrot, finely chopped

1 stick celery, finely chopped

½ leek, julienned

1 small zucchini, julienned

2 tablespoons olive oil, for final cooking

BUTTER SAUCE

70 ml dry white wine

70 ml dry vermouth (Noilly Prat)

100 g butter, cut into fine dice

salt to taste

juice of ½ lemon

2 eggs, for glazing pastry

To make the dough, combine all the ingredients in a large mixer bowl and use a dough hook to work the dough for at least 15 minutes (the more elastic the dough, the better). Transfer to a lightly oiled container that will provide enough room for the dough to double in size. Cover the container with plastic wrap and set aside in a warm part of the kitchen for 40 minutes or until doubled in size. Place on a floured work surface and knead for 5 minutes. Set aside until required.

Remove the scallops from the shell and clean six of the shells with a nail-brush in hot soapy water. Place the fish stock in a heavy-based saucepan and bring to the boil. Add the garlic and cook for a minute, then add the fennel and cook for another minute. Add the carrot, cook for one minute, then add the celery and leek. Bring to the boil, immediately remove all the vegetables from the pan and set them aside to cool. While they are still warm, add the zucchini and mix (the residual heat will cook the zucchini).

To make the butter sauce, reduce the stock used for poaching the vegetables by three-quarters. Add the white wine and vermouth, and reduce by two-thirds. Gradually whisk in the butter, a quarter at a time, until the sauce is thick, smooth and shiny. Season with salt and lemon juice, and set aside.

To assemble, heat 1 tablespoon of the olive oil in a heavy-based frying pan, add the scallop roes and fry for 30 seconds. Lightly brush the scallop shells with a thin coating of the remaining olive oil. Place the vegetables in the centre, arrange three scallops around the vegetables and season with salt and pepper. Spoon a generous amount of the butter sauce over.

Preheat the oven to 180°C.

Roll the dough into 12 thin (around 2 mm) rough circles 2 cm larger than the scallop shell and rest in the refrigerator for 10 minutes. Whisk the eggs to form an egg wash. Place a circle of dough over each shell and press down firmly around the edges to prevent the pastry separating during baking, and trim away any overhang. Brush pastry with the egg wash and place filled shells on a foil-lined baking tray (to prevent the scallops from tipping over and losing the cooking juices during baking). Bake in preheated oven for 10 minutes, or until pastry is crispy and golden.

Serves 4

Saint-Germain-des-Prés

6TH ARRONDISSEMENT

FINE DINING

For a while, it looked as if chef Jacques Cagna would take over Paris. His restaurant on rue des Grands-Augustins was constantly lauded by GaultMillau (peaking at 18/20) and by Michelin (two stars). He also opened La Rôtisserie d'en Face across the street, which was an instant hit and encouraged many other famous chefs (including Guy Savoy and Pierre Gagnaire) to open a second restaurant. There seemed to be no stopping Cagna, then suddenly his star crashed (to one star and 15/20). But that does not mean he should be forgotten.

Jacques Cagna

Chef: Jacques Cagna
14 rue des Grands-Augustins, 75006
01 43 26 49 39
jacques-cagna.com
Michelin: ★
GaultMillau: 🍴🍴🍴
Menu: 45 (lunch)/95€
À la carte: 85–155€

Scott: Cagna's main restaurant is in a historic 17th-century building in the oldest part of Paris. It is a stunning space, with exposed oak beams, Flemish paintings and wood-panelling inset with frescoes. (If you book, make sure you are not assigned one of the tables in the dingy and disgraceful area downstairs.)

Cagna is famous for many dishes, including a *Pommes surprise*, which is a plate of hollowed-out small potatoes, shaped into cylinders and then stuffed with a snail ragoût. He is especially good with pigeon, as in his dish of *pigeon de Vendée*, which consists of pigeon breasts roasted with garlic, and the legs in a pie, served with a green Chartreuse sauce. Many diners, however, clamour to get in for the choux-pastry dessert (*Le Paris-Brest de Jacques Cagna*, long considered the finest of its kind in France) or to select from his 50 000-bottle cellar, which includes some extremely rare wines. This is an old-fashioned restaurant, resolutely committed to classical cooking and not experimentation. Its glory and relevance may have faded slightly, but it is still heavily booked and expensive. **Jacques Cagna** is one of the few irreplaceable Old Paris experiences, where the food can be as compelling as the surroundings.

Relais Louis XIII

Chef: Manuel Martinez
8 rue des Grands-
Augustins, 75006
01 43 26 75 96
relaislouis13.fr
Michelin: ★★
GaultMillau: ☺☺☺
Menu: 50 (lunch)/80/125€
À la carte: 110–130€

Relais Louis XIII is probably the most controversial starred restaurant in Paris. GaultMillau didn't list it for 10 years, and in 2007 *gastroville.com* published a blistering review (scoring it just 7/20). Michelin, however, resolutely maintains its two-star rating. What no one can dispute is the beauty of the building and its exposed-beam dining-rooms. The name reflects the fact that the building, then the Saint-Augustin Convent, was where Louis XIII (aged eight) learned in 1610 that he was about to rule France. Manual Martinez's food certainly does not rule Paris, but Michelin considers the cooking 'subtle and up-to-date'.

Restaurant Hélène Darroze — La Salle à Manger

Chef: Hélène Darroze
4 rue d'Assas, 75006
01 42 22 00 11
helenedarroze.com
Michelin: ★
GaultMillau: ☺☺☺
Menu: 52 (lunch)/125/175€
(wine included)

It is extraordinary, given that most food in France is cooked by women, how few great restaurants have female chefs. One is Hélène Darroze, who has two restaurants in a building near the Le Bon Marché store. **La Salle à Manger** is the main restaurant, upstairs, while downstairs is Au Salon d'Hélène. The food and wines reflect Darroze's origins in Gascony, where her father was a famous chef. Daily the empire grows, Darroze now also running the dining-room at The Connaught Mayfair in London.

Shannon: I haven't been here yet, but I really want to. Scott gave me her first cookbook for my birthday and it is truly inspiring.

I sent friends Eddie and Carla here and they raved about it, especially the desserts and *petits fours*. Leave early if going for lunch so that you can wander through Le Bon Marché across the road. Don't miss the second-floor art exhibition that changes seasonally.

Taking its name from the secondhand booksellers beside the Seine, **Les Bouquinistes** is a charming restaurant opened by three-star chef Guy Savoy. Filled with light during the day (and offering lovely views across the river), at night it turns into one of the most romantic places to eat in Paris.

Les Bouquinistes

15 quai des Grands-
Augustins, 75006
01 43 25 45 94
lesbouquinistes.com
GaultMillau: 🍴🍴
Menu: 29 (lunch)/80€
À la carte: 60–70€

Scott: I had lunch here with sister Sue and we both loved it. The space is gorgeous and the staff are as charming as any I have met in Paris. We both had the prix-fixe menu. My entrée, a carpaccio of Salmon in aspic, was a little cold, but delicious. As a main, Sue had a huge and delicious veal kidney (*rognon*), while I had rabbit flavoured solely with marjoram flowers. It is the best rabbit dish I have eaten. Neither Sue nor I usually eat dessert, but the young waiter suggested we try one: we did, it was excellent and he did not charge for it. The wine list was small but included several excellent provincial wines. A perfect lunch.

Brasserie Lipp was once one of the most famous brasseries in Paris, but it has almost disappeared from the guidebooks and blog sites. This is a mystery, because it is still a fun place to eat on one of the great boulevards. Forget whether there is better food elsewhere, and relax. But pray you are not ushered into the Siberia upstairs.

Brasserie Lipp

151 boulevard Saint-
Germain, 75006
01 45 48 53 91
groupe-bertrand.com/lipp
GaultMillau: 🍴
À la carte: 50–80€

Shannon: I walked out after 40 minutes without food. The waiters were way too busy and rude. But the place looked great: like Paris as it used to be.

Matt: I went with a French guy who had lived in Paris for years. He loves big full-on restaurants, but he also loves the classic brasseries. Four of us went for lunch and we all had snails, with sole meunière to finish. Fantastic.

6ᵀᴴ

Le Comptoir

Chef: Yves Camdeborde
9 carrefour de l'Odéon,
75006
01 44 27 07 97
hotel-paris-relais-saint-germain.com
Menu: 50€
À la carte: 35–65€

This always-packed bistro is famous for its South-West food and its authentic 1930s Art Déco interior. After 9 p.m. you must have the Ménu Gastronomique, which GaultMillau claims demands the 'patience of an angel and a pre-booking', but don't worry: just take it easy and enjoy. Yves Camdeborde's food is very reasonably priced for its quality and justifiably high GaultMillau rating. It is part of the Relais Saint-Germain, one of the great boutique hotels of Paris.

L'Épi Dupin

Chef: François Pasteau
11 rue Dupin, 75006
01 42 22 64 56
lepidupin.com
Michelin: Bib Gourmand
GaultMillau: ☺☺
Menu: 33€

You must pre-book to get into this tiny bare-brick place, which boasts a beamed ceiling and fabulous food for the price. It is justifiably a first-choice Rive Gauche restaurant for many visitors to Paris, especially Americans. Whether foreigners order from the hand-written blackboard such specials as *Tête de veau* (calf's head) is anyone's guess, but this is certainly one of the top Paris bistros for food and atmosphere.

La Méditerranée

Chef: Denis Rippa
2 place de l'Odéon, 75006
01 43 26 02 30
la-mediterranee.com
GaultMillau: ☺
Menu: 32€
À la carte: 45–70€

Opposite the famed Théâtre de l'Éurope, **La Méditerranée** is world-famous for its fresh seafood and the artistic clientele it has served over the decades. The blue façade is by Jean Cocteau, a friend of the man who opened La Méditerranée in 1944, Jean Subrenat. Eating here is enormous fun, but the bill can add up and, despite the use of olive oil from San Guido instead of butter, the food can be rather rich. It's a perfect lunch spot, if you are prepared to write off the afternoon. There is always the Jardin du Luxembourg, 30 metres away, for a quick recovery stroll.

In the early 1990s, the then-two-starred Jacques Cagna opened a second restaurant in this listed building on rue Christine (just near the Relais Christine, a wonderful hotel). Cagna named the restaurant **La Rôtisserie d'en Face**, which led Michelin for years to ask, *'En face de quoi?'* The answer, chaps, is that it looks across the road to Cagna's main restaurant. Someone must have finally explained this to Michelin, which has now dropped the quip.

La Rôtisserie d'en Face

2 rue Christine, 75006
01 43 26 40 98
jacques-cagna.com
GaultMillau: ☙
Menu: 37€
À la carte: 39–46€

Scott: Inside, the décor is delightfully Provençal, with ochre-coloured walls, glass-panelled doors, and pretty plates on the walls. It will make you feel sunny inside, even if the weather outside is not. The food varies from simple terrines (hare, foie gras) and a *Poulet fermier label rouge* (a superb spit-roasted farm chicken) and *Côte de bœuf* to more complex but still homely dishes such as *Pintade en pastilla*, a crispy pastry filled with guinea fowl, honey-flavoured onions, eggplant and pine nuts—fabulous. This is comfort food using good-quality ingredients. A bonus is that you can taste Cagna's famous Paris-Brest dessert without having to go to the more-expensive main restaurant. The staff are relaxed and friendly, and it is a restaurant where one can feel comfortable eating alone.

Opened in 1911, this famous brasserie now has a 1930s look. It is famous for its post-theatre sittings (service lasts to 2 a.m., not common in Paris) and for once feeding the likes of Picasso, Hemingway and Trotsky.

La Rotonde

105 boulevard du
Montparnasse, 75006
01 43 26 68 84
rotondemontparnasse.com
Menu: 35€
À la carte: 40–75€

Sensing

Chef: Rémi Van Peteghem
19 rue Bréa, 75006
01 43 27 08 80
restaurantsensing.com
Michelin: ★
GaultMillau: 🍴🍴🍴
Menu: 35 (lunch)/70€
À la carte: 65–90€

This second restaurant of Le Grand Véfour's Guy Martin is a very chic affair. Chef Rémi Van Peteghem's food is modern, inventive and beautifully presented, the apparent simplicity of the dishes not quite concealing the brilliant technique involved. It looks and tastes like two-star food, but comes at bistro prices. The best bet is the 55€ four-course lunch with wine included.

Ze Kitchen Galerie

Chef: William Ledeuil
4 rue des Grands-
Augustins, 75006
01 44 32 00 32
zekitchengalerie.fr
Michelin: ★
GaultMillau: 🍴🍴🍴🍴
Menu: 39/76€
À la carte: approx. 60€

Ze Kitchen Galerie is a very hip studio-restaurant-gallery committed to 'Passion and dedication, originality and pleasure, new and common ground', all under one roof. The Asian-influenced French food (with inspirations from Thailand, Vietnam, Japan) is prepared in an open kitchen. Opened in 2001, this is still widely regarded as the hot-spot of the Rive Gauche.

Shannon: This is a tough one to review because I have mixed emotions. The Guy Savoy-trained French chef is doing some good food, but it's not mind-blowing. With Les Bouquinistes next door, it's a little distracting. The room tries too hard in its attempt to be cutting edge and modern, especially in its display of cheap artwork, and comes off in such a way that the room looks very dated and far too over-crowded. The tables are very closely planted together, similar to Benoît, but Benoît is a bistro.

I personally think if this restaurant were in Melbourne it would survive, but locals would keep it honest. In Paris, because the locals—especially the young—are wanting to see tradition evolve, they are embracing chef William Ledeuil's cuisine. Give it go if you can get in and you have a spare night, but keep your expectations to a minimum and you will enjoy. Prices are medium.

Not the best or cheapest market in Paris, but visiting it is one of the great almost-daily pleasures of staying in Saint-Germain-des-Prés.

Marché rue Buci
Monday to Sunday morning

BARS

Even though you can eat here, many people come just for a drink and to feel part of the bustling world of Saint-Germain-des-Prés. It has long been favoured by intellectuals (Sartre, Beauvoir) and filmmakers (Godard, Chabrol) over the nearby Les Deux Magots. It has been claimed that friendships were ended by people taking a drink at the 'unacceptable other' place.

Café de Flore
172 boulevard Saint-Germain, 75006
01 45 48 55 26
café-de-flore.com

Though the literati prefer Café de Flore and claim **Les Deux Magots** has sold out to tourists, this remains one of the most exquisite places in which to sit in the great city of Paris. The view across the square to the Église de Saint-Germain-des-Prés is unparalleled. (It is best early in the morning or at dusk; avoid the part of the street surrounded by hedges, which block the view.) Who cares about how much a drink costs, or how hard it can be to get a waiter's attention when you want to leave?

Les Deux Magots
6 place Saint-Germain-des-Près, 75006
01 45 48 55 25
lesdeuxmagots.com

Scott: I never visit Paris without a pilgrimage to this cinematically holy place. I have never let the non-French chatter, the brusque waiters, the pressing crowds or the exorbitant prices bother me. I don't know many ways to feel more at peace in a bustling metropolis than gazing at the Église de Saint-Germain-des-Prés. Two of the greatest films ever made were partly shot inside the church: Robert Bresson's *Le diable, probablement* (where a chair pushed out of its immaculate row spells the desolation to come) and Walerian Borowczyk's *Cérémonie d'amour* (with its grave meditation on the church's artworks contrasting with the erotic gestures of the lovers). Les Deux Magots is a place to dream.

L'Écluse

15 quai des Grands-
Augustins, 75006
01 46 33 58 74
Also at:
34 place du Marché
Saint-Honoré, 75001
01 42 96 10 18
64 rue François 1er, 75008
01 47 20 77 09
15 place de la Madeleine,
75008
01 42 65 34 69
1 rue d'Armaillé, 75017
01 47 63 88 29
leclusbaravin.com

These five wine bars across Paris offer an impressive array of quality Bordeaux wines by the glass or bottle. The food menu is classic: *Assiette autour de l'oie et du canard* (cold cuts of goose and duck), *Les joues de raies marinées* (marinated skate cheeks). The bar at the quai des Grands-Augustins has long been popular with Australian filmmakers.

La Palette

43 rue de Seine, 75006
01 43 26 68 15
cafelapaletteparis.com

La Palette, famously a haunt of Picasso and Braque, is a great place for a drink. The café was opened in 1903, but the present interior dates from 1935. It is both shabby and endearing.

 LUXURY HOTELS

Hôtel de l'Abbaye

Rating: 4★
10 rue Cassette, 75006
01 45 44 38 11
hotelabbayeparis.com
Rooms: 40
Single: 240–475€
Double: 240–475€
Suites: 4

A former convent, this gorgeous hotel was a much-sought-after address in the 1980s and 1990s but seems to have faded a little from view. While the hotel is an edifying walk from the heart of the Rive Gauche, it counters that small defect by being an oasis of civility and calm. It is no surprise the hotel's website uses the sounds of trickling water and birds rather than the obligatory music.

The public lounges are beautifully decorated with antique furniture and furnishings. Mariage Frères tea is served mid-afternoon, along with shortbread made with prized Guérande salt from Brittany. French doors lead from the lounges onto a walled garden covered in creeper. The guest rooms range from Classic (charming but a touch small) and Deluxe (the richness of the furnishings may challenge some guests) to Junior suites (the ones on the ground floor have access to a private garden) and four duplex apartments with their own terraces.

Home of the British embassy in the 18th century, the **Hôtel d'Angleterre**'s main claim to fame for many travellers is that Ernest Hemingway often stayed here. It is located on the rue Jacob (before it becomes the rue de l'Université); you enter the hotel grounds through an arched gate. French doors lead into an inviting lobby, with check-in desk, beyond which is a bar. To the left is the original staircase, one of the finest in France. The guest rooms are decorated in a variety of styles and have widely divergent footprints: some have huge bedrooms and tiny bathrooms, others are so small that a couple will have difficulty moving around if their suitcase is open. The best rooms are gorgeous, with high ceilings and exposed beams and a discreet chandelier. The furniture ranges from a comfortable country-house sofa to an antique writing desk and rattan-backed chairs. The small garden area where breakfast is served is serene.

Hôtel d'Angleterre

Rating: 4★
44 rue Jacob, 75006
01 42 60 34 72
hotel-dangleterre.com
Rooms: 23
Single: 140–260€
Double: 180–310€
Suites: 4

Scott: Alissa and I adored this hotel, with its golden drapes and French doors opening onto surely the most gorgeous street in Paris. I didn't even mind the sounds of happy people in the street till dawn. The breakfast served in the courtyard was limited (brioche, baguette and jam), but it was so peaceful there that we had absolutely no desire to wander Paris to find an alternative. Sitting calmly in an idyllic garden a few metres from your hotel room is the ideal way to start a perfect Paris day.

Shannon's Favourite Parisian Treats

Boulangeries

The best bread in Paris is made in one of two ways: naturally yeast-fermented; or with a poolish-based dough, most famously used to make baguettes. (It is a bit like a masterstock for bread, where some of the dough from the day before is kept and used the next day; roughly 50/50.) For the best butter you will ever taste, go to the small cheese shop Marie Anne Cantin and ask for the demi-sel—with warm fresh baguette, it is delicious.

Poilâne

8 rue de Cherche-Midi, 75006
01 45 48 42 59
49 boulevard de Grenelle, 75015
01 45 79 11 49
poilane.fr

Without doubt the world's most famous bread. As well as from its two bakeries, it is available all over Paris in outlets such as Le Bon Marché and selected providores.
Shannon: 'Poilâne is to bread what Paul Bocuse is to restaurants' has been quoted many times. Sadly, Lionel Poilâne passed away in 2003 following an accident, but his legacy lives on through his daughter Appolonia.

The secret to Poilâne bread is the stone-ground flour, blackish-brown in colour, and the use of a natural yeast to leaven the bread. The result is a 1.9-kg round loaf that will still satisfy three days after you've bought it. No baguettes are available at this famous bakery: the only

other products on sale are a yellow small sandwich loaf, and several types of sweet pastries and biscuits. You have to visit this shop at least once.

Eric Kayser

14 rue Monge, 75005
01 44 07 17 81
Also at:
16 rue des Petits Carreaux, 75002
10 rue de l'Ancienne Comédie, 75006
18 rue de Bac, 75007, etc.
maison-kayser.com

There are 16 Kayser outlets across Paris, including in most of the arrondissements frequented by tourists.

For the best baguette in town, it would be hard to go past Boulangerie Kayser. Eric Kayser's bread is made with a special patented machine which ensures that every baguette has the same amount of fermentation, creating a very even and crispy crust.

Du Pain et des Idées

Since 2002
34 rue Yves Toudic, 75010
01 42 40 44 52
dupainetdesidees.com

Acclaimed in 2008 by GaultMillau as the Meilleur Boulanger (best baker) in Paris, Christophe Vasseur is a former sales executive who, at 30, decided to bake bread. He is an absolute traditionalist and believes customers should taste the amount of love and friendship put into every loaf. This is also the place for a croissant, pain au chocolat, chausson aux pommes and escargot (the citron nougat version has people trekking from all over Paris). The shop, with its painted-glass ceilings, is both a historic monument and a romantic fairytale land of sweet delights. You can buy the bread by weight as well as by the loaf.

Shannon: My friend Ute took me here. There is nowhere to sit and tourists are only welcome as long as they're not a tourist's tourist! Buy the guy next door a croissant and he will let you use his tables and chairs as long as you have a coffee or drink. But do this before 10 a.m., because all the best (most popular) danishes are sold out by then! Items come out of the oven every 15–20 minutes, and the locals know at what time to collect their favourites. I love the authenticity of this place; just great. I tried the *escargot de pistache*, and fresh-from-the-oven brioche flavoured with walnuts, honey and saffron. Bloody amazing! The banana-flavoured *pain au chocolat* is also worth the trip.

Le Moulin de la Vierge

Since 1900 (shop); 1972 (bread)
166 avenue du Suffren, 75015
01 47 43 45 55
Others include:
64 rue Saint-Dominique, 75007
105 rue Vercingétorix, 75014
35 rue Violet, 75015
6 rue de Lévis, 75017
lemoulindelavierge.com

The first thing you notice about Le Moulin de la Vierge on the avenue du Suffren is the outrageous prettiness of the exterior (which developers tried to demolish in the 1970s) and the retro charm of its packaging. But don't ignore the quality of the breads baked here (and at several other Paris locations). All are made with organic flour and the same techniques as Poilâne. There is also a range of breakfast pastries.

Le Grenier à Pain

12 rue du 8 Mai 1945, 75010
01 40 35 74 07
52 avenue d'Italie, 75013
01 45 80 16 26
33 bis rue St Amand, 75015
01 45 33 01 85
134 rue Saint Charles, 75015
01 45 77 50 78
38 rue des Abbesses, 75018
01 42 23 85 36
174 rue Ordoner, 75018
01 45 33 01 85
legrenierapain.com

Michel Galloyer's **Le Grenier à Pain** has six central-Paris locations. In 2010, Djibril Bodian, the baker on rue des Abesses, won the highly coveted Meilleur Boulanger de Paris prize.

Hôtel d'Aubusson

Rating: 4★
33 rue Dauphine, 75006
01 43 29 43 43
hoteldaubusson.com
Rooms: 49
Single: 305–625€
Double: 305–625€

Located on rue Dauphine, close to the Seine in the heart of the 6th arrondissement, the **d'Aubusson** is a landmark in the opulent refitting of small Rive Gauche hotels. Given its name, it is no surprise that the hotel employs d'Aubusson tapestries to dramatic effect. But it is perhaps the warming fire in the superb Louis XV salon that will make you immediately fall head over heels for the place. It may seem a little pricey, but the discreetly elegant bedrooms are larger than usual for the area, and it has the added bonus (or negative) of live jazz being played in its Café Laurent three nights a week. Most guides will tell you this is one of the true Rive Gauche gems.

Hôtel Bel Ami

Rating: 4★
7-11 rue Saint-Benoît, 75006
01 42 61 53 53
hotel-bel-ami.com
Rooms: 108
Single: 230–620€
Double: 230–620€
Suites: 4

Running off the boulevard Saint-Germain between Les Deux Magots and Café de Flore is the tiny rue Saint-Benoît, home to this very modern hotel. Even though it feels like a boutique retreat, it is a large establishment with a spacious-for-the-area lobby, filled with modern brown couches on a pale parquet floor. Coloured glass vases are magically lit up in a wall case. There is a well-appointed bar and a sunny and strikingly contemporary café with trendy Serge Mouille lamps. The designers (one of whom remodelled the Lancaster, in the 8th) were certainly not shy, as can also be seen in their bold use of colour—such as red, orange or chartreuse—in the bedrooms. The top floors have enormous windows and are filled with light. There is an Énergie fitness centre and Harmonie spa.

- -

Hôtel de Buci

Rating: 4★
22 rue de Buci, 75006
01 55 42 74 74
buci-hotel.com
Rooms: 24
Single: 195–360€
Double: 270–570€

Located on rue Buci, in the beating heart of Saint-Germain, this hotel is so well positioned that most of what makes the Rive Gauche famous is within easy walking distance. Outside is the famous street market (open every day except Sunday afternoon and Monday), so it's certain you'll be sneaking delicious food back into your room. There are also countless cafés nearby at which to sit and observe the bustling street life. Not that you will wish to be absent too long from your room: they are not huge but they are very beautiful, with solid cherry wood, antique furniture, and quality drawings and prints; some rooms have exposed beams. The fabrics are so rich and luscious that you will want to stroke them. For those who prefer more conventional excitements, the hotel has a delightful bar.

- -

Esprit St-Germain

Rating: 4★
22 rue Saint-Sulpice, 75006
01 53 10 55 55
espritsaintgermain.com
Rooms: 28
Single: 330–590€
Double: 330–590€
Suites: 5

A pricey but charming four-star hotel between the Jardin du Luxembourg and the boulevard Saint-Germain. On a map the area may look the same as the rest of the 6th arrondissement, but it actually has an atmosphere all its own. A totally renovated 17th-century building, the hotel has a very comforting and homely feel. As it is located 60 metres from the Église Saint-Sulpice, you can have an early breakfast and beat the crowds to stand in awe (or mirth) over the mythical *Ligne Rose* ('Rose Line'), most recently given currency by Dan Brown. Just don't carry a copy of *The Da Vinci Code*; take Umberto Eco's *Foucault's Pendulum* (he got there first).

L'Hôtel

Rating: 4★
13 rue des Beaux-Arts,
75006
01 44 41 99 00
l-hotel.com
Rooms: 20
Single: 250–640€
Double: 250–640€
Suites: 4

This hotel is inextricably linked with Oscar Wilde, given he died here in November 1900. It has other virtues, of course, in that the building is round (making the rooms intriguing shapes) and dates from 1816. There is a tiny grotto in the basement and its Le Restaurant (an Empire-style masterwork) has one Michelin star. The place oozes history and charm, especially the latter since the ubiquitous Jacques Garcia spruced it up recently. The location, in a small street leading off the Beaux Arts, is perfect. You will hear American spoken more than any other language, but this remains a genuine French hotel. The website is wonderful, too, in that you can view every room before making your inspired choice.

Le Madison

Rating: 4★
143 boulevard de Saint-
Germain, 75006
01 40 51 60 00
hotel-madison.com
Rooms: 52
Single: 180–430€
Double: 240–430€

It may seem odd to recommend a hotel on the multi-lane boulevard Saint-Germain, with traffic roaring by day and night, but **Le Madison** is surprisingly quiet and restful. Set slightly back from the street, the hotel has astonishing views over the Église de Saint-Germain-des-Prés. Single rooms only face the serene inner courtyard, but all grades of doubles offer the choice of looking at the courtyard or the church (that shouldn't be a hard decision). The rooms are simply but beautifully furnished. The public rooms are particularly elegant.

On the best part of the romantic rue Jacob, the **Millésime** is an intimate hotel shaped around a small paved courtyard. The 17th-century staircase is a treasure, even if a modern lift has rather obscenely been stuck up through the middle. The Classic rooms, all with double beds, are cosy rather than large and open onto the courtyard; the more spacious Superior rooms face the street. At the top, under the mansard roof, is the one-bedroom Suite Millésime, with a view of the Église de Saint-Germain-des-Prés. Breakfast is served in a vaulted room.

Hôtel Millésime

Rating: 4★
15 rue Jacob, 75006
01 44 07 97 97
millesimehotel.com
Rooms: 22
Single: 130–285€
Double: 130–285€
Suites: 1

Shannon: The Rue Jacob is my favourite street in Paris. The Millésime is a very small, sweet hotel, tastefully decorated in Provençal style. The rooms are a little small, but you really do get what you pay for; and you can consistently get good prices online. Negotiate a room rate exclusive of breakfast and walk across the road to Ladurée each morning: what you save will surely, and happily, be spent in the bars and bistros of the 6th and 7th arrondissements. The staff in this hotel are very friendly.

Scott: This is a lovely hotel. Classic rooms can be small, but they are very comfortable. There is a certain airlessness in the rooms facing the patio, but they are quiet and if you are on the ground floor the courtyard feels like your own private space. The small sitting area at the front is charming. As for the area around the hotel, it is my favourite part of Paris. Walking down the rue Jacob past the book and antique shops and galleries is one of life's great joys. The Millésime's staff are wonderful. When Shannon, Simon and Madeleine arrived, tired and frustrated after discovering the only vacant parking spot was at least a kilometre from the hotel, the staff immediately offered to look up the public garage closest to their car. They then printed out a map of the area and drew arrows to highlight the safest and fastest way through the maze of one-way streets. Try to get such service, unrequested, at most five-star hotels.

Le Placide

Rating: 4★
6 rue Saint-Placide, 75006
01 42 84 34 60
leplacidehotel.com
Rooms: 11
Single: 154–515€
Double: 154–515€

A new boutique hotel in a 19th-century residence not far from Le Bon Marché department store and Hélène Darroze's restaurant. It was designed by Bruno Borrione of the Philippe Starck studio and employs white Moroccan leather, glass and chrome—plus, of course, typically Starckian bursts of red.

Relais Christine

Rating: 4★
3 rue Christine, 75006
01 40 51 60 80
relais-christine.com
Rooms: 51
Single: 325–840€
Double: 325–840€
Suites: 16

The **Relais Christine**, occupying a beautiful townhouse built on the site of a 13th-century convent, has been a top choice in the Saint-Germain area for decades. It has an imposing presence on the rue Christine, with a wide gate leading via a cobblestone path through a courtyard garden to the welcoming entrance. The downstairs areas have a club-like feel, with comfortable armchairs, soft wood panelling and the odd chessboard lying about. The lower two grades of room (Standard and Superior) are pleasant, but small and hardly cutting-edge; Deluxe and above are lovely. The bathrooms are trendier than the rooms.

Hôtel Relais Saint-Germain

Rating: 4★
9 carrefour de l'Odéon, 75006
01 44 27 07 97
hotel-paris-relais-saint-germain.com
Rooms: 22
Single: 198–220€
Double: 255–395€

Located on the busy intersection known as the carrefour de l'Odéon, 50 metres from the boulevard Saint-Germain and the Odéon Métro station, this is one of Paris's great hotels. Its elongated rooms are enormous, with a separate seating area furnished with a round table, chairs and a plush sofa. A small balcony overlooks the junction, as do the full-length glass doors. Despite the location, however, the rooms are whisper-quiet and totally restful. The décor is not as opulent as in some boutique hotels, but this is a place to feel totally at home in. And if hunger hits, either go to the always-busy restaurant Le Comptoir (part of the hotel: guests get precedence) or walk up the rue de l'Odéon to La Méditerranée and eat some of the best seafood in Paris.

Scott: Along with the **Duc de Saint-Simon**, this is my favourite boutique hotel in Paris. You know you are entering a special place when you open the 17th-century building's Chinese-style front door. The lobby may be tiny, but the rooms are wonderfully spacious, their shape allowing you to do what is impossible in most Paris hotel rooms: walk around. The separate sitting area is a wonderful relaxation zone, and particularly good for a calm study of the books or whatever else you have just bought. But it is probably best for just observing, in eerie silence, life on the intersection below. The décor of the rooms is warmly embracing, with exposed beams and elegant fabrics. One room I had featured a huge mirror on the wall facing the foot of the bed, which did nothing thrilling for a solitary guest like myself, but added to the sense of spaciousness. The breakfast room is small but cosy. The Relais Saint-Germain is not the cheapest small hotel in Paris, but is one of the best. I could live there forever.

....

Résidence des Arts

14 rue Gît-le-Coeur
01 55 42 71 11
hotelresidencedesarts
paris.com
Rooms: 11
Single: 185–350€
Double: 185–350€
Suites: 1

In a quiet cobbled street between the River Seine and the rue St-André des Arts is this luxurious boutique hotel. It's sister hotel, Villa d'Éstrées, is directly across the street. The 17th century buildings have lost none of their charm. The double rooms are large by Left Bank standards, while the neo-classical Junior suites are huge. Few Parisian hotels are as gorgeous as this, but noise can be an issue from the street's two Irish pubs. When football matches are broadcast, you will be thinking dark thoughts about the vocal fans.

....

Victoria Palace Hotel

Rating: 5★
6 rue Blaise-Desgoffe,
75006
01 45 49 70 00
victoriapalace.com
Rooms: 62
Single: 268–756€
Double: 268–756€

Located on a tiny street between rue de Rennes and rue Vaugirard, near the boulevard Montparnasse, this is a charming small luxury hotel. Once home to James Joyce and surrealist artist Giorgio de Chirico, it has been a landmark in the area since 1913. The public rooms are opulent, with Louis XVI-style furniture and an abundance of toile de Jouy. The standard rooms, however, while pretty, are rather uninspired; you may prefer a Junior suite.

Villa d'Éstrées

Rating: 4★
17 rue Gît-le-Coeur
01 55 42 71 11
villadestrees.com
Rooms: 10
Single: 195–365€
Double: 195–365€
Suites: 1

Villa d'Éstrées (sister hotel of the Résidence des Arts) has a dazzling Napoléon III lounge, refreshed with modern touches from Jacques Garcia, naturally. If anything, the guest rooms—especially those with blue lined wallpaper—are even more impressive than those at the Résidence. An apartment can be made up of a Junior suite and a Deluxe Double. The same warning as at the Résidence regarding Irish pub noise holds.

 OTHER HOTEL

Hôtel Le Sainte-Beuve

Rating: 3★
9 rue Sainte-Beuve, 75006
01 45 48 20 07
hotel-sainte-beuve.fr
Rooms: 22
Single: 169–317€
Double: 169–317€

One of the highest-rated Paris hotels on *booking.com* (9.4), the **Sainte-Beuve** is a treasure of the 6th arrondissement. Decorated (like the Hôtel Montalembert and Hôtel Le Tourville) by British designer David Hicks, the hotel has his trademark sense of harmony and calm. But you must like the colour green. The guest rooms are modern, but with unusual period touches. The hotel is off the bustling boulevard Raspail, near the Jardin du Luxembourg. It's a bit of a walk to the Rive Gauche hot spots, but it takes you along some of the finest and most fascinating streets in Paris.

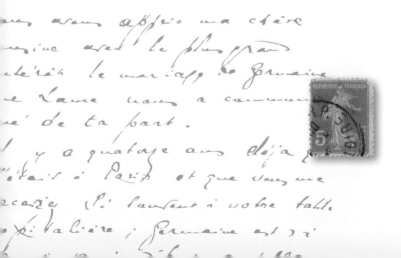

The freedom afforded by your own apartment in Paris is invaluable. *Comme ça*, you are a part of the community rather than a faceless number in a hotel. ApartRental has an easy-to-use website with a feature every such site should have but doesn't: the ability to search with specific dates over the entire portfolio in one go.

ApartRental

33 9 63 22 85 58

apartrental.com

Bryan: I had a few criteria to satisfy when booking accommodation in Paris. I wanted it to be comfortable, central—but not too central!—within easy reach of everything else I wanted to do, and reasonably priced. The pre-eminent consideration was space: I wanted to be able to move about without bumping into another faux antique. And I am not a great fan of hotels; I find them relatively soulless places.

The ideal solution was an apartment, and I took one in the 6th at 18 rue des Grands-Augustins. This is the street where Picasso painted *Guernica* and chef Jean Cagna established his reputation. Now, it is also home to more contemporary concerns, such as **Ze Kitchen Galerie**. It is an ideal spot that met all my aforementioned requirements. Its position four blocks from Nôtre Dame in one direction, and one-and-a-half blocks from the Pont Neuf in the other, gives some indication of its amenity. In comparison to a hotel of any quality in the area, it was remarkably cheap, and even more cost-effective if taken for seven days or more (dropping by approximately 85€ per night).

While it probably wouldn't be considered for the latest edition of *Vogue*, the apartment was comfortable, and there was definitely enough room to swing the proverbial cat with some enthusiasm. It included a mezzanine and open-plan living/dining area with a dining table for eight, presumably in case you proved a hit with the locals. I didn't throw any extravagant dinner parties on this occasion, but the table proved most useful for spreading out maps, etc. The kitchen and bathrooms were also separate, which was convenient. Storage was fairly good, but strangely there was an iron *sans* ironing board—maybe the reason for the large table. It was what might be termed a traditional interior, with exposed beams and brickwork.

Shannon's Favourite Parisian Treats

Pâtisseries

Parisians have been making exquisite pastries and cakes for centuries. There is a delicacy, a refinement, that is quite unique.

La Chocolaterie de Jacques Genin

133 rue de Turenne, 75003
01 45 77 29 01
no website

Shannon: Jacques Genin actually claims that he is not a chocolate maker but a chocolate former, and to the true meaning of the term he is correct and logical. His very modern shop is just around the corner from the great boutique department store, Merci. His specialties are chocolates, but I really think his made-to-order millefeuille, *Gâteau St Honoré* and his amazing caramels, with flavours such as mango and passion fruit, are the way to go.

Relax here for at least forty minutes and have a really interesting cup of tea. His list is unique and well thought through to match each different gâteau.

Reinventing the simple makes this pâtisserie a must. It's not ever going to be the place to be seen, but that's what I like about it.

Ute: Genin makes the best chocolate and caramel éclairs in Paris. But the pièce de la résistance is the millefeuille. If you don't see it in the display cabinet, ask for it and you will be presented with a choice of six flavours.

Ladurée

As well as macarons (page 44), Ladurée has an astonishing array of pâtisseries, which match perfectly the range of rare teas. Sample the *Mont Blanc*, the *Gâteau Saint Honoré*, the *Savarin chantilly au vieux rhum*, or try one of the millefeuilles or viennoiseries.

Sue: One day, I went into the rue Royale shop and asked for a *tarte au citron*. The saleslady insisted that Ladurée sold no such thing, to which I replied that they must because there was one in the window. When the saleslady calmly requested that I show it to her, I motioned towards the tart. 'But, Madame, that is not a tarte. It is a flan!'

Pain de Sucre

Since 2004
14 rue Rambuteau, 75003
01 45 74 68 92
patisseriepaindesucre.com

A traditional *boulangerie* with modern-style pâtisseries.

Shannon: Didier Mathray and Nathalie Robert, who used to work for the creative three-star chef Pierre Gagnaire, have opened their own pastry shop. Their cakes are highly original, intelligently using herbs like jasmine, rosemary and coriander, and all look very beautiful. If you're a chef, this is a must-visit place. They don't open until 10 a.m. (except at weekends, when they open just before

9 a.m.), which has disappointed more than a few people.

La Pâtisserie des Rêves par Philippe Conticini

93, rue du Bac, 75007
01 42 84 00 82
111 rue de Longchamp, 75016
01 42 84 00 82
lapatisseriedesreves.com

Here are two locations to make every pastry fan's heart beat faster, with modern interpretations of classic traditional French patisseries by master pâtissier Philippe Conticini. He makes the best Paris–Brest and, on Sunday only, Le Millefeuille du Dimanche.

The first address is the small boutique and the second a combination of boutique and beautiful tearoom, with garden access in summer.

Shannon: This guy is doing the classic and simple really well. It's a foodie traveller's heaven. All his desserts are presented in glass domes, as if they were on display in an art gallery, with amazing results to one's senses. The take-away packaging is inventive and decadent. There is nothing like this in Australia.

Pâtisserie Sadaharu Aoki

Since 2001
35 rue de Vaugirard, 75006
01 45 44 48 90
Also at:
56 boulevard de Port Royal, 75005
72 rue Bonaparte, 75006
Galeries Lafayette Gourmet
40 boulevard Haussmann, 75009
25 rue Pérignon, 75015, etc.
sadaharuaoki.com

Sadaharu Aoki, chef pâtissier here, was born in Tokyo but migrated to France in 1991. Having worked in several Paris restaurants and with the great Fredy Girardet in Switzerland, he opened his first atelier in 1998, serving his pastries at shows by fashion designers Kenzo, Yohji Yamamoto and Chanel, among others. Aoki opened his first Paris boutique in 2001 (he now has three, along with a presence in Galeries Lafayette) and has two outlets in Tokyo. His pâtisseries are as delicious and refined as you would expect.

Pierre Hermé

Since 1998 (Tokyo), 2001 (Paris)
72 rue Bonaparte, 75006
01 43 54 47 77
Also at:
4 rue Cambon, 75001
publicisdrugstore, 133 avenue des Champs-Élysées, 75008
Galeries Lafayette, 40 boulevard Haussmann, 75009
185 rue Vaugirard, 75015
58 avenue Paul Doumer, 75016
pierreherme.com

Shannon: What can I say about the guy who has made his seasonal macarons, such as foie gras, available to the world? His shops are like clothing boutiques, not pastry shops. A visit to Paris is not complete with a visit to his flagship store.

Guillaume Brahimi's Paris

Frédéric Vardon

Chef: Frédéric Vardon
39 avenue George V, 75008
01 56 62 39 05
le39v.com
Vardon trained under Alain Chapel and
Alain Ducasse.

La Cantine du Troquet

Chef: Christian Etchebest
101 rue de l'Ouest, 75014
Christian Etchebest trained under
Christian Constant. There is a strong
Basque influence in his cooking.

Fromagerie Laurent Dubois

47ter boulevard Saint-Germain, 75005
01 43 54 50 93
2 rue Lourmel, 75015
01 45 78 50 58
The aged Comté from affineur Laurent
Dubois is sublime.

Patrick Roger

108 boulevard Saint-Germain, 75006
12 cité Berryer, Village Royal, 75008
199 rue du faubourg Saint-Honoré,
75008
45 avenue Victor Hugo, 75016
patrickroger.com
Be transported around the world in one
mouthful when you visit chocolatier
Patrick Roger's boutiques. Marvel at
his seasonal windows before venturing
inside to indulge in some of his
exquisite creations.

L'Avant Comptoir

9 carrefour de l'Odéon, 75006
01 44 27 07 97
Unfortunately it's not a secret anymore,
but if you are lucky enough to get a
table at Yves Camdeborde's bistro, Le
Comptoir, pop next door first to his tiny
wine bar, L'Avant Comptoir, for a glass
of Morgon and the deep-fried chorizo or
sample a plate of charcuterie made by
Yves' brother in the Basque country.

Bread? Make sure you dine somewhere
that serves the bread by Jean-Luc
Poujauran, accompanied by a hand-
shaped pyramid of Jean Yves Bordier's
butter from Normandy.
　　If you can't get to Brittany, find Henri le
Roux's salted caramels and the exquisite
chocolate from Bernachon in Lyon at
Denise Acabo's famous shop.

À l'Étoile d'Or

30 rue Fontaine, 75009
01 48 74 59 55

Guillaume's Perfect Parisian Day:

Breakfast at Les Deux Magots

Walk through the Jardin du Luxembourg

An exhibition at the Musée d'Orsay

Lunch at Benoît

An exhibition at the Grand Palais

A quick macaron at Pierre Hermé

Dinner at Restaurant Alain Ducasse au
Plaza Athénée

Shannon's Parisian Recipes

Sourdough

. . . .

Famous bakeries have their own secret recipes for sourdough ferments, which are never revealed! It can be made at home by making a bread dough and then leaving it out for a few days so that the natural yeast grows.

400 g rye flour, sifted
200 g organic spelt flour, sifted
20 g salt
20 g cocoa powder
300 g sourdough starter
40 g butter
400 ml tepid water
2 tablespoons polenta

Place some banana peels or mouldy grapes in muslin. Mix equal quantities of flour and water until it forms a thick paste. Submerge the muslin in the flour and water. Let it ferment in a cool dry place no hotter than 17°C for a few days, until it bubbles. Keep adding flour and water for three weeks; this process is called 'feeding'. When ready to make bread, separate the 'starter' into the desired weights and continue to feed the original 'mother' every day and store in the fridge.

Combine the dry ingredients with the starter, butter and water in a large mixing bowl. Using a mixer with the dough hook attached, start mixing on low, gradually increasing the speed to high. Mix for at least 10 minutes (the more the gluten is worked, the better the texture will be after baking).

Place the ball of dough on a lightly oiled tray, cover loosely with cling wrap, and leave in a warm spot in the kitchen for 2 hours, or until the dough has doubled in size. Knead and knock out the air in the dough, then shape it into one large round loaf. Place the dough on a greased baking tray, cut a deep cross in the top and dust with some polenta, using a sieve. Cover the tray with plastic wrap, return to the warm place, and leave to prove until doubled in size (around 50 minutes).

Preheat the oven to 200°C.

Place the loaf in the oven, throw a cupful of water into the bottom of the oven to create some steam, and shut the door immediately. Bake for 30–35 minutes, or until crisp and golden. Tap the loaf with your fingertips: when ready, it should sound hollow.

Invalides, Tour Eiffel, École Militaire

FINE DINING (WITH HOTEL)

The new fine-dining restaurant of acclaimed chef Jean-François Piège (ex Les Ambassadeurs) seats just twenty guests and is on the first floor of the revitalized Thoumieux complex (jointly owned by Piège and Thierry Costes of the Hôtel Costes). Michelin wasted no time and gave the restaurant two stars in its 2011 guide. That is because, by anyone's reckoning, Piège is one of the finest chefs in Paris.

Le Restaurant de Jean-François Piège

Chef: Jean-François Piège
79 rue Saint-Dominique, 75007
01 47 05 79 79
thoumieux.fr
Michelin: ★★
À la carte: 40–65€

One of the older brasseries of Paris (1923), on one of the best streets in Paris (rue Saint-Dominique), **Thoumieux** has the added attraction of a new superstar chef, an ultra-exclusive upstairs area (Le Restaurant de Jean-François Piège) and a hotel (L'Hôtel Thoumieux). How can you have a better Parisian experience than sleeping above your own brasserie? GaultMillau voted Thoumieux the best Parisian bistro in 2010.

La Brasserie Thoumieux

Chef: Jean-François Piège
79 rue Saint-Dominique, 75007
01 47 05 49 75
thoumieux.fr
GaultMillau: 🍴🍴
À la carte: 40–65€

Shannon: Thoumieux has a long history in the brassiere world. Since being 'quietly' taken over by the Costes hotel group in 2009, the dining room has had a transformation of sorts. Well-known chef Jean-François Piège, formally of the Hôtel de Crillon's Les Ambassadeurs, has become a consultant to the group and has revamped the menu here.

There is a tendency to make guests wait unnecessarily for a table if you walk in without a reservation. Avoid this by booking a table. That's what I did, but I did still turn up to the barrage of 'Pourquoi? Pourquoi?' and something I just didn't quite catch as arms flailed around like a mosquito with Tourette syndrome for two to three minutes. All I said was 'Je suis desolé' over and over again to Ute! At the end of the performance, the man simply smiled and asked how many we were and sat us down.

To my shock, the dining room was only half full, yet there would have to have been twenty-five people lining up at the door without a booking, waiting. Avoid Friday and Saturday evenings here. The seating and tables are very close together.

The Costes touch includes attractive models roaming up and down the aisles, sometimes taking orders and I'm not sure what else, but they definitely added to the atmosphere. It kept all the old men busy, pulling neck muscles, including my mate Simon, and ordering more expensive bottles of wine than they most probably wanted to!

The menu had plenty of choice and was very well priced. Entrées included home-smoked Salmon, calamari thinly julienned to look like pasta in a carbonara sauce, and cèps from Chataignier served raw in a frissé lettuce salad. Prices ranged from 12–22€ for entrées and 22€ for mains such as beef tartare with 'allumette'-cut French fries and confit of Scottish Salmon with provencal vegetables, and then up to 30€ for a roast palombe, a type of pigeon which was very generous in its portion size, deboned and served with artichokes and a well-crafted meaty sauce.

Desserts were all takes on such classics as a crème caramel but served in a glass rather than de-moulded. The top of the caramel had been brûléed and the caramel at the bottom had been lightly salted. I would also highly recommend the *Vacherin glacé* that was served with banana.

The wine list is not huge but well chosen. One can drink very well and cheaply here. There is also a very good choice of beers and cocktails. You will love the atmosphere as well as the great food. I highly recommend it.

. . . .

L'Hôtel Thoumieux

79 rue Saint-Dominique, 75007
01 47 05 79 00
thoumieux.fr
Rooms: 10
Single: 130€
Double: 130€

Thoumieux has always had rooms to rent, but not before done up by Thierry Costes. Overnight it became one of the hottest residential addresses in Paris.

Alain Passard's **L'Arpège** is where Alain Senderens had his famous restaurant L'Archestrate. (The connection is important because Passard trained under Senderens on this very spot; and, just as Senderens returned as chef to Lucas Carton, where he had trained, so Passard returned as master of the place where he started.) The main room is modern and rather trendy, but beware the cellar below. Many consider Passard the best chef in Paris, and for a while there was a concentrated effort to pressure Michelin into making him the world's first four-star chef. Then, at the height of the campaign, he astonished everyone by abandoning most of his meat, fish and fowl dishes to become a temple of vegetarianism (the vegetables, by the way, come from his farm in the Sarthe region).

L'Arpège

Chef: Alain Passard
84 rue de Varenne, 75007
01 47 05 09 06
alain-passard.com
Michelin: ★★★
GaultMillau: ♔♔♔♔
Menu: 120 (lunch)/320€
À la carte: 190–290€

Shannon: My meal here was disappointing in many ways. L'Arpège is famous for focusing on vegetables, which I found intriguing and is why I had long wanted to go there. When we arrived, we were seated in a basement cellar where there were only three tables, which I found claustrophobic as the ceilings were very low. Also it was difficult to have a private conversation: I found that confronting and our conversation was rather subdued as a result.

The first course was a series of *amuse-bouches*, which you used your fingers to eat. They were all very small, very delicate and delicious (an avocado tartare served on a potato chip was lovely). On receiving a menu, I was gobsmacked at how much a plate of vegetables cost (we are talking 40€) and was therefore expecting something like the *Gargouillou de jeunes légumes* from Michel Bras, which has layers and layers of flavours and complexity, with many hidden sauces that merge and change as you eat the dish. We didn't go with the dégustation menu, which I usually do, because it was almost 9 p.m. when we arrived. But we were in a very happy mood and the service was excellent.

I ordered the plate of vegetables and Madeleine had a radish soup. It was a clear cucumber-based cold soup containing little daikon ravioli (only three) filled with something we couldn't identify but which seemed like water chestnut and mushrooms. It was about 34€, so there must be good profit in that dish! I was astounded that this was a three-star dish: it's all about simplicity, I guess, and perfection, but I just didn't get it. My plate of vegetables, some raw and some cooked, was very boring. There was a sauce and some edible flowers, but it is something I could have done at home.

The wine list is extensive, with some good choices available by the glass and it was very reasonable.

I had read a lot about L'Arpège, but it was not very accurate: a lot of the reviews said there were no red-meat dishes on the menu, but we were offered a special of a veal chop and another of venison, which surprised me. I chose the Turbot, which was baked whole, removed from the bone at the table ('*au guéridon*') and served with a lovely sauce and some braised baby leeks. It was nice, but again not something I would expect from a Michelin-starred restaurant. Madeleine had the venison, which was also nice but nothing exceptional.

Passard is very famous for a tomato dessert: a sweet confit of tomatoes with 14 spices, served with pistachio ice-cream. I was tempted to have that, but it wasn't available when I dined—his most famous dish! The idea of the soufflé I ordered instead—avocado with a bitter-chocolate sorbet—intrigued me, but all I could taste was sugar, the sorbet overpowering any taste of avocado I could have hoped to find. There were, though, some beautifully made *petits fours* to finish. It cost around 210€ per person, and that was four years ago. I was disappointed, but there are many people who have raved about what a good time they have had there.

David: I have eaten some fantastic meals at L'Arpège: for example, a sensational vibrant-green lettuce soup with snails.

Geoff: One of the greatest dining experiences of my life was at L'Arpège, a lunch with four friends celebrating a birthday. All of us took the dégustation menu. It was lunchtime: by about 3 p.m. we were the only people left in the place, and the final, exquisite dessert (Passard's specialty) was yet to arrive. Passard himself appeared at our table with a bottle of one of his finest dessert wines and the six of us proceeded to demolish it. He asked where we came from: one was from England, one from Switzerland, one from Chicago via England, and two from Australia. 'Et moi, je suis Breton', boomed the happy chef, acknowledging that not a single soul around the table was 'French'! We left at 5 p.m.

Scott: Maria, a film producer, kindly took me and her partner Ian to dinner at L'Arpège. This is a restaurant I had long dreamed of visiting, having closely followed the rise and rise of Alain Passard. My dear friend Geoff had been several times and raved about the food, though he warned me to insist on a table on the main floor (street level), not in the cellar below. Our preference was confirmed at the time of booking and again when I reconfirmed (which you always have to do with three-star restaurants), yet on arrival we were quickly escorted (I almost wrote 'shunted', but that is going too far) to the dungeon below. Attempts to demand our rights were imperiously rebuffed.

The cellar is like the breakfast room of a tiny Rive Gauche hotel, devoid of headroom, windows and oxygen. The waiters don't appear that often (you feel like yelling up the stairs for help), adding to the sense of being abandoned. All this would have been bearable, however, if the food were great. It was not.

Though the restaurant abruptly became 'vegetarian', it has always had the odd meat or poultry dish, like the *Dragée de pigeonneau à l'hydromel*, on the menu. The proportion of non-vegetarian dishes seems to be gradually increasing. After the *amuse-bouches*, the dégustation began with Passard's famous egg. It is lightly poached and served with crème fraîche, maple syrup and sherry vinegar inside an eggshell mounted on a silver eggcup. Maria and Ian thought they had gone to heaven; I felt it was way too sweet. But then I thought that about much of the meal. The langoustine (memory says it was the famous one on a bed of mâche and candied carrot quenelle with orange) was overcooked, dry, stringy ... and sweet. The pigeon was also too sweet because of the hydromel (a fermented beverage made from honey). And so on.

Maria and Ian still claim it to be the finest meal they have ever eaten. But they, too, will insist on being upstairs next time.

L'Atelier de Joël Robuchon

Chefs: Éric Lecerf,
Philippe Braun
5 rue Montalembert, 75007
01 42 22 56 56
joel-robuchon.net
Michelin: ★★
GaultMillau: ☺☺☺
Menu: 150€
À la carte: 60–120€

Before giving up his place at the stove, Joël Robuchon was one of the finest chefs in Paris, his three-star Jamin acclaimed by many as the pinnacle of fine dining. Since closing it, Robuchon has worked non-stop, running restaurants in Tokyo and Monte-Carlo, advising a veritable multitude of restaurateurs and opening two casual but trend-setting L'Atelier restaurants in Paris (the other is on the Champs-Éylsées). Designed by Pierre-Yves Robuchon (it's a family affair), L'Atelier has no tables and essentially no reservations: just red-leather stools at an elegant bar and long queues outside. For those who hate stools, La Table carries the same rating and has tables.

Shannon: The best way to describe L'Atelier would be as a French version of a tapas bar, combined with the practicality of a teppanyaki bar and touches of decadent French décor. The restaurant is designed with a central kitchen at its heart. The eating section has two arms, mirror images of each other, and the waiter is on the opposite side of the bar from the guests.

The toughest aspect of dining here is choosing between the menus ('Découverte' or à la carte). Then 98€ for nine courses (it is now 110€), the 'Découverte' was a bargain. My first memory is of a cold soup of puréed avocado garnished with fresh almonds dipped in chilli oil. This was followed by a floured and then fried chicken winglet on a carpaccio of pineapple marinated in mint and basil, with a sweet-and-sour sauce. It was the very definition of modern French dining.

The waiters are very knowledgeable about food and I found interacting with them essential to the experience. The wine matching, while not cheap, was something of a revelation, as I generally believe wine matching in Paris lags behind other cities, especially Melbourne.

Desserts were spectacular, safe and agreeable. I tried the lychee coulis with grapefruit sorbet and wild strawberries. You can serve me these at any time in Paris! I followed it with a chocolate mousse served with white chocolate ice-cream, tonka bean and biscotti.

Robuchon now has a L'Atelier chain around the world. It may not be the best way to experience the true Paris, as expanding brands do change the nature of the dining experience, but now and then it is good to have a change from the opulent three-star establishments that Paris is known for.

Matt: I love L'Atelier, just love it. I have been to most of the Ateliers around the world, but I love the one in Paris because you invariably sit next to someone you don't know and end up having a great conversation. Last November, I sat next to a quirky Texan girl and her husband; filthy-rich.

You can't beat the langoustine wrapped in pastry and then deep-fried. I also had a small piece of Bresse chicken, with a little bit of cabbage; and the foie gras, which is always fantastic.

I just love how you sit there and have all these different dishes and share them all. But the trick is to book for 6.30 p.m. because you can't get in otherwise.

Ute: This is one of my favourite restaurants in Paris. I recently had an outstanding meal there: it was an innovative, very relaxed and sophisticated experience—exquisite food served in an environment without any of the stuffiness that often goes with that kind of food. It is a winning concept that is very appropriate for the current culinary climate in Paris.

Gaya Rive Gauche par Pierre Gagnaire

44 rue du Bac, 75007
01 45 44 73 73
pierre-gagnaire.com
Michelin: ★
GaultMillau: 🍷🍷
Menu: 29/38/45€ (lunch)
À la carte: 45–110€

Gaya Rive Gauche is the most famous of the 'second' restaurants in Paris run by a noted chef. It opened in September 2005 and has become one of the major food destinations on the Rive Gauche, which has the prettiest buildings and streets in Paris but generally disappointing food. With one bold stroke, Pierre Gagnaire changed that. His modern dining-room is also unusual in an area noted for exposed-beam ceilings and bare-brick walls. It follows on from Gagnaire's successful Sketch restaurant in London.

Le Jules Verne

Chef: Pascal Féraud
2nd floor, south pillar,
Tour Eiffel
Champ-de-Mars, 75007
01 45 55 61 44
lejulesverne-paris.com
Michelin: ★
GaultMillau: 🍷🍷🍷
Menu: 85 (weekday lunch)/
165/200€
À la carte: 165–205€

Some 125 metres above the ground, this spectacular restaurant in the Tour Eiffel has been featured in several films, including the James Bond movie *A View to a Kill* (where a fake butterfly does the killing). The restaurant once had two stars, but fell on hard times and closed. It was taken over by Alain Ducasse and reopened to great publicity in 2007: the chef, 34-year-old Pascal Féraud, ran Spoon in London for Ducasse, and before that worked at Restaurant Louis XV–Alain Ducasse in Monte-Carlo.

The view here is extraordinary, the design a little bizarre, with chairs that could have been stolen from some boardroom. The food is modern Mediterranean, ranging from roasted langoustines with truffled vegetables and a shellfish vinaigrette to a confit of duck foie gras with a black-pepper and citrus jelly. Book at least three months in advance.

David: I haven't eaten at **Le Jules Verne** since the change, but I always thought it over-the-top in every sense—décor, service and food.

Vin sur Vin

Chef: Pascal Toulza
20 rue de Monttessuy,
75007
01 47 05 14 20
No website
Michelin: ★
À la carte: 80–120€

Rated one star in the Michelin guide, this restaurant, a few steps from the Tour Eiffel, is not the sort most tourists seek out; it seems to exist for those who live a short stroll away. Eating here feels a little like being at a small soirée in someone's home, with the other guests looking as if they could each buy the neighbourhood without getting financially stressed. There is also likely to be a large dog or two (a Borzoi, perhaps) lying at someone's feet and, as you would expect, behaving exquisitely.

Scott: This gorgeous, profoundly bourgeois restaurant has just seven tables for a maximum of 15 guests. The tables are beautifully set with fine linen, decorated with trails of dark spices in geometric patterns: this is unusual and highly effective, but it is hard not to fiddle and, as the night wears on, the table becomes a little messy.

The restaurant is owned by Patrice and Sylvie Vidal, who often both manage the floor. Immaculately bearded, Patrice looks like an elegant university professor (as might be played by the great Anglo-French actor Michel Lonsdale). As the menu is extremely simple—Lamb from Lozère, Chicken from Bresse—you'll need Patrice to fill in the details. Better yet, just be brave and order.

The cooking itself is unfussy and classical rather than adventurous or thrilling.

Fortunately, Patrice's knowledge of his wonderful 400-label cellar (especially strong on unusual Burgundies) is remarkable. We started with an excellent Beaune Premier Crus and, when it was finished, Patrice asked if we wanted more of the same or something similar but different. Though we ultimately preferred the first, we were grateful for the opportunity to compare. If you are not a wine expert (we had one at our table), just leave the choice to Patrice, first explaining clearly what you feel comfortable spending. Dealing with Patrice was a great relief after restaurants where you have 30-odd staff at various times surrounding and questioning you. All in all, it was a truly relaxing experience, but you must pre-book.

Liz: Make sure you go to the toilet during the course of the dinner, because you have to walk though part of the cellar to get there. It is well worth the journey, just to see all those beautiful wines.

There is a little-discussed trend emerging among top French chefs and that is the desire to lead simpler lives. Alain Senderens is famous for sending his three stars back to Michelin and announcing to the world he was going to cook simpler food. A man who took a similar path long before him is Christian Constant, who had two stars at Les Ambassadeurs at the Hôtel de Crillon but gave all that away on his 45th birthday to open this simpler, more intimate restaurant on the rue Saint-Dominique in a gracious residential area. Constant named his restaurant **Le Violon d'Ingres** to pay homage to the painter Ingres, who came from Constant's home town of Montauban, while also cheekily borrowing the French term for an artistic hobby.

But if Constant was looking for a quieter life, he didn't get it. Overnight, Le Violon became the coolest and most-difficult-to-get-into restaurant in Paris: Michelin gave it two stars, and critics and diners clamoured for it to receive the ultimate accolade. This, however, was at odds with what Constant had in mind: a neighbourhood restaurant that would feel cosy, where regulars could be assured of nourishing comfort food and a friendly welcome. To reinforce the point, Constant slashed his prices and redid the décor to make it feel even more relaxed. He did not seek stars and critical acclaim, and the guides predictably reacted by downgrading him (GaultMillau no longer lists the restaurant and Michelin lowered its rating from two stars to one) and by making subtle digs at what they saw as his lack of ambition. But all Constant was doing was being true to himself, and it is working. He has opened two more restaurants—Les Cocottes and Café Constant—all at the same address. He is a man who sought to trade glory for happiness and achieved it.

And in 2010, Constant decided to wind back even more. After Le Violon was dramatically redesigned, Constant largely handed over the cooking to chef Stéphane Schmidt.

Le Violon d'Ingres

Chefs: Christian Constant, Stéphane Schmidt
135 rue Saint-Dominique, 75007
01 45 55 15 05
leviolondingres.com
Michelin: ★
Menu: 39 (lunch)/49/70€
À la carte: 55–65€

Auberge "d'chez eux"

2 avenue Lowendal, 75007
01 47 05 52 55
chezeux.com
GaultMillau: ⊤
Menu: 43€
À la carte: 55–80€

This is a traditional bistro serving classic food from South-West France. A favourite of *The New York Times'* Patricia Wells, it is well known for its snails, frogs' legs and *Salade de foie gras à l'Armagnac.*

Café de l'Esplanade

52 rue Fabert, 75007
01 47 05 38 80
Menu: 46€
À la carte: 40–85€

Located on a corner opposite Les Invalides, this trendy brasserie is owned by Jean-Louis Costes (of Le Café Marly and Hôtel Costes).

Café du Marché

38 rue Cler, 70007
01 47 05 51 27
À la carte: 15–30€

On the 7th arrondissement's iconic rue Cler, with its bustling market, is the area's busiest local hang-out, the **Café du Marché**. You can't book, so get there early. The *Confit de canard* is famous (and cheap); and the oysters and seafood in season are magnificent and extremely well priced. The service is friendly and welcoming, despite the place at times being invaded by loud Americans (though this has been less the case in recent times).

Right in the heart of the 7th, this simple and authentic bistro serves up subtle variations of classic dishes.

Le Florimond

Chef: Pascal Guillaumin
19 avenue La Motte-Piquet, 75007
01 45 55 40 38
GaultMillau: 🍞
Menu: 21 (weekday lunch)/36€
À la carte: 35–55€

STRANGE FACT

Did you know that a wild hare is not a direct member of the rabbit family? It is actually a small deer! Many of you will not believe this fact, but I am happy to argue this point because it's true!

Liz's and Craig's 7th

See main text for restaurant details.

Auberge "d'chez eux"

Liz: When you step in the door, waiters (who I am sure have been there since it opened) hand you a piece of sausage hacked off from a whole one with an oversized knife. Banish thoughts of Australian and New Zealand food-safety standards, and enjoy. The seating is in very cosy booths and I did feel a little penned in by the table. But once in the seat, you're in for a great ride through the South-West.

The food is rich and comforting, particularly on a cold night. The chicken with morels, skilfully carved and served at the table, was memorable.

My sister Catherine and I were spending a couple of days in Paris on a girls' escape. We found the restaurant delectable and welcoming, and felt at ease and comfortable while experiencing new tastes. Neither of us will forget sitting trapped by the most extraordinary dessert trolley we had ever seen, with bowls of home-glazed fruits, decadent trifles, chocolate mousse and mountains of berries.

Craig: I ordered the bouillabaisse and the confit of duck. The bouillabaisse was so good I could not stop myself from having more when asked. The serves were rather large; and, at the same time, my wine glass was constantly refilled. The only problem was that I ran out of gas to properly enjoy the confit. We took our six-month-old son Max, and the staff could not have been more helpful.

Café de l'Esplanade

Liz: I loved l'Esplanade. It is certainly not traditional French (as with the red-and-white-chequered tablecloths), but it is still a wonderful Paris experience. First, there is the view of the Invalides dome; second, there is the view of the very groovy people turning up in very expensive cars. The chairs are plush and velvety, in rich tones, but the food is light, with a lot of seafood (including some fish I had never heard of). I don't remember anything particular about the service, which probably means it was perfect for a couple on a romantic break in Paris, away from the kids.

Craig: I enjoyed the meal and the service, but give me Le Florimond any day!

Café du Marché

Liz: On the corner of rue de Champ de Mars and rue Cler, this café is in a prime position for watching the shops open up onto the pavement and turn rue Cler into a vibrant market. The *Omelette avec fromage* is a must; even the lettuce garnish has a fabulous dressing drizzled over it. The coffee is average, but have a *pain au chocolat* with it and you'll become very forgiving.

Le Florimond

Liz: Talk about a sweet local haunt. It is very small and the owner was genuinely welcoming: you really feel as if he is grateful that you are there. We brought our six-month-old son in a pram, asleep, and there were a number of 'Here we go' looks from the other diners, but he was so quiet that towards the end of the evening people were curious whether there was a baby in the pram at all. The food was surprising: sophisticated and refined, yet lovingly home-cooked.

Craig: I absolutely love this restaurant. The owner is young and vibrant and enthusiastic, the menu is small but interesting, the wine list is surprisingly varied, and the service and attention are outstanding. I have recommended Florimond to a number of first-time Paris-goers and every one of them has loved it, too.

Marché rue Cler

Monday to Saturday (all day),
Sunday (morning)

Liz: Surely this is the best street market of all. To me, this is Paris. The colours: tomatoes, wild strawberries, melons, mint. The smells: saucissons, foie gras, cooked pheasant and, of course, freshly baked baguettes. The shapes: pyramids of chèvres, discs of Rocamadour, triangles of Pont-l'Évêque. Apart from the fresh produce, there are other food shops that make this area: an unbelievable deli, Davoli–La Maison du Jambon, sells incredible cold meats, smoked fish, cheese, dips and a homemade choucroute; there are always lines of people down the street. Who needs restaurants? Indulge, then return to your apartment. Life's good.

There are interesting non-food shops, too. Once, we had booked to go to Lucas Carton (before its reincarnation as Senderens) and Craig had bought a new shirt: he stopped at a drycleaner and asked if the shirt could be pressed, whereupon the woman pressed it on the spot and refused to let him pay.

Craig: The seafood! The fish shop La Sablaise Poissonnerie has the most extraordinary range of delicate crustaceans. Going to the tank and selecting a lobster, then coming back half an hour later to collect it—cleaned and cooked—is a highlight. One Bastille Day we did this, getting a baguette and a bottle of Sancerre, and heading off on a short walk to the Tour Eiffel. It does not get any better than this.

La Sablaise Poisonnerie

28 rue Cler, 75007
01 45 51 61 78
lasablaiseparis.fr

Duc de Saint-Simon

Rating: 4★
14 rue Saint-Simon, 75007
01 44 39 20 20
hotelducdesaintsimon.com
Rooms: 29
Single: 225–290€
Double: 225–290€
Suites: 5

The **Duc de Saint-Simon** is a ravishing *domain perdu* just metres from the chaotic boulevard Saint-Germain. The wide entrance leads to a cobblestone courtyard, the wisteria that blankets the walls filling the air with sweet scent. Inside, the décor is a picture-book dream. None of the rooms are exactly huge, so a suite (complete with a crystal chandelier over the bed, and a separate sitting-room), or a Deluxe room with a private terrace, are good options. A lift takes you down to a 17th-century cellar where breakfast is served year-round, though in summer you can have it in the tiny courtyard at the front.

Scott: Probably the finest boutique hotel in Paris. The rooms are small (a tiny 12 m² for the basic doubles), but several of the larger ones have terraces or look out onto a gorgeous courtyard garden. The Lauren Bacall Suite would suit anyone. All guest rooms are exquisitely decorated—the best having rich wallpapers, coverings and drapes—as are the public areas. Having a cooling drink in the cobbled courtyard is sheer bliss after a tiring stroll around Paris.

Hôtel Montalembert

Rating: 4★
3 rue de Montalembert, 75007
01 45 49 68 68
montalembert.com
Rooms: 52
Single: 300–440€
Double: 300–440€
Suites: 4

The **Montalembert** proudly sits on a street with the same name, having long reigned as one of the premier hotels of the 7th arrondissement. Its supremacy has now been challenged by the Hôtel Pont Royal next door, with its super-trendy L'Atelier de Joël Robuchon (not that the Montalembert would want anything so vulgar as a 'chain' restaurant within its hallowed space). The Montalembert is the epitome of discreet elegance, a place in which you speak in hushed tones as if it were your own personal club. Full of dark wood and leather, this understated and slightly retro hotel draws a famously loyal clientele.

Adjacent to the Hôtel Montalembert, just north of the intersection of boulevard Saint-Germain and rue de Bac (forever linked with Parisian naughtiness since W. Somerset Maugham published *The Razor's Edge*), stands the recently remodelled **Pont Royal**. Variously the haunt of Zelda and Scott Fitzgerald, André Gide and Guillaume Apollinaire (let's hope he didn't research *Les Onze Milles Verges* while staying here), today the hotel is very refined and chic in a quite different way. The circular lobby, with its modern touches (and ubiquitous pink cushions), is framed with many photographs of famous past guests. The spacious Superior and Deluxe rooms face the street, but if you're a romantic you'll want to be in a Prestige room, with a separate living area and a balcony affording one of the best views in Paris (including the Tour Eiffel lit up at night). The hotel is also home to the acclaimed two-star restaurant L'Atelier de Joël Robuchon.

Hôtel Pont Royal

Rating: 4★
7 rue de Montalembert, 75007
01 42 84 70 00
hotel-pont-royal.com
Rooms: 65
Single: 260–550€
Double: 260–550€
Suites: 10

Shannon: The Pont Royal pitches itself between a tiny boutique hotel and a five-star. It has the feel of a boutique hotel but the facilities of an international five-star. It is very well priced for Paris. Rue de l'Université, which is just around the corner, is one of my favourite addresses in this city. The Musée d'Orsay is almost at your doorstep, and having L'Atelier de Joël Robuchon as your local is more than a bonus. This is total luxury at an affordable price, but some of the rooms are small and a bit plain.

Le Bellechasse

Rating: 3★+
8 rue de Bellechasse, 75007
01 45 50 22 31
lebellechasse.com
Rooms: 34
Single: 159–390€
Double: 159–390€

If Jacques Garcia has a near stranglehold on five-star-hotel interior design in Paris, fashion designer Christian Lacroix is making dramatic inroads with mid-range retreats—**Le Bellechasse** is one. You don't have to be as brave as those venturing to Lacroix's Hôtel du Petit Moulin in the Marais, but you do need to love colour (especially pink) if you enter this hotel's portal. You probably also need a PhD in graphic arts to be able to properly describe it (Michelin tries with 'baroque, romantic, "arty", contemporary and neo-classical'). Let's just say there are a lot of butterflies. The Privilege rooms are the best and you should stay for at least three days, because the rates drop noticeably. There is nothing else like this in Paris (not even Du Petit Moulin).

Bourgogne & Montana

Rating: 3★
3 rue de Bourgogne, 75007
01 45 51 20 22
bourgogne-montana.com
Rooms: 28
Single: 210€
Double: 210€
Suites: 4

At the northern end of the rue Bourgogne (which leads south to the Musée Rodin) is the **Bourgogne & Montana**. Though it has been praised for decades in various guidebooks, it seems to be mostly visited by regulars and friends of regulars. Handily located opposite the Assemblèe Nationale (should you wish to check out if French parliamentarians behave any better than our own), this 18th-century building is a bastion of elegance and calm. The staircase, wrapped around a mesh-encased lift, is wondrous.

Hôtel Les Jardins d'Eiffel

Rating: 3★
8 rue Amélie, 75007
01 47 05 46 21
hoteljardinseiffel.com
Rooms: 80
Single: 190–250€
Double: 190–250€

Located in a quiet street off the rue Saint-Dominique, east of the Tour Eiffel, the **Jardins d'Eiffel** actually comprises two (fairly nondescript) buildings linked by a breakfast patio. The guest rooms are colourful and comfortable, but feel a little like those in an upmarket chain hotel.

Scott: Alissa often stays here when in Paris on business. She loves the balconies (where you can smoke), the Wi-Fi (which in Paris is not as common as one would like) and, most of all, the location in her favourite part of the city. Alissa dislikes boutique hotels, which she finds offer décor and charm and very little else: this for her is a dependable and homely Parisian choice.

....

This is a lovely hotel on the rue de l'Université, the continuation of the rue Jacob (or vice versa). It has a glistening Art Déco lobby and a Jazzy Bar, which in no way prepare you for the fact some rooms have Egyptian-style frescoes. The angular corridors and basic (Classic) rooms certainly aren't big, but the hotel's rates are more than generous. Book a larger double (they are generally spacious and are done out in 'Saint-Germain' style) or one of the three attic rooms; there are also duplexes. The views from the top rooms are spectacular, and the hotel's location in the heart of Saint-Germain is unbeatable. It's a short and fascinating walk to Les Deux Magots.

Hôtel Lenox Saint-Germain

Rating: 3★
9 rue de l'Université, 75007
01 42 96 10 95
lenoxsaintgermain.com
Rooms: 34
Single: 150–190€
Double: 190–240€

Scott: I have stayed here several times and always love it. The staff are wonderful, and the compactness of the building (the corridors and staircase are magnificently narrow) give guests the feeling of 'We're all in this together.' If you want space, airiness and luxury, go somewhere else (such as the **Relais Saint-Germain**). If you want a genuine Rive Gauche experience in a charming and eccentric hotel, at admirably low prices, this is the one.

Hôtel Le Tourville

Rating: 3★+
16 avenue de Tourville,
75007
01 47 05 62 62
paris-hotel-tourville.com
Rooms: 30
Single: 140–280€
Double: 140–280€
Suites: 2

Le Tourville is a discreet hotel on avenue Tourville, which runs along the south edge of the Hôtel des Invalides (where Napoléon is buried). The design is by the David Hicks studio, so expect a lot of clean white space. Like most Parisian hotels, it has a wide range of rooms, from the Standard overlooking the avenue (it would be a Deluxe room in most hotels) to the Superior (some face the lovely courtyard; others have a private terrace) to the suites. They all have a Balneo whirlpool bath, which is extremely relaxing after hours of walking on Paris's cobblestone streets (there aren't as many as in, say, Prague, but still plenty). The rates are very reasonable, especially as discounted on the hotel website.

Hôtel de Varenne

Rating: 3★
44 rue de Bourgogne,
75007
01 45 51 45 55
varenne-hotel-paris.com
Rooms: 25
Single: 129–280€
Double: 129–280€

Located on a relatively quiet street with the Musée Rodin at one end and L'Arpège on the corner, amazingly this hotel is rated by the government as a two-star, even though it is roomier and far more luxurious than many with three. The 19th-century building has been decorated in Louis XVI and Empire styles, though the entrance has all the light and delicacy of Provence. The rooms range from a cosy Standard to a spacious and elegant Deluxe double. This is a truly gorgeous hotel, its tiny garden along the side the perfect place for breakfast.

Scott: This is one of my favourite hotels in Paris and I stayed here almost every year in the 1980s after the Cannes Film Festival. More recently, Alissa and I stayed here after we were married in the garden of the Australian embassy. It is a bit of a walk to a Métro station, but I love the serene semi-residential feel of the area. The staff are always friendly and help make the hotel feel like a home away from home. It is also a preferred haunt of writers and academics, especially from America. I love the place.

Liz and Craig: We love the 7th. This apartment is close to great restaurants (**Florimond**, **Auberge "d'chez eux"** and others) and, best of all, rue Cler. There is no better way of experiencing living in Paris than heading down to the market there and choosing some fresh produce for lunch or dinner, and then enjoying the meal while looking out over the rooftops to the Tour Eiffel. On one particular visit, we booked five nights at **Hôtel de Crillon** but ended up staying for just two. We adored the hotel but missed the opportunity of picking up some foie gras and a fresh baguette and heading back to our apartment. So we checked out (the Crillon was utterly charming about it), grabbed a taxi and headed to the Parissimo Apartments office, whose owner, Franz Lalieux, was dumbfounded that we preferred one of his apartments to staying at the Crillon. He found us an apartment on the boulevard de la Tour-Maubourg, from which we could see the top third of the Tour Eiffel. Simply stunning.

Parissimo
9 avenue de la Motte-Picquet, 75007
01 45 51 11 11
parissimo.fr

Shannon's Favourite Parisian Treats

Take-home Meals

Shannon: For take-home pre-cooked meals, there are only two places I know of with great reputations. One is La Grande Épicerie at Le Bon Marché, and the other is Dubernet Foie Gras (2 rue Augereau, 75007; 01 45 55 50 71).

You could also try Hédiard and Comptoir de la Gastronomie (34 rue Montmartre, 75001; 01 42 33 31 32; *comptoir-gastronomie.com*). And don't forget the *homard* from La Sablaise Poissonnerie.

Jeremy's Paris

Les Papilles
30 rue Gay-Lussac, 75005
01 43 25 20 79
lespapillesparis.fr

Aussie wine journalist Nick Stock was in Paris and sent us a text demanding that we go to this wine bar in the 5th arrondissement. We duly obliged. It is, however, unfair to deem this establishment a wine bar, as it is serving some of the most outstanding bistro food in Paris.

We met up with some friends from Geelong and chose two bottles from the shelves on the wall. 7€ corkage is added for drinking within the restaurant.

The 2007 Domaine Latour Giraud Cuvee Charles Maxime Meursault was restrained, emitting the faintest whiff of straw and lemons.

As red Burgundy vintages go, 1992 is generally maligned by the so-called wine cognoscenti. Don't be fooled: there are some splendid drinks from this year and the Dominique Laurent Chambolle-Musigny Derriere la Grange is a case in point. It has beautiful aromatics of red fruits, decaying leaf, freshly tilled earth and pine needle sap.

The thing to do here is order the chef's degustation. For 35€ you get a starter, main, cheese and dessert, and are left in the hands of the chef.

Our starter was a carrot soup that had the most brilliant broth laden with shredded carrot and bacon. A large casserole dish was then placed in the centre for us to help ourselves to

a wonderful slow braise of pork with tomatoes, potatoes and thyme. As the lid was lifted, an intoxicating, earthy aroma filled the room.

Goats curd was served with freshly chopped chives and a perfectly dressed bunch of greens. Dessert was the most rich, dark chocolate mousse with a caramel foam on top. Words can't describe how good it was. An accompanying 2008 Uroulat Jurancon burst with honeyed fruits.

This is an outstanding place with great service, atmosphere and food. The best-quality ingredients are prepared simply but perfectly, and all the food is incredibly wine friendly. We will be returning soon.

Cinq-Mars
51 rue de Verneuil, 75007
01 45 44 69 13
lecinqmars.com

Directly opposite the apartment we were renting on rue de Verneuil is this stylish, small locals' bistro. They do simple food well and we had a delicious lunch here. A glass of Auge Blanc de Blancs was fresh, crammed full of green apples and citrus, and got the gastric juices well and truly flowing. We also ordered a Marcel Lapierre MMIII, a vin de table from the cult Beaujolais producer.

My partner Heidi's Œuf en cocotte was masterfully simple with the most wonderful egg served with a little cream and fresh herbs. My cèp mushrooms with parsley were, again, a study in understatement, but thoroughly satisfying and a cracking match with the Lapierre.

Heidi wanted something light for main, so I suggested we share the *Côte de bœuf*. It was of the highest quality, prepared perfectly, and served with wickedly good roast potatoes and a little green salad, perfectly dressed.

A splendid crème brûlée for me for dessert and an *Île flotante* for Heidi, a kind of floating pavlova on a bed of vanilla cream. Service here is prompt and friendly, and we would certainly return again.

Restaurant Auguste
54 rue Bourgogne, 75007
01 45 51 61 09
restaurantauguste.fr

It is a daunting task contemplating taking a couple of very excited children under the age of five to a fine-dining restaurant. It must be even more daunting to accept the aforementioned children as the restaurateur, but the staff at the one-star **Restaurant Auguste** did so with aplomb. We were heartily greeted and immediately put at ease. A glass each of Billecart-Salmon Rose also helped unfray the nerves.

We decided upon the three-course 35€ menu. A choice of an entrée, main and dessert from two options has to be one of the better-value dining propositions in the city. Heidi and the kids had a wonderful creamy chestnut soup with a soft poached egg. I had what in less skilled hands could have been a train wreck, but was indeed fresh, vibrant and quite engaging: a sashimi of sardines with sweet chilli sauce and avocado mousse.

The 2007 Amiot Servelle Chambolle Musigny Les Bas Doix was selected to accompany the protein course: perfectly roasted Guinea fowl breast on mashed potato. The mash was so rich and silky we're sure it had been passed through a sieve with about a kilo of butter. The wine

was crammed full of tart red berries and had a pretty waft of violets coupled with a little moss.

The wine list here is rather limited but one can get a drink, albeit one that won't have much more than a couple of years bottle age on it.

Some Chambolle remained after our main, so we called up a cheese course, consisting of a delightful hard cheese called Laguiole, similar in character to Comté, and a perfectly ripened, oozy St Marcellin.

Dessert for me was lychees with crème fraiche, a lovely mix of sweet and savoury, and Heidi had the most marvellous apple cider soufflé. Coffee was good and we left relaxed and thoroughly satiated, vowing to return and try a few more things from the à la carte menu.

Tan Dinh
60 rue Verneuil, 75007
01 45 44 04 84

Protein overload can happen easily in Paris and one needs to wedge in something of the Asian persuasion if one is to keep the digestive system in balance. **Tan Dinh** has been on our radar for several years but we have never got around to eating there, so it was fortuitous that it was located three doors down from our apartment.

It is a strange restaurant: Vietnamese fusion food, a slightly chintzy-looking dining room full of Americans the night we were there and a fabulous wine list

that has been picked over by the wine vultures. There are still some hidden gems at the right price and we ordered a 1993 Anne et Francois Gros Chambolle-Musigny La Combe d'Orveau. The waiter tried to dissuade us, telling us that older wine is lighter. I responded with, 'I like light and older wine.' I think he sensed that he believed me and duly found us a bottle. The wine was 'á point' with some tertiary notes of mushroom and earth sneaking in.

The food was good but not outstanding. Entrées of spring rolls and goose hot rolls were good. The star was steamed Sea Bass that had been lightly spiced and was served with cauliflower. It was delicious with the Chambolle. Mixed vegetables with seaweed was cleansing and we finished with green tea.

I'd recommend this place to the wine savvy who want to enjoy some decent Asian food and raid a well-stored bargain from the wine list.

La Cagouille
10 place Constantin Brancusi, 75014
01 43 22 09 01
la-cagouille.fr

Five years ago, we sat next to a food journalist from *Le Monde* at a dinner in Paris and the question was posed, 'Where do you eat?' His response was, 'La Cagouille. It's the best seafood in Paris.' Since that time, we have made La Cagouille our 'go to' bistro each time we hit Paris, eating there a couple of times per trip. It serves great seafood, done simply.

One is presented with a splendid bowl of cockles on arrival, just warmed through till they open and bathed in a beurre blanc—quite sublime. The wine list here is not deep or wide, but is serious if you love white Burgundy. Ramonet, Domaine Leflaive, Raveneau, Dauvissat, Sauzet and Coche-Dury are all well represented, and you'll drink them for under Australian retail prices. We initially ordered a 2000 Vincent Dancer Meursault-Perrières, but some premature oxidation had set in, and a 2005 Raveneau Chablis Clos was called up off the bench. What a wine in waiting! If you want to drink a 1996 red, La Tache and Grands-Echezeaux are on the list at well below the current Australian auction price.

For entrée, my razor clams were grilled simply and served with a butter and garlic sauce. Heidi's grilled sardines were delicious and butter again featured heavily in the sauce. A main course of a simple whole St-Pierre (John Dory) for me and Mackerel in a mustard sauce for Heidi: both fish were of the highest quality and cooked to perfection.

This may be the best seafood in Paris, but La Cagouille can also do dessert. Heidi's *Chocolate mœlleux* literally burst with an oozing chocolate lava and was sublime. My pear tart was classic and imminently satisfying. Coffee here is also good and, if you feel inclined, there is an amazing selection of Cognac and Armagnac.

This is a true locals' restaurant with very few tourists inside. It is a bit of a hike to get here, as its out in the back blocks of Montparnasse, but is worth the effort.

Bistro d'Hubert
41 boulevard Pasteur, 75015
01 47 34 15 50
bistrodhubert.com

Our experience here was a mixed bag. The place is quaint, service is excellent and tables are well spaced. A starter of tuna pâté was serviceable and a glass of 1995 Veuve Clicquot Rose was drinking very well. The wine list is not great, and our food was up and down. Unfortunately, Heidi's two dishes were a letdown and she had a sour look as I bragged about my two very good plates.

The two offending dishes were an entrée of beef cheek and foie gras, with crème fraîche, curry and almonds. It didn't really gel and was nondescript. Her main of chicken breast with various spices was overdone.

My cured Salmon with crème fraîche, dill and tomato was fresh and vibrant, and the simple entrecôte de bœuf for main was correct and utterly delicious. The accompanying wine, a 2006 Tortochot Gevrey-Chambertin Champerrier Vieilles Vignes, was delicious. The kids had an excellent confit of duck served similar to a *poule au pot*, with tasty root vegetables in a clear broth.

We skipped dessert, had two good coffees and departed.

Shannon's Favourite Parisian Treats

Chocolatiers

Belgium has long been regarded as producing the world's finest chocolates, but several *chocolatiers* in Paris are challenging that notion.

Chocolat Debauve & Gallais

Since 1800
30 rue des Saints-Pères, 75007
01 45 48 54 67
debauve-et-gallais.com

Chocolat Debauve & Gallais started in 1800 when Sulpice Debauve, pharmacist to Louis XVI, opened a chocolate factory. The distinguished connection didn't stop there: the shop on rue des Saints-Pères was designed by Empress Joséphine's architects; it is now a listed historical monument. But it is what is inside that really counts, and the super-fine *palets ganaches*, *truffes* and *bouchées*, all beautifully packaged, appear on many people's lists of the most delectable chocolates in Paris.

La Chocolaterie de Jacques Genin

133 rue de Turenne, 75003

Ute: The freshest and most divine chocolates in Paris, with caramels like you have never tasted them before and *pâte de fruits* with a purity of flavour. All are made on the premises by the master chocolate melter, who is also one of Paris' top pâtissiers.

Christian Constant

37 rue d'Assas, 75006
01 53 63 15 15
christianconstant.com

Not to be confused with the Christian Constant who runs Le Violon d'Ingres, this one is a master *chocolatier*. A scholar as well as a skilled artisan, Constant travels the world seeking out new and better ingredients, and has written two award-winning histories of chocolate. Some of his famous ganache chocolates include ingredients such as roses and Corinthian raisins, Yemen jasmine and green teas, Tahitian vanilla flowers, cardamom from Malabar, cherry with eau de vie, and hazelnuts with honey and cinnamon. If that weren't enough, there is a fabulous range of crystallised fruits.

Jean-Paul Hévin

Since 1988 (La Petit Boulé), 2002 (Hévin 2)
231 rue Saint-Honoré, 75001
01 55 35 35 96
3 rue Vavin, 75006
23 bis avenue la Motte-Picquet, 75007
jphevin.com

For many, Jean-Paul Hévin is the king of Parisian *chocolatiers*. His creations have the imaginative scope of a Picasso or Dali. Hévin trained under Joël Robuchon in Tokyo, but did Robuchon ever imagine that one day his disciple would flavour

chocolate with such powerful cheeses as
Époisses and Pont l'Évêque (you serve
them as an apéritif with wine) or that he
would reinvent the classics with such
delicacy? Honoured as Meilleur Ouvrier de
France (best artisan in France) in 1986,
he remains a master who has never stood
still. Some of his creations may confront;
none will be forgotten.

Joséphine Vannier
4 rue du Pas de la Mule, 75003
01 44 54 03 09
chocolats-vannier.com
Joséphine Vannier, based in the Marais,
loves to sculpt with chocolate and her shop
is filled with extraordinary artistic creations
(a miniature grand piano, for example).
Apart from a wide range of ganaches,
pralines and nougats (including orange-
blossom water, Sicilian pistachios), Vannier
makes gourmet ice-cream. She has a
devoted following.

Shannon's Favourite Parisian Treats

Chocolatiers (continued)

La Maison du Chocolat
Since 1977
225 rue du faubourg Saint-Honoré, 75008
01 42 27 39 44
Also at:
99 rue de Rivoli, 75001
19 rue des Sèvres, 75006
52 rue François 1er, 75008
8 boulevard de la Madeleine, 75009
Printemps Haussmann, 75009
120 avenue Victor Hugo, 75116
lamaisonduchocolat.com

La Maison du Chocolat was opened in 1977 by Robert Linxe, who had settled in Paris in 1955 from the Basque region. Linxe did his apprenticeship in Switzerland, but it was at his La Maison du Chocolat, located on the rue du faubourg Saint-Honoré in the basement of a former wine shop, that he truly began experimenting with ganache. He was obviously successful, for in 1987 he opened a second shop (rue François 1er). Today there are six shops and a boutique (Printemps Haussmann) in Paris, and others in Cannes, London, New York, Tokyo and Hong Kong. Gilles Marchal, formerly head pastry chef at Hôtel Le Bristol, succeeded Linxe in 2007 and is responsible for the 'Haute Couture' range, which includes a replica of a Boucheron necklace.

Michel Chaudun
149 rue de l'Université, 75007
01 47 53 74 40
michel-chaudun.jp

Once the head *chocolatier* at La Maison du Chocolat, Michel Chaudun struck out on his own 20 years ago and his shop on the rue de l'Université is a must for visitors to the Saint-Germain-des-Prés area. His fans swear by the simple tiny squares of ganache known as *pavés*. Like many other top chocolate artisans, Chaudun has a shop in Tokyo; he also has a passion for sculpting in chocolate. But the best news is that he is regarded by one and all as running the friendliest chocolate shop in Paris.

Michel Cluizel
Since 1987
201 rue Saint Honoré, 75001
01 42 44 11 66
cluizel.com

A chocolate specialist since 1948, Michel Cluizel has been on a self-proclaimed mission of producing chocolate that reflects the principle of *terroir* (as with wines). His chocolate bars, now widely available outside France, rival those of Valhrona. The Cluizel shop (managed by his daughter Cathérine) and online boutique offer five different macarons and various types of crystallised fruit. But it is the ganache-centred chocolates that draw most people in, especially the new 'Los Anconès' (made with cacao beans from Saint-Dominique).

Patrick Roger

Since 2004
108 boulevard Saint-Germain, 75006
01 43 29 38 42
Also at:
91 rue de Rennes, 75006
12 cité Berryer Village Royal, 75008
45 avenue Victor Hugo, 75016
patrickroger.com
Patrick Roger is a Meilleur Ouvrier de France–Chocolatier (best chocolate artisan in France) and in 2007 was voted producer of the best chocolate in Paris. His website is like an art installation, making light of the stock-market travails and, in the process, promoting chocolate as a tonic to lift people's spirits. Some of the chocolates that may tempt are praline *feuilleté*; and ganaches of peppery mint with citronella, or of Sichuan peppercorns. There are also *pavés* and orangettes (for which the fruit comes from Corsica) and some flavoured with fresh ginger. The packaging, a green version of Tiffany's blue, is stunning.

Pierre Hermé

Since 1998 (Tokyo), 2001 (Paris)
72 rue Bonaparte, 75006
01 48 74 59 55
Also at:
4 rue Cambon, 75001
publicisdrugstore, 133 avenue des Champs-Élysées, 75008
Galleries Lafayette, 40 boulevard Haussmann, 75009
185 rue Vaugirard, 75015
58 avenue Paul Doumer, 75106
pierreherme.com
The world's best maker of macarons also makes fine chocolates. Try the white-truffle hazelnut or the passionfruit ganache made with milk chocolate, the pink rose-petal ganache, or the Americano Pamplemousse (with Campari and grapefruit), or … Book a ticket to Paris, now!

Pierre Marcolini

Since 1994 (Brussels)
89 rue de Seine, 75006
01 44 07 39 07
Also at:
9 rue Scribe, 75009
marcolini.be
Most agree the Belgians make the best chocolate in the world, and it is a fair bet Belgian Pierre Marcolini would agree. Having now adopted Paris as his home, Marcolini is one of five European craftsmen who still manufacture their own couverture from raw cacao beans. He only uses fair-trade beans he personally sources from around the globe, one reason why he has so many dedicated fans, who claim he is easily the best *chocolatier* in Paris. However, Marcolini does not only produce chocolate: he also creates pâtisseries, biscuits, ice-creams and sorbets. In 1995, he was acclaimed Champion du Monde de Pâtisserie and, in 2000, Champion d'Europe de Pâtisserie.

Sunday Markets

Sunday is the market day with the most vibrant atmosphere. The following three markets are open on Sunday:

Marché Raspail

boulevard Raspail between rue du Cherche-Midi and ru de Rennes, 75006
Tuesday, Friday and Sunday: 7 a.m.–2.30 p.m.
On Sundays, the market turns 100 percent organic and offers the largest selection of organic produce. On Tuesday and Friday the selection is traditional, with a few organic stalls amongst the traders.

Marché Bastille

boulevard Richard Lenoir, north of Bastille, 75011
Thursday and Sunday: 7 a.m.–2.30 p.m.
This is the largest outdoor market in Paris, with 248 traders to choose from, including horse butchers and offal specialists. In season, there is the most amazing range of mushrooms.

Marché Couvert Beauveau and the Marché Aligre

place d'Aligre, 75012
Tuesday to Saturday: 9 a.m.–1 p.m. and 4 p.m.–7.30 p.m.; Sunday: 9 a.m.–1.30 p.m.
A historic undercover market surrounded by a local market with a true neighbourhood feel.

Shannon's Parisian Recipes

Truffle Omelette

The perfect omelette is light and fluffy, evenly yellow with no indication of any colour or crispiness from the pan, and a little bit translucent in the centre. To serve, fold it in half, or in a cigar shape, and fill with a minute amount of quality filling: normally this is just one specific flavour. Cheese, mushroom and herb are the three most popular, and the ones I would most recommend. An omelette should be cooked 'à la minute': I know that a lot of bistros actually cook something like a frittata, but a real omelette should be cooked on order, and at the last minute, by the chef. It's a real skill. Make sure there is no flavouring or garnish through the egg: these should be added once the omelette is cooked. If you want good French fries to go with that, they should be thin, crispy and light-golden, and well seasoned with good-quality sea salt.

2 tablespoons olive oil	In a small non-stick frying pan, heat the olive oil with the butter.
10 g French butter, unsalted	When the butter is frothing, add the eggs. Using a firm rubber
3 large free-range eggs, lightly beaten	spatula, beat the eggs as they cook, scraping down the edges. When the egg mix is half-cooked, remove from the heat, sprinkle
50 g Gruyère cheese, grated	the cheese in the middle. Follow with three shavings of truffle, and gently fold the omelette over until it's a smooth sausage
5 g truffle	shape. Shave the rest of the truffle over the omelette, season
salt	with salt, and serve with French fries.

Serves 1

Truffles Grown in Australia

Shannon: When a typical black winter truffle is fully ripe, it dispels a long-aged myth amongst food snobs and so-called experts that there is a noticeable difference in smell and taste. Truffles do not taste of their environment; they are a fungus and use the conditions of the environment to feed and grow successfully on different species of oak, walnut and hazelnut trees. Some people say they can taste the difference between what tree root a truffle grows off; what a load of nonsense.

Italians consider the white truffle to be superior in taste to the black truffle. The latter cost around $2000 per kilo.

The Australian season for truffles is late May to late August, with the best truffles coming from Manjimup in south-western Australia. They are also grown with good success in regions around Canberra and Melbourne, and all over Tasmania.

The French season starts from late December to early March. French chefs are starting to recognise that Australian truffles are just as good, so look out for them at the Hôtel Plaza Athénée soon.

Montparnasse

14TH ARRONDISSEMENT

Built in 1927, **La Coupole** has an Art Déco interior which has recently been restored by Groupe Flo. Every brasserie in Paris has a history, but who can top Picasso, Man Ray, Hemingway, Alberto Giacometti, Josephine Baker and Georges Simenon? With its famous 24 pillars, this is a remarkable space. The food is actually quite inventive, ranging from crunchy prawns with fresh herbs and mango chutney to a fricassée of Bresse chicken with a yabbie sauce and spring vegetables. Classicists can have the pepper steak.

La Coupole

102 boulevard du
Montparnasse, 75014
01 43 20 14 20
lacoupoleparis.com
GaultMillau: 🍴
Menu: 24 (lunch)/32€
À la carte: 40–80€

This famous bistro was frequented by Jean-Paul Sartre. Then again, which one wasn't? Regulars (long known as Dômiers) also included Henry Miller, Aleister Crowley, Paul Gaugin, Wassily Kandinsky and Vladimir Ilyich Ulyanov (aka Lenin). It has a classic location on one of those acute-angled corners of Paris. Long renowned for its seafood (*Turbot hollandaise, Sole de l'Île d'Yeu*), it also has a sufficiently tempting selection for meat-eaters. It also features in Hemingway's *A Moveable Feast*.

Le Dôme

108 boulevard du
Montparnasse, 75014
01 43 35 25 81
no website
GaultMillau: 🍴🍴
Menu: 75–145€

 LUXURY HOTEL

A glass-and-concrete blob near the Montparnasse railway station, it was recently restored and has reasonably sized (and priced) rooms. Some have stunning views, but it is not a place for romantics.

Pullman Paris Montparnasse

Rating: 5★
19 rue de Commandant
Mouchotte, 75014
01 44 36 44 36
pullmanhotels.com
Rooms: 918
Single: 179–499€
Double: 179–499€
Suites: 35

Marché rue du Grenelle (15th)

Wednesday and Sunday
till 2.30 p.m.

This is a wonderful down-to-earth market, with a huge range of fresh fruit and vegetables, meat and fish.

Shannon's Parisian Recipes
Zopf Bread

Zopf bread is an Austrian recipe, a 'poor-man's brioche'. You can get away with proving the bread only once, which is a great help to the dinner-party host. I like to use Zopf bread as the base for excellent Wagyu beef burgers.

2 cups water	Combine the water, powdered milk, sugar, salt, yeast, butter and flour in a large mixing bowl. Using a mixer with dough hook attached, beat on a medium speed for 10–15 minutes or until the dough is smooth and shiny but somewhat sticky. Transfer to a lightly oiled container that will accommodate the dough when it has doubled in size. Cover with a large plastic bag and set aside to prove in a warm place for 2 hours, or until doubled in size.
70 g powdered milk	
¼ cup sugar	
15 g salt	
40 g fresh yeast	
100 g butter	
900 g plain flour, sifted	
100 ml egg yolk, lightly beaten	

Knock down the dough, releasing all the air. Divide into 40-g portions and roll into balls using the palms of your hands. Place on a greased baking tray, cover the tray with the plastic bag, and set aside for 30 minutes, or until doubled in size.

Preheat the oven to 220°C.

Gently brush the dough with the beaten egg yolk. Place tray in preheated oven and bake for 10 minutes or until golden and slightly crusted. Cool on a wire rack.

Makes 24 rolls

Outside Paris

As rural France is comprehensively covered in
Shannon Bennett's France (The Miegunyah Press, 2011),
here are some lists of Shannon's places to stay and eat,
just to tantalise the senses.

Shannon's Favourite French Restaurants

Le Petit Nice
Chef: Gérald Passédat
Anse de Maldormé
(Corniche J. F. Kennedy), Marseille
04 91 59 25 92
passedat.fr
Michelin: ★★★
GaultMillau: ♙♙♙♙
Menu: 85 (weekday lunch)/130/250€
À la carte: 135–230€

La Bastide de Capelongue
Chef: Edouard Loubet
route de Lourmarin, 2km from Bonnieux
04 90 75 89 78
capelongue.com
Michelin: ★★
GaultMillau: ♙♙♙♙
Menu: 70 (weekday lunch)/140/190€
À la carte: 130/220€

Bras
Chef: Sébastien Bras
route de l'Aubrac, outside Laguiole
05 65 51 18 20
michel-bras.com
Michelin: ★★★
GaultMillau: ♙♙♙♙
Menu: 111/136/179€

Restaurant Régis et Jacques Marcon
Chefs: Régis and Jacques Marcon
Saint-Bonnet-Le-Froid, at the top
of the village
04 71 59 93 72
regismarcon.fr
Michelin: ★★★
GaultMillau: ♙♙♙♙♙
Menu: 140/175€
À la carte: 130–210€

L'Auberge du Pont de Collonges
Chef: Paul Bocuse
40 rue de la Plage, Collonges au
Mont d'Or, 12km north on the banks
of the Saône, Lyon
04 72 42 90 90
bocuse.fr
Michelin: ★★★
GaultMillau: ♙♙♙♙
Menu: 140/175/220€
À la carte: 113–167€

Pic
Chef: Anne-Sophie Pic
285 avenue Victor-Hugo, Valence
04 75 44 15 32
pic-valence.com
Michelin: ★★★
GaultMillau: ♙♙♙♙
Menu: 90 (weekday lunch)/210/330€
À la carte: 144–268€

Maison Troisgros

Chef: Michel Troigros
place de la Gare, Roanne
04 77 71 66 97
troisgros.com
Michelin: ★★★
GaultMillau: ♟♟♟♟
Menu: 95 (weekday lunch)/165/200€
À la carte: 160–220€

Chez Paul

11 rue Major Martin, Lyon
04 78 28 35 83
chezpaul.fr
Menu: 19 (lunch)/25€

Joël Robuchon Monte-Carlo

Chefs: Joël Robuchon, Christophe Cussac
Hôtel Métropole
4 avenue de la Madone, Monte-Carlo
377 93 15 15 15
metropole.com
Michelin: ★★
GaultMillau: ♟♟♟♟
Menu: 60 (weekday lunch, wine
included)/180€
À la carte: 71–360€

Le Surcouf

7 quai Gambetta, Cancale
02 99 89 61 75
restaurantlesurcouf.com
Michelin: Bib Gourmand
Menu: 15.50 (weekdays)/26/44€
À la carte: 50–65€

Shannon's Favourite French Hotels

Le Petit Nice
Anse de Maldormé
(Corniche J. F. Kennedy), Marseille
04 91 59 25 92
passedat.fr
Rating: 4★+
Rooms: 13
Single: 190–750€
Double: 210–750€

La Bastide de Capelongue
route de Lourmarin,
2km outside Bonnieux
04 90 75 89 78
capelongue.com
Rating: 4★
Rooms: 17
Single: 190–380€
Double: 190–380€

Château de la Chèvre d'Or
Rue du Barri, Èze
04 92 10 66 66
chevredor.com
Rating: 5★+
Rooms: 30
Single: 280–870€
Double: 280–870€
Suites: 6

Hôtel Métropole
4 avenue de la Madone, Monte-Carlo
377 93 15 15 15
metropole.com
Rating: 5★+
Rooms: 126
Single: 420–800€
Double: 420–800€
Suites: 39

Royal Champagne

Champillon-Bellevue, near Épernay
03 26 52 87 11
royalchampagne.com
Rating: 4★+
Rooms: 24
Single: 260–410€
Double: 260–410€
Suites: 4

Cour des Loges

2, 4, 6 and 8 rue du Bœuf, Lyon
04 72 77 44 44
courdesloges.com
Rating: 5★+
Rooms: 57
Single: 240–505€
Double: 240–505€
Suites: 4

Châteaux Richeux

Point-du-Jour, Saint-Meloir-des-Ondes,
Cancale
02 99 89 64 76
maisons-de-bricourt.com
Rating: 4★+
Rooms: 11
Single: 165–310€
Double: 165–310€
Suites: 2

L'Hôtel Régis et Jacques Marcon

Saint-Bonnet-Le-Froid,
at the top of the village
04 71 59 93 72
regismarcon.fr
Michelin: 5★
Rooms: 10
Single: 355€
Double: 355€

Maison Troisgros

place de la Gare, Roanne
04 77 71 66 97
troisgros.com
Rating: 5★
Rooms: 11
Single: 190–390€
Double: 190–390€
Suites: 5

La Lucarne aux Chouettes

quai Bretoche, Villeneuve-sur-Yonne
03 86 87 18 26
lalucarneauxchouettes.fr
Rating: 3★
Rooms: 3
Rates: 55–99€
Suite: 1

Picture Credits

pp. ii–iii Gautier Willaume/iStock Photo; **p. iv** Nic Taylor/iStock Photo; **p. v** top right: Bryce Kroll/Graffizone/iStock Photo, bottom left: Catherine dée Auvil/iStock Photo; **p. x** Evgeny Murtola/iStock Photo; **p. xi** Tom Samek; p. xii Catherine Jones/iStock Photo; **p. 15** Elena Elisseeva/iStock Photo; **p. 18** Neil Farrin/JAI/Corbis; **p. 20** Eugenie Baulch; **p. 26** Scott Murray; **p. 28** Tom Samek; **p. 30** Nikontiger/iStock Photo; **p. 31** Madeleine West; **p. 32** Marisa Allegra Williams/Corbis; **p. 33** Stefan Ataman/iStock Photo; **p. 37** left: Graffizone/iStock Photo, right: Hilden/Corbis; **p. 38** Bryce Kroll/Catherine dée Auvil/iStock Photo; **p. 39** Ljiljana Pavkov/iStock Photo; **p. 40** Catherine dée Auvil/Anja Hild/iStock Photo; **p. 45** gprentice/iStock Photo; **p. 47** Ivan Bastien/iStock Photo; **p. 49** Bettmann/Corbis; **p. 50** Marco Beretta/iStock Photo; **p. 51** left: Bryce Kroll/iStock Photo, right: Seth Joel/Corbis; **p. 54** Franck Boston/iStock Photo; **p. 58** Dan Moore/iStock Photo; **p. 66** Qi Zhou/iStock Photo; **p. 69** Sarah Zagami and Matthew Vaughan; **p. 79** Eugenie Baulch; **p. 81** Hilden/Corbis; **p. 86** left: Graffizone/iStock Photo, right: Bryce Kroll/iStock Photo; **p. 89** left: Bryce Kroll/iStock Photo, right: Cussotti/Corbis; **p. 93** Matthew Dixon/iStock Photo; **p. 97** left: Bryce Kroll/iStock Photo; **p. 104** Tom Samek; **p. 107** Rhiannon Harris and Andrew Paranavitana; **p. 110** imagetwo/iStock Photo; **p. 112** left: Catherine dée Auvil/ iStock Photo, right: Anja Hild/iStock Photo; **p. 115** Sarah Zagami and Matthew Vaughan; **p. 118** Roscoe Darshan Grover; **p. 129** Seth Joel/Corbis; **p. 131** Bettmann/Corbis; **p. 133** Ingenui/ iStock Photo; **p. 135** Eugenie Baulch; **p. 138** Tom Samek; **pp. 142–3** Skip Nall/ Corbis; **p. 145** Tom Samek; **p. 149** Bryce Kroll/iStock Photo; **p. 151** Roscoe Darshan Grover; **p. 153** Emilie Duchesne/iStock Photo; **p. 154** Rhiannon Harris and Andrew Paranavitana; **p. 157** left: Bryce Kroll/iStock Photo, right: Seth Joel/Corbis; **p. 159** Tom Samek; **p. 161** Eugenie Baulch; **p. 164** Tom Samek; **p. 168** Consuelo Almazán Carretero/iStock Photo; **p. 176** Michael DeWeese-Frank/ iStock Photo; **p. 179** Nikada/iStock Photo; **p. 180** Catherine Jones/iStock Photo; **p. 185** Tom Samek; **p. 188** left: Graffizone/iStock Photo, right: Bryce Kroll/iStock Photo; **p. 189** Eugenie Baulch; **p. 190** Rhiannon Harris and Andrew Paranavitana; **p. 191** Steve Burger/iStock Photo; **p. 193** Barbara Hoogendoorn/iStock Photo; **p. 197** Bryce Kroll/iStock Photo; **p. 198** Rhiannon Harris and Andrew Paranavitana; **p. 200** Pierre Vauthey/Corbis Sygma; **p. 201** Eugenie Baulch; **p. 206** Eugenie Baulch; **p. 209** Bryce Kroll/iStock Photo; **p. 211** parema/iStock Photo; **p. 213** Emil Huston/iStock Photo; **p. 214** left: Catherine dée Auvil/iStock Photo, right: Anja Hild/iStock Photo; **p. 217** Alexander Walther/iStock Photo; **p. 218** Roscoe Darshan Grover; **p. 229** left: Bryce Kroll/iStock Photo, right: Anja Hild/iStock Photo; **p. 232** Arpad Benedek/iStock Photo; **p. 234** Rosoce Darshan Grover; **p. 238** Bryce Kroll/iStock Photo; **p. 253** Andrea Pistolesi/The Image Bank/Getty Images; **p. 256** Bryce Kroll/iStock Photo; **p. 257** Roscoe Darshan Grover; **p. 261** Catherine dée Auvil/iStock Photo; **p. 263** left: Bryce Kroll/iStock Photo, right: Seth Joel/Corbis; **p. 267** calvio/iStock Photo; **p. 271** GMVozd/iStock Photo; **p. 274** Alison Stieglitz/iStock Photo; **p. 279** Roscoe Darshan Grover; **pp. 280–1** Gordon Bell/iStock Photo; **p. 283** Scott Murray; **p. 284** Alexandre Ménard/iStock Photo.

Index